God's Strategy

in Human History

Roger Forster & Paul Marston

Volume 1

God's Path to Victory

FSC
www.fsc.org
MIX
Paper from
responsible sources
FSC® C005094

Cover design and typesetting by Joseph Laycock
Printed by Cambrian Printers Ltd, Aberystwyth

Contents

Foreword by Howard Marshall vii
Foreword by Greg Boyd ix
Preface to the 3rd Edition xiii
  Acknowledgements xiv
  Bible versions used xv
  About the Authors xvi

Introduction 1

Part 1 | The Nature of the Conflict

  1 Righteous Job – Human Battlefield 7
  2 Prayerful Daniel – Human Combatant 31
  3 The Church – Weapons, Methods & Banners . 39
  4 Jesus the Messiah – God's Glory in the Battle . . 45
  5 The Conflict is Real 49

Part 2 | The History of the Conflict

  6 How War Was Declared – Genesis 59
  7 Israel and God's Plan – Introduction 63
  8 Israel and God's Plan – Abraham & Isaac 71
  9 Israel and God's Plan – Jacob & Esau 77
  10 Israel and God's Plan – Moses 83
  11 Israel and God's Plan – Pharaoh 91
  12 Objectors and Vessels 97
  13 The Effects of the Cross 111
  14 God's Great Project and the Final Battle 125
  15 Eternity 141

  16 Key Concepts and Definitions 181

  Bibliography 199
  General Index 202
  Index of Verses Cited 204

Commendations for the 1st Edition

This is a long awaited treatment of the mystifying problem of predestination and freedom... The work is sound, biblically and exegetically...

Dr Harold J Ockenga *President of Gordon College and Gordon-Conwell Theological Seminary*

I congratulate you on the many excellent features of the book; in particular its style is crystal clear. I like the presentation of the material and short chapters that make the argument very easy to follow. There are many splendid insights offered on important aspects of Biblical teaching throughout the book. I also think it a very good idea to place in the study sections material which strengthens the argument, without asking the reader to stop in his tracks and consider in detail the meaning of the key concepts which are alluded to.

Rev Dr GR Beasley Murray, *Principal of Spurgeon's College, London.*

This is a book to read with an open mind. I have learnt a lot from it, and I am grateful to the authors for daring to take a fresh look at questions which most of us have too easily considered closed.

Rev Derek Kidner, M.A., *Warden, Tyndale House, Cambridge.*

Here is a book which gets to grips with some of life's baffling problems – dealing particularly with the Christian's spiritual warfare. It deals both with the nature of the warfare and with its history. In the second part of the book we see how God's purposes find their culmination in Christ, with the final overthrow of evil. The authors reveal not only a profound knowledge and understanding of the Scriptures, but a refreshing realism as regards human nature, and the situation in the world generally. Here is a book to be warmly commended as meeting a real need.

Rev GW Kirby, *Principal, London Bible College*

Within the Biblically minded community this book should be much appreciated. You have stated the case for human responsibility very forcibly, and this is needed. I like the "grand design" of the book and trust that it will be successful.

Rev A Morgan Derham, *Secretary for Information, United Bible Societies.*

This is a most worthwhile study on an important and relevant theme. I have thoroughly enjoyed reading it, and consider that it deserves a wide circulation. It is on beam for today, and interprets the Divine strategy in meaningful terms.

Rev Dr A Skevington Wood, *Senior Lecturer in Theology, Cliff College, Calver.*

Foreword

by Howard Marshall

We are sometimes given the impression that the only viable meta-framework for evangelical biblical theology is an Augustinian-Calvinist one in which everything that happens is predestined by God as the total sovereign over the universe; a rigid determinism controls everything. The Bible is then interpreted in accordance with this presupposition. Such an approach is not free from difficulties, especially in regard to the doctrine of God as a being who predestines some to salvation and others to condemnation in what appears to us to be an arbitrary fashion but is due to his unfathomable purpose. Other possible frameworks are rejected by the dominant school of theology.

Yet there is a strong alternative which is less well-known. A detailed exposition and defence of it was published by Paul Marston and Roger Forster in 1973, but has not been well-known in this country. It has now been thoroughly updated in the light of contemporary biblical study to provide an exposition of the biblical understanding of human history in the light of God's purposes and a critique of the weaknesses of the Calvinist alternative.

There is a basis here for an understanding of God that is more satisfying and true to Scripture. It deserves careful attention by those who struggle with the problems of the dominant approach and are looking for a better way. Upholders of the Augustinian-Calvinist approach need to reconsider their position in view of the cogent criticisms of it that are offered here.

It may well be that there are areas in this book where there are tensions between different understandings of God and evil that would tempt readers to dismiss the whole approach. But, whatever our school of theology, there are always going to be tensions as finite human minds attempt to understand the ways of God, and the problem is to locate correctly where the real tensions exist. To ascribe all our difficulties to the incomprehensibility of God may be the wrong approach; it may be better to identify the source of our problems in the incomprehensibility of evil and thus to be able to develop a doctrine of God that is freed from the moral difficulties that many of us find in the alternative picture.

I am delighted to see Paul and Roger's careful, clearly and simply written contribution to this area of biblical exegesis and systematic theology revised and updated to serve a new generation of readers and warmly welcome its publication.

I. Howard Marshall

Professor Emeritus of New Testament,
University of Aberdeen, Scotland

Foreword
by Greg Boyd

Many who know me as a passionate defender of human free will and the open nature of the future may find this hard to believe, but for several years while attending seminary, I embraced five-point Calvinism. My reasons were entirely exegetical. The Calvinist interpretation of Romans 9 along with their interpretation of other biblical passages dealing with 'predestination', 'election' and 'providence' struck me as stronger than any Arminian interpretation I could find. Even when I believed it, however, I have to honestly confess that I never really liked it, despite my sincere attempts to feel otherwise. I was never able to sincerely join my fellow Calvinists as they proclaimed the 'glory', 'beauty' and 'justice' of a God who damned people to suffer eternally for committing the sins he predestined them to commit. Nor was I ever able to sincerely join the chorus of those who expressed 'joy' over being one of God's elect, all the while acknowledging that my adorable newborn child may very well have been created for the purpose of 'glorifying God' by suffering his wrath for all eternity.

As I learned from Jonathan Edwards and other Calvinists that one 'sign of election' is that a person sincerely sees the 'glory', 'beauty' and 'justice' of this all-controlling portrait of God and sincerely finds 'joy' in their election, I began to wonder if I was truly one of God's elect – despite the fact that I at this time truly believed this view to be true. This in turn led me to question why God would predestine someone like myself to believe Calvinism to be true and yet withhold from me the accompanying grace to sincerely see the beauty of this truth. What kind of God would create a person to be tormented in this fashion?

Yet, over time I came to see that this is more or less what the God of Calvinism does to every non-elect person. He decrees that they eternally long for what he himself decrees they can never have, and according to most Calvinists, he does this with the vast majority of humans throughout history! And if you don't see this as 'glorious,' 'beautiful' and 'just,' then it simply means you (and I) aren't one of his 'elect'. As a result of this line of thinking, I found that, throughout the three to four years I embraced Calvinism, I was increasingly revolted by, and damned by, the very belief system that I, on strictly exegetical grounds, believed to be true.

Fortunately for me, I eventually encountered several biblical and theology works by Arminians that offered interpretations of the crucial Calvinistic passages that struck me as more persuasive than what the Calvinists had offered me. And among the works that exercised the most powerful influence on me at this time was the book that you are presently reading and that I now have the great honor of writing a Foreword for: *God's Strategy in Human History*. For me – and I have firsthand knowledge that I am far from alone in having this experience – reading Marston's and Forster's masterful work was like finally acquiring the picture for a puzzle you've been unsuccessfully trying to piece together for several years without knowing what picture you were trying to construct. In fact, while the several pieces that Calvinism had helped me put together pointed in the direction of what Marston and Forster boldly call 'a monster deity', once *God's Strategy in Human History* helped me get the true big-picture the pieces were meant to form, I discovered that all the pieces, properly placed together, present a God of breathtaking beauty who has a beautiful plan for humanity and his creation.

I could not be more delighted that Marston and Forster decided to offer us this 3rd, updated and revised edition of this important work. So far as I can see, the timing could not be more perfect! The religion of Christendom with its vision of the 'church triumphant' is on its way out! This is the religion that came about when Eusebius, Augustine and other church fathers unwisely accepted from the emperor Constantine the power of the sword, thereby embracing as a divine gift the very kind of power that Jesus had renounced as a temptation from Satan (Luke 4:5-7)! This religion has been dying a slow death for several centuries, and – God be praised! – all indications are that, despite a recent resurgence of very vocal and aggressive defenders, it's demise is drawing nigh.

This militant version of Christianity exchanged the image of Jesus as the humble crucified Savior for the image of Jesus as a conquering Caesar, thereby transforming the conception of God's power from the power of self-sacrificial love revealed on the cross into the controlling power of a tyrant's decree and the coercive power of his enforcing sword. The Augustinian/Calvinistic portrait of God unilaterally determining by divine decree all that comes to pass, whether good or evil, is simply the quintessential expression of the Caesar-looking God of this dying religion.

While some bemoan the death of this religion, I see it as a cause for celebrating! For out of the rubble of this decaying religion is rising, all around the world, a new generation of kingdom revolutionaries who are catching the vision that the true God and the true kingdom look like the crucified Messiah, not a reigning Caesar! Freed from the blinding shackles of the old, triumphalist, sword-wielding religion of Christendom, these rising revolutionaries are grasping the profound biblical truth that God's 'glory' is about the radiance of his other-oriented, self-sacrificial love that was revealed on Calvary, not about the twisted, human-made 'glory' of a narcissistic, self-absorbed, deity who only loves himself. So too, these rising revolutionaries are seeing the profound biblical truth that the true God is a confident, self-assured God who shares power while loving all people, not a petty, insecure god who monopolizes power to control people. And this new tribe of kingdom people is increasingly receiving the revelation that the true God calls on and empowers the Church to manifest his loving character by sacrificially serving the world, not to manifest the power of a warrior god by trying to conquer the world.

The 1st edition of *God's Strategy in Human History* helped plant the seeds for this beautiful, rising revolution, but I believe this new and expanded edition will begin to reap the harvest. My sense is that there is far more openness to the profound, biblical concepts that are so clearly, and so thoroughly, communicated in this work than there was 40 years ago when the 1st edition appeared. In the two volumes of the revised edition of this masterpiece, kingdom people will find a clear, thoroughly biblical theology that removes the many layers of unnecessary, human-made contradictions – illegitimately passed off as 'mysteries' – that have plagued the theology of Christendom for centuries. And in this work, kingdom people will find a coherent and compelling presentation of the 'big picture' that finally makes sense of all the individual pieces they have found in Scripture and/or perhaps inherited from the Church.

Most important, in this work followers of the Lamb will find – as I myself found more than 30 years ago – that this 'big picture' is not a portrait of an ugly, tyrannical god that one must confess out of fear to be altogether 'glorious,' 'beautiful' and 'just: they will rather find a portrait of God whom their heart can't help but see as actually altogether 'glorious,' 'beautiful' and 'just'.

My prayer – and I know it's the prayer of Marston and Forster as well – is that this new, updated edition of *God's Strategy in Human History* will reap the full harvest of the magnificent kingdom seeds that were planted with the previous editions. Lord bless this work and all who read it!

Greg Boyd

Senior Pastor, Woodland Hills Church,
Maplewood, MN, USA

Preface to the 3rd Edition

It is four decades since *God's Strategy in Human History* first appeared. It was reprinted several times in the UK and USA (and in mandarin Chinese), and a second edition came out in 2000. This book, *Volume 1: God's Path to Victory* is part of a two-volume set under the original title, which expands similar materials in the light of deeper study and more recent New Testament scholarship. This has involved substantial revision and much new material. This first volume can be read on its own, and brief word studies at the end outline some of key concepts which can be studied in much greater depth by reading *Volume 2: Reconsidering Key Biblical Ideas.*

God's whole plan and way of dealing with humanity is centred on 'Jesus the Messiah', which in the Greek used in the New Testament is translated 'Jesus the Christ' or 'Jesus Christ'. From the garden of Eden God looked forward to the time when the offspring of the woman would crush the serpent at Calvary. The choice of Abraham and Israel was a preparation for the Messiah, and the New Covenant is the outworking of his Kingdom plan through the Church, which is the body of Jesus the Messiah on earth. This is the exciting theme of this book.

Our theological position in all we write is unchanged: we are conservative evangelicals, committed only to the authority of Scripture. We stand in the great traditions of for example the Early Church teachers, the Anabaptists, and Wesleyan holiness theology, only because we find in them a teaching which is closer to Scripture and the heart of the Gospel of Jesus the Messiah than some of the other theologies that have arisen. In understanding Scripture we seek to follow the best principles of biblical interpretation – of *hermeneutics*. This involves close analysis of verses in their context, but also of the backgrounds of language and culture in which they were written. In our lifetimes, the availability of a wealth of new New Testament scholarship has enriched and deepened our understanding of the key concepts of God's unfolding plans, and these new volumes seek to share this with the readers.

Our commitment remains to what (in the Wesleyan context) might be called 'theology on horseback'. Our God chose not to given us a single book of 'systematic theology', but revealed himself in the context of history, relationship and action as recorded in the multiple books of Scripture. The great theologian, Paul, was a missionary not an 'academic', and Jesus himself never even wrote a treatise. What we would like is to be able to contribute towards a biblical and theological understanding for those who are already active in the spiritual conflict, and to stimulate others to get the vision and join it.

This approach is in line with the theology of the Bible. The biblical God in whom we believe is relational with those made in his image. He himself acts, reacts, and interacts with us. He is not immovable, impassive, immutable, and locked in rigid timelessness where nothing ever happens. Rather he can be angry, disappointed, glad, well pleased, and may change his mind according to the reactions of those with whom he is in relationship. In short, he is a person who is able to love and feel emotion.

The approach is also practical, because God calls upon those who love him, who are called according to his purpose, to be co-workers with him in his world in the power of his Spirit.

Some theologians have only *interpreted* the world in various ways – the point is to *change* it! Jesus' commission was about making disciples, not belief systems.

Acknowledgments

The responsibility of anything said in this book remains that of the authors alone. We would, however, like to thank the many scholars who have commented on the various editions of this work. These include Dr GR Beasley Murray, Dr Mark Bonnington, Professor FF Bruce, Mr Geoffrey Bull, Rev A Morgan Derham, Mr HL Ellison, Mr T Harpur, Rev Derek Kidner, Dr and Mrs A Kinnear, Rev GW Kirby, Dr Leon Morris, Mr FN Martin, Dr T Martin, Canon Alan Neech, Dr Harold J Ockenga, Mr DF Payne, Dr Meic Pearse, Rev KFW Prior, Dr A Skevington Wood, Mr Alan Storkey and Dr Stephen Travis.

For this totally revised two volume work our particular thanks go to Dr Joseph Laycock for his detailed work on the text and useful comments.

Bible versions used

For a work like this, we wanted to use an accurate modern version, and unless indicated quotations will be from the New King James Version (NKJV).

Where other versions have been cited, the abbreviations used are as follows:

o   English Standard Version (ESV)

o   King James/Authorised Version (KJV)

o   Revised Standard Version (RSV)

o   Revised Version (RV)

o   New American Standard Version (NASB)

o   New English Bible (NEB)

o   New International Version (NIV)

o   Jerusalem Bible (JB)

The Septuagint (LXX) is the Greek translation of the Hebrew Old Testament, completed in the second century BC. The LXX was the version in common use in apostolic times. The New Testament writers sometimes quoted it, and it may help us to understand something of the implications of various Greek expressions used by them. It also includes twelve books of the Old Testament Apocrypha which may give insight into ancient Hebrew thinking.

About the Authors

Roger Forster

Roger studied mathematics and theology at St John's College, Cambridge. After a period in the Royal Air Force, he worked as an itinerant evangelist before starting Ichthus Christian Fellowship, with his wife Faith, in 1974. Roger was one of the founders of March for Jesus, was on the board of the AD2000 Movement and the Council of the Evangelical Missionary Alliance for many years. He has been involved with the Evangelical Alliance since the early 1970s as a member of the Council, and has served on a number of EA committees.

Among his many responsibilities he has been Chairman of the Council for the UK Evangelical Alliance and honorary Vice President of Tearfund, and is honoured to be on the Council of Reference for Aglow International (Britain), and together with Faith is a patron of Springs Dance Company.

Roger and Faith have a son and two daughters: Christen, Juliet and Deborah.

Together Roger and Faith have written *Women and the Kingdom*, and his solo books include *Suffering and the Love of God: The Book of Job, Prayer: Living in the Breath of God, The Kingdom of Jesus, Trinity, Saving Faith, Fasting*, and *Saturday Night, Sunday Morning…*

Paul Marston

Paul's initial studies included philosophy and the history and philosophy of science and scientific methodology at London University's LSE, where his tutors included the philosophers of science Karl Popper, Imre Lakatos and Paul Feyerabend. He has a PhD and three Masters degrees: in theoretical statistics, in the history and philosophy of science, and in theology. He has lectured on courses at the Nazarene Theological College, and is currently a Senior Lecturer (now part time) in the University of Central Lancashire.

Paul and his wife Janice have a daughter Christel, and a son Justin.

His solo books include *The Biblical Family, God and the Family, Christians, Divorce and Remarriage, Understanding the Biblical Creation Passages, Women in Church Leadership and in Marriage*, and *Gay Christians and the Jesus Centred Church*.

Paul and Roger have co-authored a number of books including: *Yes But…, That's A Good Question, Reason and Faith, Christianity, Evidence and Truth*, and *Reason, Science and Faith*.

Introduction

In this book we explore what the Bible says about how God is working in human history. We look at the conflict between good and evil and at our role within God's plans and purposes, both as individuals and together as the Church. This is not a book of sermons on Christian living, nor a self-help guide – instead we hope that it will help you establish a framework for interpreting the Bible and understanding how your personal relationship with God fits into his bigger strategy of bringing in the Kingdom. We look at the history of God's plan not only in the Bible, but also at what this means for us today and into the future.

By developing this bigger picture of God's strategy in human history many questions that may otherwise seem obscure, come alive with fresh meaning:

o   If God is good, why do suffering and evil exist?

o   Is God in control of the future?

o   Do my prayers make a difference?

o   Why did God choose Israel? And is Israel still chosen?

o   What is God's purpose for the Church today?

By looking at these important topics in the context of God's strategy we see how they start to make sense to our Christian lives in the 21st Century.

We believe that theology should be 'holistic' – that is, it should give a complete and consistent explanation for all of Scripture as well as our own christian experience. We feel that ignoring or distorting particular verses or words in order to make the Bible fit our theology is not an acceptable approach. In *God's Strategy in Human History* we set out our theology, which we believe consistently and comprehensively describes all of God's dealings with mankind throughout the Bible and Church history, without having to compromise the word of God.

This is the 3rd edition of this book and since the last edition it has been thoroughly revised to make it easier to read and navigate. We have updated it to include new perspectives and up-to-date scholarship, as well as including new material to help complete the picture. We have also restructured the book by dividing it into two separate volumes. *Volume 1: God's Path to Victory* (the one you are reading now!) describes the main thrust of our thesis, and is purposefully compact, accessible, and easy to follow. This first volume can be read on its own, but we hope that many will want to go on to explore the ideas in more depth in volume 2.

The second volume of this book, *Reconsidering Key Biblical Ideas* looks in much greater depth and scholarship at some of the key concepts in God's strategy that have often been misunderstood in popular theology. It also contains an outline showing the historical sources for these misconceptions and how they have come into being.

Volume 1: God's Path to Victory

In the first part of Volume 1, *The Nature of the Conflict,* we set out the reality of the war between God and the forces of evil in rebellion against him, and look at the way in which God planned his strategy for Jesus the Messiah to rescue humanity. Then in the second part, we outline *The History of the Conflict* in Scripture: from the declaration of war in Genesis 3 through to the final battle when God will establish the New Heaven and New Earth in Revelation 21.

We look at what God's sovereignty means in this context and how it influences his actions in the world, and then use this as a starting point to explain how often-misunderstood terms like 'justification', 'predestination' and 'election' should be understood in the framework of God's future plans. We end with a look at what the Bible says about eternity and the ultimate destiny of the righteous and the unrighteous.

Volume 1 finishes with an easy reference guide to the key concepts and definitions involved in this book which are further expanded upon in *Volume 2: Reconsidering Key Biblical Ideas.* These topics include:

o   God's will, plans and sovereignty

o   Justification and righteousness

o   God's election and foreknowledge

o Works and faithfulness

o The hardening of Pharaoh's heart and unbelief

o God's will and man's freewill

The concepts in this book are simple and easy to grasp for all believers. However, some arguments require more complicated explanation, and if you are interested in studying these ideas in more depth, we recommend you read or refer to Volume 2. These studies support and reinforce the points we make in Volume 1, and can either be read alongside or individually to explore particular topics in more depth.

God's Strategy for you!

This book is academic in that it draws upon critical biblical scholarship, but we are aware that theology *is not*, and *should not be*, a purely academic subject – it is tremendously exciting to grasp a little of God's purposes in history. It enables us to see the whole movement of which we are a tiny part – the whole history into which our lives fit. We begin to discover how our day-to-day actions, sufferings and attitudes have repercussions for eternity, and start to realise the great future destiny God has in store for his children.

We hope you enjoy reading this new edition of the book and that it will inspire you to seek what God's strategy is in your life and how you can play your part to work together with him to help bring in the Kingdom!

Part 1

The Nature
of the Conflict

or 'what the Bible says about the
battle between Good and Evil'

1

Righteous Job – Human Battlefield

God is, of course, the reason why *everything* came to exist and continues to exist (Hebrews 1:3); he is author of all reality. The God of the Bible, however, is also clearly shown as one who *acts in special ways* in his world. He is not only *author* but *participant*, and to us this seems to be central to Christian faith. The biblical picture of a God who *acts in particular situations* is completely inconsistent both with a kind of deistic absentee landlord (who created the universe and then just left it to get on with things by itself), and with a God who determines *everything* which happens. The biblical God is a *personal God*, a person in whose image we are made. This is not of course in the sense of shape or physicality, but of emotion and volition. He has particular intentions and plans, and he acts to fulfil them.

The Bible also speaks of other spiritual forces at work, like angels, demons and the devil. We are well aware that some believers take this as purely figurative personification, but in our view this is not the most natural way to interpret either Scripture or our own experience. It may be unhealthy to become over-preoccupied with this, but as Christians we may need to be more aware of spiritual forces in the heavenlies.

Many things which are hinted at in the Old Testament become clear in the New, and before we look at what is happening in the book of Job we need to explore some ideas in the New Testament. Spiritual warfare is the subject of Ephesians 6, and we will use this well-known passage to introduce this and the following two chapters of the book. To begin with, let's look at the last part of Ephesians 6:11:

> Put on the whole armour of God that you may be able to stand against the wiles of the devil.

Who is the Devil?

So who exactly is *the* devil? The word 'devil' (*diabolos*) is a Greek word meaning a slanderer or accuser. In 1 Timothy 3:11 and 2 Timothy 3:3 the word is used of human slanderers, and Jesus says in John 6:70 that Judas is 'a devil' (even though Jesus had chosen him in the same way as the other eleven disciples and he shared in their early ministry).

But the New Testament also refers to '*the* devil', as a *spiritual* force and person who is behind much of evil. Jesus himself was tempted by *the* devil. In two of the temptations the devil sought to bring doubt into Jesus' mind as to whether he really was the Son of God – doubt of the truth of God's words when the Spirit descended on Jesus at his recent baptism. This is reminiscent of the serpent's words in Eden: 'Has God really said…?' (Genesis 3:1). The serpent in Genesis 3 is not meant to be seen as a physical snake, rather the serpent is a spiritual entity, which is how Jesus identifies him:

> You are of your father the devil, and the desires of your father you want to do. He was a murderer from the beginning, and does not stand in the truth, because there is no truth in him. When he speaks a lie, he speaks from his own resources, for he is a liar and the father of it. (John 8:44)

In his teaching, Jesus constantly used symbolic language to explain spiritual things – for example being 'born again', 'living water' and giving 'his body' to eat. Even his friends often took him *literally* when he was speaking symbolically, a mistake repeated by Christians in the modern 'literalist' movements (as Paul Marston explores in *Understanding the Biblical Creation Passages*). The devil/Satan is sometimes portrayed in Scripture as a 'seven headed dragon' or a 'serpent', but this is no more literal than Jesus being an actual 'lamb', or the Church a 'bride'.

We may remember that in Genesis God said to the serpent:

> And I will put enmity between you and the woman, and between your seed and her Seed; he shall bruise your head, and you shall bruise his heel. (Genesis 3:15)

Jesus sees the serpent as a spiritual force/person, and his 'seed' or offspring as the human opponents of truth who choose to follow the urgings of the devil.

As such Jesus calls his human opponents the 'seed' or 'brood' of the serpent:

> Brood of vipers! How can you, being evil, speak good things? For out of the abundance of the heart the mouth speaks. (Matthew 12:34)

God's prophecy in Genesis 3:15 was not about literal snakes, but about the spiritual influence of the devil who would finally be crushed by Jesus the Messiah – the 'seed' of the woman – on the cross. As John puts it:

> He who sins is of the devil, for the devil has sinned from the beginning. For this purpose the Son of God was manifested, that He might destroy the works of the devil. (1 John 3:8)

Judas chose to allow the devil to put it into his heart to betray Jesus (John 13:2). People can allow themselves to be taken captive by the devil to do his will (2 Timothy 2:26). However, James warns us against blaming other agents when we sin: 'each one is tempted when he is drawn away by his own desires and enticed' (James 1:14). We have a way to resist the devil, not by gritting our teeth and making an effort in our own flesh, but by turning to God:

> Therefore *submit to God*. Resist the devil and he will flee from you. Draw near to God and he will draw near to you. (James 4:7-8)

God is always faithful, he will always draw near to us and drive away the devil and his lies if we turn to him day by day.

The word *diabolos* is Greek, and there is no exact Old Testament Hebrew equivalent. The nearest Hebrew word is *satan,* meaning 'opponent' or 'adversary', and Jesus uses this word in its general sense when he rebukes Peter in Mark 8:33 (and Matthew 16:23) for opposing God. Often however, 'Satan' seems to mean the devil. Jesus addresses the devil during the temptations by the Hebrew *Satan* (Matthew 4:10). Then, in the book of Revelation, we read:

> He laid hold of the dragon, that serpent of old, who is the Devil and Satan, and bound him for a thousand years; and he cast him into the bottomless pit, and shut him up, and set a seal on him, so that he should deceive the nations no more till the thousand years were finished. (Revelation 20:2-3)

Again, Satan/the devil is not *literally* a seven headed dragon, nor a serpent, but this is the symbolism used from Genesis to Revelation.

We began this chapter with the words in Ephesians – 'Put on the whole armour of God that you may be able to stand against the wiles of the devil.' There is a warfare between God and the spiritual forces of Satan (the opponent)/ the devil (the accuser). The book of Revelation is full of this, for example:

> And war broke out in heaven: Michael and his angels fought with the dragon; and the dragon and his angels fought. (Revelation 12:7)

Words and ideas are part of this spiritual warfare. Satan accuses God to mankind (Genesis 3:5) and accuses mankind to God (Job 1:11). Although Satan is mentioned very little in the Old Testament, this role of being an adversary is seen very clearly in the book of Job. This is further explored in Roger Forster's book *Suffering and the Love of God*.

Job is Afflicted

The time setting of the book of Job is unclear. David Clines says:

> Most scholars would date the composition of the book of Job to some point between the seventh and second centuries BCE, with the probability that a prose folktale of a pious sufferer existed long before the largely poetic book itself was written… the narrator is clearly depicting an archaic age and not writing of his own time. (*Job 1-20*, p lvii)

In all probability Job lived in the age of the patriarchs, and the Jewish narrator who wrote up the story assumed that *Elohim* (a word coming from the original Canaanite word for God, *El)* was to be identified with *Yahweh,* their covenant God. This seems likely because, like Abraham, Job's wealth is in his flocks, and although he sacrifices (1:5) there is no mention of a priest as there should be if he were Jewish. None of the participants mention any Jewish Law or covenant, dietary laws or anything specifically Jewish. In Job 1:1, Job is introduced as one who fears *Elohim*, and the comforters refer to God by this name – but the narrator has Job use the covenant name *Yahweh* in 1:21 perhaps to identify his faith as genuinely in the Jewish One God, and it is *Yahweh* who answers Job out of the whirlwind in 38:1. All this indicates that the story was set down by Jewish people, but the setting of the account is likely in the era contemporary to Abraham.

The book starts with a setting in which the 'sons of God', 'came and presented themselves' before *Yahweh*. John Hartley explains:

> On this occasion the Satan also came among them. Here the Hebrew word *haśśāṭān* has the [definite] article so it functions as a title rather than as a personal name. (*The Book of Job*, p 71)

Here and in Zechariah 3:1 it is 'the Satan', but the Septuagint (LXX) translates it as *diabolos*, and we can clearly identify him with 'Satan' or 'the devil' in the Gospels. (The Septuagint is the Greek translation of the Old Testament, started in the 3rd century BC and completed by 132 BC, which was in common use by Greek-speaking Jews at the time of Christ and Paul. While it is sometimes quoted by the Gospels and Paul, it is not considered to be 'inspired' but can give indications of how early Jewish scholars understood the Hebrew Old Testament, and also how certain New Testament Greek words were understood at that time.) Hartley explains that scholars differ as to whether *the Satan* was one of the 'sons of God', though traditionally he has been seen as such (and Clines seems to agree).

The Hebrew root for *satan* is a word for a kind of prosecuting lawyer, though how far he was acting as God's agent is disputed. Some commentators have suggested that *Satan* is a direct agent of God, and is an opponent of *Job* rather than of God. However, this does not do justice to Satan's sneering attitude to God, to the LXX rendering of *satan* as *diabolos* as noted above, or to Jesus' identification of Satan/the devil as opposing God's will.

God's Fatherly Pride In Job's Righteousness

The drama begins with *Yahweh* boasting about the uprightness of his servant:

> Then the Lord said to Satan, 'Have you considered my servant Job, that there is none like him on the earth, a blameless and upright man, one who fears God and shuns evil?' (Job 1:8)

Although God says Job is 'blameless', he is *not* saying that Job is ethically perfect or sinless. Indeed we see that Job wasn't perfect, as he refers to his own sin, transgression and iniquity in 14:16-17. But Job's life of faith and consequent uprightness pleases God, who shows a fatherly pride in his servant.

The question of whether someone can be 'upright', or 'righteous', before God is an interesting and important one.

Paul famously wrote in Romans 3:10 'There is none righteous not even one'. Some Christians take this literally, and, assuming that 'righteous' means sinless, claim that only Christ is righteous. But this is taking the verse out of context. Paul is using hyperbole and neither he nor Psalm 14 which he is quoting are saying that no-one can be called 'righteous'. Psalm 14 is about those who do not really believe in their hearts there is a God, and in their ignorance oppress God's people (v4), and the generation of the 'righteous' (v5), and it is of these corrupt crypto-atheists and 'workers of iniquity' that none is righteous. In fact, right throughout the Psalms a contrast is made of the 'righteous' and 'sinners' (see also on this the *Dictionary of Old Testament Theology and Exegesis*, Ed Van Gemeren, vol 3 p 1202)

So Who are 'The 'Righteous' and 'Sinners'?

In Scripture, 'righteous' really means someone in rightstanding with God, and a 'sinner' is someone who is in rebellion against God and in a sinful lifestyle. Not just in the Psalms but throughout Scripture 'sinners' are consistently contrasted with 'the righteous'. This is true both for the Hebrew and the Greek equivalent words. So modern preachers who may stand up in church and say: 'Everyone here is a sinner in the sight of God', are not using the term in the usual biblical sense. In biblical terms the Christians in the audience are 'righteous' and are not 'sinners'.

In biblical terms a 'righteous' person is not someone who is sinless. We have all sinned (Romans 3:23), and if we say we have not then we have no truth in us (1 John 1:10).

> Righteousness in the Old Testament is not a matter of actions conforming to a given set of absolute legal standards, but of behaviour which is in keeping with the two-way relationship between God and man. (*Dictionary of New Testament Theology*, Ed Colin Brown, vol 3, p 355)

Noah (who was certainly not sinless) was 'righteous' (Genesis 6:9). Abraham was looking for ten righteous men in Sodom (Genesis 18). In the New Testament Lot is referred to as 'righteous' (2 Peter 2:2-9) and is contrasted with 'the wicked'. The Lord 'will bless the righteous' (Psalm 5:12), and 'is with the generation of the righteous' (Psalm 14:5). Psalm 32:11 and 33:1 tell the righteous to rejoice in the Lord.

Jesus uses the Greek word 'righteous' (*dikaios*) in exactly the same way (for example Matthew 10:41, 23:35, 25:37). In Luke 6:32 he contrasts his disciples with 'sinners', and in Matthew 9:10 'sinner' does not mean everyone but specifically those leading a godless lifestyle. In Matthew 23:28 Jesus speaks of Pharisees who *outwardly appear* righteous to men, but in the same passage speaks of Old Testament prophets who *really were* righteous. Pharisaic 'righteousness', as Paul also later noted, was based on the wrong things – ritual and ceremony. To Jesus though, the righteous are those whose lives show the spontaneous acts of love to others that indicate real relationship with God (Matthew 25:46). It is their lifestyle not merely their beliefs that shows them to be righteous.

Universally in both Old and New Testaments it is assumed that a 'righteous' person behaves in a particular way – it is not about keeping ceremonial 'works of the Law', but spontaneous love and compassion (see Matthew 25). John is quite adamant that Jesus is the righteous one, but:

> ... let no one deceive you. He who practices righteousness is righteous, just as he is righteous. (1 John 3:7 – also 2:29)

John would clearly have rejected the idea of some Reformation theologians that our only righteousness in God's sight is Jesus' sinlessness 'imputed to us'. John insists that we have all sinned, and that sometimes still as Christians we sin and need to repent and confess to be forgiven and cleansed through the sacrifice of Jesus (1 John 1:9). But 1 John 3:9 says:

> Whoever has been born of God does not sin.

A truly born again Christian does not lead a sinful lifestyle. In biblical terms he or she is not a 'sinner' or 'wicked'.

The only possible place where believers may be called 'sinners' is in James 4:8. Here, though, James is talking to those who by their lifestyle are making themselves 'enemies of God' who are 'double minded'. These are surely in contrast to the 'righteous' man of 5:16 whose prayers are effective, and James has already said that 'faith' without a loving lifestyle is dead and cannot save them (2:14). To call these people 'sinners' is saying much the same thing – their 'belief' is nominal and cannot save them.

In general, then, in Scripture the 'righteous' are contrasted with 'sinners' or 'the wicked'.

Job is Righteous

So going back to Job, although he admits to sin (14:16) he insists that he is not 'wicked':

> You know that I am not wicked,… If I am wicked, woe to me;
> Even if I am righteous, I cannot lift up my head. (Job 10:7,15)

The righteousness of Job is implied by God, and affirmed in Ezekiel 14:14,20. However, the comforters, as we shall see, did not believe that Job *was* righteous, but even if he were, Eliphaz says in 22:2-3:

> Can a man be profitable to God, though he who is wise may be profitable to himself? Is it any pleasure to the Almighty that you are righteous? Or is it gain to him that you make your ways blameless?

We have heard preachers (rather like Eliphaz) say things like 'Nothing we can do will be pleasing to God', whereas in fact Paul says:

> And we pray this in order that you may live a life worthy of the Lord and may please him in every way: bearing fruit in every good work, growing in the knowledge of God. (Colossians 1:10, NIV, see also 2 Corinthians 5:9)

Why pray for people to live lives worthy of and pleasing to God if it is impossible? Even before Pentecost, Job was evidently living a life 'fully pleasing to God' and the Lord, in a sense, staked his reputation on him.

Satan's Accusation and Job's Suffering

Then we get the key background to the book of Job – Satan's fundamental accusation is that people fear God solely because he has shown them some special favour:

> Does Job fear God for nothing? Have you not made a hedge around him, around his household, and around all that he has on every side? (Job 1:9-10)

Satan is saying that God's kingdom is based on expediency, and that just as some people worship Satan to gain power and favour, so others worship God because he is more powerful. God takes up this challenge of Satan, and a battle is declared, with the battleground being Job's heart, mind and being.

Job however was unaware of the spiritual backdrop to Job 1–2, so most of the book hardly mentions Satan, while Job struggles to maintain his faith in the face of what are to him incomprehensible circumstances.

The most obvious temptation for Job is the temptation to turn away from God and embrace godlessness – to 'renounce God and die' (2:9). Job did not do this, and so Satan's prediction was confounded. However, Satan still has a more subtle line of attack: how will Job stand up against his friends appealing to him from seemingly orthodox traditions (Job 8:8,9; 15:10; 20:4)? Surely Job has heard that a person suffers only because of his or her own unfaithfulness (Job 4:7,8; 8:8-20; 20:4, etc)? The fundamental view of the comforters is that only 'sinners' or 'the wicked' suffer, not the righteous, so Job must have led a sinful lifestyle in some way. When young Elihu sees that Job is 'righteous in his own eyes' (Job 32:1) he insists:

> [God] does not withdraw his eyes from the righteous; but they are on the throne with kings, for he has seated them forever, and they are exalted. (Job 36:7)

Another fundamental assumption in all the speeches of Job's three comforters and young Elihu is that it is *God* who binds up, who smites and heals (5:18), and who enters into judgment (22:4-5), and even then he is punishing wicked Job less than he deserves (11:6). They fail to understand that Job is not suffering because of his own sin, but because in the conflict Satan is allowed to afflict one of God's blameless and upright servants. The comforters and young Elihu remain convinced that it is *God* who is afflicting Job, and that he is doing so because of Job's sin (Job 8:4-6; 11:5,14; 15:5; 25:4; 28:42; 34:7-11,37). 'God is so holy', they say, 'that he does not even trust the angels' (4:18; 15:15), whereas 'man is abominable and corrupt' (4:17; 15:16), 'a mere worm' (25:6). 'God is so high that a man's righteousness can never bring pleasure to him' (22:3).

Notice how misled Eliphaz, Bildad, Zophar and Elihu were when they imagined themselves to be proclaiming God's truth! They believed that God was too exalted for Job's righteousness to mean anything to him.

The Cause of Job's Suffering

Some commentators argue that although the hardships Job endured were not punishment for his sin, God allowed them, or even brought them on him either as a form of chastening, or for his own spiritual development. Eliphaz actually suggests this:

> Behold, happy is the man whom God corrects; therefore do not despise the chastening of the Almighty (Job 5:17)

The Hebrew word translated here as 'chastening' means 'discipline', 'instruction' or 'correction', and appears to be something that God initiates to halt his people's involvement with sin. But note carefully what God says about Job:

> Have you considered my servant Job, that there is none like him on the earth, a blameless and upright man, one who fears God and shuns evil? And still he holds fast to his integrity, although you incited me against him, to destroy him *without cause*. (Job 2:3)

God's motive for allowing Job's misfortunes was not chastening, nor to 'teach Job something', the kind of suggestion Greg Boyd rightly criticizes in his book *Is God to Blame*. Of course we *can* learn things from suffering, and Job did come out with an enhanced spiritual experience because of his reactions. But there is no indication that anything in Job's lifestyle was displeasing to God and needed 'chastening', nor that this was God's motive in allowing it. It was not God but Satan who instigated and effected Job's misfortunes. It was Satan who first suggested that Job should suffer physically and materially.

It is important to note that although Satan suggested that God should 'put forth his hand' against Job there is no indication that God did so. God says: 'You incited me against him to destroy him', but there is nothing that says he complied with the request. Rather, God said: 'He is in your hand, but spare his life', and it was Satan who destroyed Job's possessions and health. It is enlightening for us to see that God was in no sense, either directly or via Satan, the *cause* of Job's afflictions. In fact James explicitly says that God does not use evil things to tempt or test anyone (James 1:13). God *allowed* Satan's actions, but this is another matter.

But couldn't God have stopped Job's suffering? We must be clear exactly what we mean if we say that God 'could have stopped' it. We may indeed accept that he had the sheer power to stop or even destroy Satan. The problem is that in this case, even as Satan sank under God's wrath and destruction, he would have gone with a sneer on his lips as though to say, 'I told you so'. Such a solution would have left Satan's accusation that God's kingdom was based (like his own) on force and expediency unrefuted forever. It was not lack of power that prevented God from crushing Satan – it was a matter of principle. It is, perhaps, comparable to the moral restraint that makes it impossible for God to lie (Hebrews 6:18). Satan's accusations must be answered, but they cannot be truly answered by a force that simply crushes the accuser. They can only be fully answered by the method God adopts – by allowing Satan to remove Job's privileges. God must show that the servant in whom he trusts loves God for who he is and not for what he can get out of him.

God may have various reasons for allowing suffering in different cases, but in this particular instance it seems that he allowed Job to be afflicted in order to prove to Satan (and everyone else) that someone could love God without any reward, and even in the midst of misunderstanding about him. Implicit in this is the Hebrew notion that Job had a choice in how to react to the calamities in his life. The Lord's fatherly boast in his servant Job would hardly have any point if Job was faithful only because God was secretly forcing him to be. Job is dependent, Job recognizes his need for a redeemer, but Job also has real responsibility and choice.

Job's Response to Suffering

God had confidence in Job, but did God know for certain how Job would react? All evangelical Christians accept that God is 'omniscient' – he knows everything that can be known – but does this include all the details of the future? There are three main theological views on omniscience:

1) *The Outside-of-Time God*: God gave humans genuine freewill, but as he is 'outside time' he knows all the future, without determining it

2) *The Inside-of-Time God*: God knows everything that can be known, and knows the general pattern of the future because he has decided how he will act, but does not know how each individual will exercise freewill in moral choices

3) *The All-Determining God*: God determines everything that happens and human freewill is an illusion, so God knows the future because he has decided every detail of it

As we will look at in chapter 15, the Hebrew mindset was less obsessed with abstract theories of time than the Greek philosophies which became more prevalent in Church history. View 1) started with the 1st century Philo, a devout Jewish philosopher who was also a follower of the Greek philosopher Plato. This Greek idea was later adopted by Christians like Boethius (480-524 AD). The Early Church believed in human freewill and so their view would have been somewhere between views 1) and 2), but it is hard to determine exactly what they thought about whether God was inside or outside of time, or indeed if this was a relevant concept. In the case of view 3), the philosophical genius of Augustine is shown in his sophisticated discussion of time, but his rejection of human freewill was a clear departure from all earlier Christian leaders (as we show in chapter 7 of *Volume 2: Reconsidering Key Biblical Ideas,* see also chapter 16 of this volume).

David Clines in his two-volume commentary on Job sees the text of Job as being in line with the second view of God being inside time, which is increasingly being espoused as more biblical by many theologians today:

> God can agree to the proposal to 'smite' all that is Job's only because he too, like everyone else, does not know what the outcome will be. The *Yahweh* of this tale is not the absolutely omniscient God of later systematic or speculative theology. He is wise beyond human comprehension… But not even Yahweh knows what has not yet happened… (*Job 1-20*, p 28-29)

We tend to agree with Clines on this, although the 'outside time' view of God's omniscience is also possible. But we would also go on to say that part of God's omniscience means that he knows all the possible outcomes that could occur, and what he will do in each case. Nothing takes God by surprise. That is why we as his children can have full faith and confidence in him. Clines goes on to say that:

> [God has] confidence in Job, but not a confidence which would enable him to use Job as an object lesson to refute the Satan's aspersions… The Satan has the right to ask the question, and *Yahweh* is in the right in having the problem solved. (p 28-9)

Clines comments that if *Yahweh* really did know for certain how Job would react, then:

> Job's suffering serves only to prove God right in the eyes of one of his subordinates. Affirm that *Yahweh* knows that Job will not waver and you cannot explain why *Yahweh* takes the slightest notice of Satan's questions or why he does not dismiss them out of hand from superior knowledge. (p 29)

This is a version of an 'inside time' view of God, a view today sometimes referred to as 'Openness Theology'. God's omniscience is to know all that there is to be known, but this doesn't include aspects of the future concerning moral choices of individuals – those individuals have not made those decisions yet, and there may also be effects of the moral choices of others!

Our own view, which could be called 'Relational Theology' has similarities to this, though we would want to say that on issues in which there is no moral choice involved God may well overrule human decisions. The key is that relationship is a fundamental property of God himself in the Trinity, and his desire to have relationship with humans made in his image means that he interacts with them according to their own moral choices. This is what God says in Jeremiah 18, as we will explore in chapter 10.

The God of Job is a personal God with emotions and reactions, as shown throughout the Bible. He is not the immutable, impassive God of abstract theology adopted later by many christian traditions. God had confidence in Job as he had confidence in Abraham, but it was only after Abraham actually showed that he really *did* trust God enough to sacrifice Isaac that God said:

> *Now I know* that you fear God, since you have not withheld your son, your only son, from me. (Genesis 22:12)

So God allows Job to be tested...

Was God's confidence in Job vindicated? If we read through the book we find that Job, like his friends, mistakenly ascribed his misfortune to God. Yet Job remained certain of his own righteousness and innocence, and cried out for an opportunity to bring his case for trial. He seemed to have felt that something somewhere had gone wrong – there had been an anomaly in the justice of the universe. We see therefore that Job did not understand the situation he was in. Satan had ruined Job's fortunes and, through the comforters, had multiplied Job's doubt and confusion. Would Job, as Satan had predicted, renounce God to his face?

The comforters are single-minded – their theology is simple, linear and clear. Job is all over the place, in each of his speeches moving, searching, confused, as indeed many of us might be when faced with such calamity in our lives. Yet Job, albeit without much understanding, vindicated his Lord's trust. He said: 'though he slay me, yet will I trust him. Even so, I will defend my own ways before him'. Job would serve God come what may. God showed through Job that his Kingdom is not based on the obedience of expediency or self-interest, but the obedience of love.

We have no problem with God commending Job's attitudes in spite of his having a mistaken belief that God (not Satan) was the direct cause of his affliction. That Job was 'righteous' did not mean that he made no mistakes or had no misunderstandings. The point is for us (like Job) to maintain faith *even when* we do not understand what is going on and struggle to make sense of it. It was Job's ignorance of the underlying drama which made his words all the more praiseworthy.

God vs the 'Comforters'

To highlight the contrast between what God says about Job, and what the comforters and young Elihu say, we have set them out side by side:

a) God has confidence in his servant

God says:

> Have you considered my servant Job?... for there is none like him in the earth. (1:8; 2:3)

But the comforters say:

> He puts no trust in his servants. (Eliphaz, 4:18)

> Can a man be profitable to God... Is it any pleasure to the Almighty that you are righteous? Or is it gain to him that you make your ways blameless? (Eliphaz, 22:2-3)

> If you are righteous, what do you give him? Or what does he receive from your hand? (Elihu, 35:7)

b) Job is perfect (ie complete) and upright (righteous)

God says Job is:

> A blameless and upright man. (Job 1:8; 2:3)

But the comforters say:

> If you were pure and upright, surely now he would awake for you, and prosper your rightful dwelling place. (Bildad, 8:6)

> Behold God will not cast away the blameless. (Bildad, 8:20)

> Remember now, whoever perished being innocent? Or where were

the upright ever cut off? (Eliphaz, 4:7)

And I have heard the sound of your words, saying, 'I am pure, without transgression; I am innocent, and there is no iniquity in me … Look, in this you are not righteous. (Elihu, 33:5-12)

What man is like Job, who drinks scorn like water, who goes in company with the workers of iniquity, and walks with wicked men? (Elihu, 34:7)

How then can man be righteous before God? Or how can he be pure who is born of a woman? (Bildad, 25:4)

What is man, that he could be pure? And he who is born of a woman, that he could be righteous? (Eliphaz, 15:14)

For you have said, 'My doctrine is pure, and I am clean in your eyes.' But oh, that God would speak … Know therefore that God exacts from you less than your iniquity deserves. (Zophar, 11:4-6)

c) Job's attitudes to God and to evil are right

God says Job is:

One who fears God and shuns evil. (1:8;2:3)

But the comforters say:

Yes, you cast off fear, and restrain prayer before God. (Eliphaz, 15:4)

Is it because of your fear of him that he corrects you, and enters into judgment with you? Is not your wickedness great, and your iniquity without end? (Eliphaz, 22:4-5)

d) The Innocent do Suffer 'Without Cause'

God says:

And still he holds fast to his integrity, although you [Satan] incited me against him, to destroy him without cause. (2:3)

But the comforters say:

If you were pure and upright, surely now he would awake for you, and prosper your rightful dwelling place. (Bildad, 8:6)

Know therefore that God exacts from you less than your iniquity deserves. (Zophar, 11:6)

Remember now, who ever perished being innocent? ... Those who plough iniquity, and sow trouble reap the same. By the blast of God they perish. (Eliphaz, 4:7-9)

For Job has said, 'I am righteous... Should I lie concerning my right? My wound is incurable, though I am without transgression'. What man is like Job, who drinks scorn like water ... For he has said, 'It profits a man nothing that he should delight in God'. Therefore listen to me, you men of understanding: far be it from God to do wickedness... For he repays man according to his work, And makes man to find a reward according to his way. (Elihu, 34:5-11)

e) Job's Affliction is Caused by Satan and not by God

The truth is:

So Satan went out from the presence of the LORD, and struck Job with painful boils from the sole of his foot to the crown of his head. (Job 2:7)

But the comforters say:

Therefore do not despise the chastening of the Almighty. For he bruises, but he binds up; he wounds, but his hands make whole. (Eliphaz, 5:17-8)

Know therefore that God exacts from you less than your iniquity deserves. (Zophar, 11:6)

Is it because of your fear of him that he corrects you, and enters into judgment with you? (Eliphaz, 22:4)

God is mighty, but despises no one... He does not preserve the life of the wicked, but gives justice to the oppressed. (Elihu, 36:5-6)

Indeed he would have brought you out of dire distress, into a broad place where there is no restraint; and what is set on your table would be full of richness. But you are filled with the judgment due the wicked. (Elihu, 36:16-17)

f) Job's Words are Acceptable to God

God says:

My wrath is aroused against you (Eliphaz) and your two friends, for you have not spoken of me what is right, as my servant Job has. (42:7)

But the comforters say:

How long will you speak these things, and the words of your mouth be like a strong wind? (Bildad, 8:2)

Should not the multitude of words be answered? And should a man full of talk be vindicated? (Zophar, 11:2)

For your iniquity teaches your mouth, and you choose the tongue of the crafty. (Eliphaz, 15:5)

How long till you put an end to words? (Bildad, 18:2)

And I have heard the sound of your words, saying, 'I am pure, without transgression...' In this you are not righteous. (Elihu, 33:8,12)

Job speaks without knowledge, his words are without wisdom. Oh, that Job were tried to the utmost, because his answers are like those of wicked men! For he adds rebellion to his sin; he claps his hands among us, and multiplies his words against God. (Elihu, 34:35-37)

Therefore Job opens his mouth in vain; he multiplies words without knowledge. (Elihu, 35:16)

John Hartley comments:

Although Job has lacked insight, *Yahweh* does not say that Job has sinned. He never rebukes Job for swearing his avowal of innocence. But he contends that Job's limited understanding hinders him from disputing wisely with his Creator about his own fate. (*The Book of Job*, p 491)

David Clines comments:

The purpose of God's parade of unknown and unknowable features of the natural world can hardly be to browbeat Job with dazzling displays of his power and intelligence – for Job has not for a minute doubted that God was wise and strong... Rather God invites Job to reconsider the mystery and complexity – and often the sheer unfathomableness – of the world that God has created. (*Job*, vol 1, p xlv)

Our Attitudes to Suffering

What lessons can we draw from the story of Job? Clearly the hardships Job endured are not a punishment for his sin, and there is no indication that God brought them on him or even allowed them to come on him for his own spiritual development.

Chastening?

When we suffer, some people may suggest (like Job's comforters) that our suffering is because God is 'chastening' us. While it is clear from the text that this is not true in Job's case, could it be true for us? And what should we make of Hebrews 12:5-11 concerning 'the chastening of the LORD'?

The Greek word translated in Hebrews 12 as 'chastening' is *paedia* and is rendered in Ephesians 6:4 as 'nurture' (KJV), 'discipline' (ESV), 'training' (NIV) and in 2 Timothy 3:16 as 'training' or 'instruction', and is probably best translated as 'child training'.

So how does God train his children? Sometimes we suffer because of our sin – there is grief and pain (physical, mental and spiritual) caused by the consequences of our sin and we can lose our sense of blessing (Galatians 4:15). God can use this grief and pain and our consciences to give us 'instruction in righteousness' to help us to lay aside 'the sin that so easily ensnares' and cleanse our conscience (2 Timothy 3:16; Hebrews 12:1,11; 10:22). God nurtures and disciplines us as our loving Father, so that 'we may be partakers of his holiness' (Hebrews 12:10) – he does not seek to destroy our lives and families like Satan did to Job.

So when we suffer we should examine our hearts and ask the LORD if we are suffering because of our own sin – if we come to the conclusion we are not, then we are likely suffering in the battle against Satan, just as Job did. There can be a sense in which we 'glory in tribulations, knowing that tribulation produces perseverance; and perseverance, character; and character, hope' (Romans 5:3-4). But this does not mean that the tribulation has been brought on us because 'God needs to teach us something', as though a good human father would apparently randomly cause suffering in his child to 'teach him something' without even telling him what it was. Rather, we can choose to view tribulation positively as an opportunity to develop character and reliance on God.

Working Together with God

Job's comforters seem to imagine that God is determining everything that happens in the world, foreshadowing the later theology introduced by Augustine in the 5th century. If they were right in this, then it would be logical to expect suffering always to be either for pure punishment or for punitive chastisement. If everything happened as God willed, and if he is just, then the innocent could never suffer. 'Who ever perished being innocent?' asked Eliphaz, and based on his own presuppositions it would be difficult to disagree with him – Job must be guilty. But in fact there is a battle involved, and so it may often happen that one of God's perfect and upright servants suffers. Like Job we too may suffer even though we are living a life pleasing to God and in continuing close relationship with him. It was not God but Satan who instigated Job's sufferings. Nevertheless, God could *use* Job's sufferings to bring him into a deeper relationship with himself.

Paul's famous 'thorn in the flesh' in 2 Corinthians 12:7 also came from Satan and Paul does not suggest that God instigated it, though God allowed it to continue to encourage Paul's reliance on him rather than trusting in his own abilities.

Romans 8:28 is an important verse to help us understand that when suffering arises we should not just say 'Everything happens for a reason – God knows what he's doing' or 'It's all part of God's bigger picture'. Instead we can pray 'God, show me how you want me to work together with you to bring good from *these* circumstances'. However, different Bible translations have radically different interpretations of this verse, and some obscure its meaning:

> NKJV: All things work together for good to those who love God, to those who are the called according to his purpose. (KJV is similar)

> ESV: And we know that for those who love God all things work together for good.

> RSV: In everything God works for good with those who love him, who are called according to his purpose.

> NASB: God causes all things to work together for good to those who love God, to those who are the called according to his purpose.

> NIV: In all things God works for the good of those who love him, who have been called according to his purpose.

NIV Margin: In all things God works together with those who love him to bring about what is good.

NEB: In everything, as we know, [the Spirit] cooperates for good with those who love God.

These interpretations broadly fall into two camps: those who think that 'all things working together' means that God is behind the scenes of all things that happen (even suffering) and those who see God's work as breaking in to bring good, even out of bad situations.

The first issue is whether it is 'things' or 'God' who 'works'? There is nothing anywhere else in Scripture to indicate 'things' somehow work together, but we do clearly find the idea of God at work in his world and working together with his people. The Early Church understood that it was a personal God, rather than abstract 'things' at work in this verse, and some important early manuscripts contain an extra nominative 'God' (*ho theos*) to put this beyond doubt (which we can see in the RSV, NASB and NIV translations). The KJV/NKJV and ESV renderings are therefore misleading.

This extra *ho theos* also makes the NEB rendering attractive, because the strong trinitarian understanding of the Early Church would make working with the Spirit the same as working with God – and working together with the Spirit in prayer was the topic in Romans 8:26.

One key term in the verse is 'work *together*' – *sunergei* (*ergei*, work + *sun*, together). The NIV main rendering seems inadequate because it completely leaves out the word 'together'.

So we are left with this key issue: is God 'causing all things to work together' exclusively for the good of those who love him (NASB) or it is that he is working in all things, together with those who love him, for good in general (RSV and NIV Margin)? This is not a trivial difference as it affects our view both of God and of our own role in his plans.

The word *energia* is the word from which we get 'energy', but it does not mean 'cause' as it is translated in the NASB. Rather, the picture is of God 'energising'. Indeed, in Ephesians we find that God is *energising* in things (1:11). God *energises* in us (3:20), but we also read that Satan *energises* in the children of disobedience (2:2). We also find that the prayer of a person in right-standing with God is an effective *energising* power (James 5:16). The idea of Christians working together with God to *energize* for good is therefore an obvious one.

Moreover, would the God who loved the world and sent Jesus, who told us to love our enemies and do good to those who treat us badly, want to do good *only* to those who love him at present? While it is undeniable that:

> ... the eyes of the LORD are on the righteous, and his ears are open to their prayers; but the face of the LORD is against those who do evil. (1 Peter 3:12)

... surely God still wants to bring good even to those who do not love him, because he would rather they turn and repent.

The NASB not only gives a misleading picture of God, but it encourages Christians simply to sit back and feel smug – 'Don't worry, God is working all things for your good, you don't need to do anything!' Actually the verse is a call to action, for those 'called according to his purpose' are called to be the body of Christ seeking to work with God to bring good into the world.

What makes the NIV margin (or the RSV) the most sensible rendering is that the idea of Christians as God's fellow energisers, or co-workers, appears elsewhere. In Mark 16:20 we find that as the disciples preached, the Lord 'worked together' with them. In 1 Corinthians 3:9 Paul says that 'we are God's fellow workers'. In 2 Corinthians 6:1 he again describes himself as 'working together' with God using the same term as in Romans 8:28.

Also significant is that the preceding two verses in Romans 8 speak precisely of such a co-working in prayerful intercession between Christians and the Holy Spirit. For God to be *energising* together with Christians in verse 28 is therefore a natural progression of ideas.

Sadly, the widely quoted mistranslations of Romans 8:28 can not only cause Christians to be apathetic, but also cause some to fall into doubt or despair: when tragedy or disaster strikes they have to try to convince themselves that 'things' are somehow working for their best good, or God's 'secret' will is causing things to happen to them for good. Indeed, things may *not* be working for their good, and Satan rather than God may be behind events. Nevertheless, what any Christian *can* be sure of is that, whatever disaster may strike and however bad the situation may be, God will be there, wanting to work together with that Christian and with other believers, to bring good into the situation.

Reacting to Suffering

Interestingly, the LORD restored Job's losses *when he prayed for his friends.* (Job 42:10). In the book of Job we do not see God causing all things to work for Job's good, but we do see Job begin to work together with God through prayer to bring good into the situation, and in doing so himself get blessed.

It is therefore important that we react rightly to situations of suffering or tragedy. Remember the incident when Jesus and his disciples saw the tragic sight of a man born blind:

> Now as Jesus passed by, he saw a man who was blind from birth. And his disciples asked him, saying, 'Rabbi, who sinned, this man or his parents, that he was born blind?' Jesus answered, 'Neither this man nor his parents sinned...' (John 9:1-2)

Sin is the ultimate cause of all suffering and sickness. The disciples tried to raise a theological question: 'Who sinned, this man or his parents, that he was born blind?' They were trying to unravel the causal chain ultimately linking suffering to sin. Jesus' reply indicates the futility of their question – the man's blindness was not simply a result of his own sins nor those of his parents. It was pointless for them to try to unravel its causes.

But what did Jesus mean by the next part, which the NKJV renders:

> Neither this man nor his parents sinned, but that the works of God should be revealed in him. I must work the works of him who sent me while it is day; the night is coming when no one can work. As long as I am in the world, I am the light of the world. (John 9:3-5)

New Testament Greek does not use punctuation marks like English does, so the punctuation in our translations can be up for interpretation, and we believe that most versions put the punctuation marks in the wrong place in translating Jesus' reply. The NIV is particularly misleading here, even adding words that are not there (shown in italics): 'but *this happened* so that the work of God might be displayed in his *life.*' This makes it sound as though God purposely ordained this man to be born and spend most of his life blind just so that God could show his power.

So how should it be translated? There are a number of Greek words for 'but', and the one used here, *alla,* is a 'strong disjunctive', that is, it is commonly used to begin a new idea, statement or even paragraph (eg John

7:27). Therefore, it is more likely that there is a full stop after 'sinned'. Some argue against this, saying that the word for 'that' (*hinna*) only ever indicates purpose, ie 'this happened *so that...*' However, this is simply not true in the *Koine* Greek dialect used by the Gospel writers, where *hinna* is often used as a general word for 'that', for example in Matthew 4:3.

So putting all this together, the passage most naturally reads:

> Jesus answered, 'Neither this man nor his parents sinned. But so that the works of God should be revealed in him, we must work the works of him who sent me while it is day; the night is coming when no one can work.'

Not only is this a natural and acceptable way to read the Greek text, it is consistent with the rest of Jesus' teaching and ministry about a loving God. God did not organise it so that the poor man was born blind just to show off by healing him. This does not sound like the God and Father of our Lord Jesus Christ.

Rather, Jesus is saying that the disciples are asking the wrong question. The real question should be not 'What caused the suffering?', but rather 'How can I cooperate with God to bring good into this situation?' Or in other words: 'How does God want to work together for good with those who love him?'

Christ did not see suffering as an intellectual challenge but as a need and opportunity to show the works of God in healing. Sometimes a person *may* be suffering because he or she has sinned, but more commonly the causes are too complex to unravel. Our primary task is to seek to cooperate with God in alleviating suffering, rather than endlessly trying to work out what the causes are – our reactions to suffering are important.

Like Job we too can suffer even though we are living a life pleasing to God and in continuing faith in him. God can heal miraculously, and 'the prayer of faith will save the sick, and the Lord will raise him up. And if he has committed sins, he will be forgiven' (James 5:15). Sometimes, however, we find that people of great faith and close walk with God (like Stephen Jeffries, David Watson, Kathryn Kulmann and John Wimber) have died painful deaths (also Smith Wigglesworth had years of pain from kidney stones and sciatica). We should not conclude that they have some secret sin in their lives any more than Job did. It would be wrong to emulate Job's comforters and try to add a guilt trip to Christians who are ill and suffering but who God has not healed miraculously in spite of the fervent prayer of themselves and others.

Our attitude when *we* suffer is equally important. If Job had 'cursed God and died', he would neither have received blessing himself nor been a channel of blessing to others. Job did not curse God, and neither was he content with pious platitudes. He was real with God in the situation, and therefore God commended his words. Job confessed his doubts, his confusion, and yet he knew he had not done the wickedness his friends imagined. God commended this, and then commanded Job to stand up and answer his questions (Job 40:7). In times of trouble we need to be open for God to reveal more of himself to us. Many people, like Job, have found a deeper experience of God through suffering – the Lord is ready to exploit any situation to bring in blessing.

We read further that:

> ... the Lord restored Job's losses when he prayed for his friends...
> (Job 42:10)

As Job turned from his own needs to those of others and began to work together with God to bring in blessing, he found that his bondage to despair began to lift. It often happens that as a person becomes a channel for blessing, his own burdens seem lightened. At the end of the book Job may have realised something of the conflict that had been going on, for through prayer he himself became a participant in the battle.

So Job was a battlefield in which God proved to Satan that his servants could love him for himself, and not merely for what he could give them. Perhaps, as a result of his experience, Job himself began to realise what was happening, and actually participate, through prayer, in the bringing in of blessing.

For more insight into Job's suffering and why God allows bad things to happen to good people, see Roger Forster's book *Suffering and the God of Love: The book of Job.*

2

Prayerful Daniel – Human Combatant

Job was a battlefield in the conflict between God and Satan, but he himself was largely unaware that this conflict was happening, even though his own reactions were a key part of it. At the end of the book, however, God says he is angry with the comforters and their false theology, and that they themselves must offer sacrifice, but also:

> My servant Job shall pray for you. For I will accept him, lest I deal with you according to your folly; because you have not spoken of me what is right, as my servant Job has. (Job 42:8)

Through intercessory prayer, Job becomes God's agent to bring in blessing and redemption. Ephesians 6 explains further how we can be more than unwitting individual battlefields. God wants us to understand that through prayer we form part of the larger spiritual battle, and actually fight in it:

> For we do not wrestle against flesh and blood, but against principalities, against powers, against the rulers of the darkness of this age, against spiritual hosts of wickedness in the heavenly places. (Ephesians 6:12)

From the book of Daniel, we get a vivid prophetic picture of the spiritual battle and how we can participate in the struggle against such 'spiritual hosts of wickedness'.

Daniel as Combatant

In Daniel chapter 1, Daniel is introduced as a young but disciplined exile captive, who together with his three friends was determined to practise what we now call a *Daniel fast* – eating only vegetables and drinking only water. His abstinence from wine as well as meat may indicate that this was not only to do with the prohibitions of Israel's laws, but was also a self-imposed distancing from the pressures and values of the surrounding world. Some such a distancing is necessary for a life of listening to God.

God's response to Daniel's fellowship and prayer was to give him and his friends knowledge, skill and wisdom (v17, see also Ezekiel 28:3). In particular, God gave Daniel revelation, which is one of the spiritual gifts we are encouraged to seek *now* in the Church Age (1 Corinthians 14:1,26). Self-discipline can lead to communion with God, which leads to the gifts necessary for engagement in spiritual warfare.

Revelations are part of God's way of bringing us into participation with his kingdom rule. Amos 3:7 tells us that 'the Lord God does nothing, unless he reveals his secret to his servants the prophets', and in the Bible pronouncement of a prophecy is often essential for its fulfilment. By proclaiming God's word, Daniel is working together with God in bringing in the Kingdom.

Through Daniel's life of prayer we can say with confidence that:

> He [God] reveals deep and secret things... I thank you and praise you, O God of my fathers; you have given me wisdom and might, and have now made known to me what we asked of you. (Daniel 2:22-23)

Daniel said this when he received revelation from God regarding Nebuchadnezzar's dream. While it was Daniel who personally received the answer, he magnanimously says it was because of his and his friends' prayers together (v17). This resulted in the preservation of Babylon's wise men, and it is possible that heirs of some of those wise men were the Magi who came from the East in Matthew 2:1. The revelation also meant that Daniel and his friends were placed in important positions in Babylon's administration when Nebuchadnezzar's spiritual and mental breakdown took place (Daniel 4). God was manoeuvring his troops into a position for the future by working together with Daniel. Incidentally, Daniel's friends were willing to suffer and lose everything, including their lives in the fiery furnace, but in so doing provided the situation for Nebuchadnezzar to get a revelation of God's Son (3:25). God was clearly wanting to do a work in Nebuchadnezzar.

Nebuchadnezzar responded:

> Blessed be the God of Shadrach, Meshach and Abed-Nego, who sent his angel and delivered his servants who trusted in him, and they have frustrated the king's word, and yielded their bodies, that they should not serve nor worship any god except their own God! (3:28)

In Daniel 4:1-3 Nebuchadnezzar praises the Lord and declares God's Kingdom 'to all peoples, nations, and languages that dwell in all the earth'. This shows God's intention to bless all the families of the earth, just as was promised to Abraham, and was accomplished by Jesus 500 years later.

Later in chapter 4, Daniel's bravery in speaking out the revelation of the King's dream – the prophecy of his temporary madness – ultimately leads to Nebuchadnezzar praising the Lord again and declaring God's Kingdom reign, despite his own attempts at 'playing God' (Daniel 4:34-37).

In chapter 5 Daniel is in the era of King Nabonidas, dealing with Belshazzar, a new 'king' (probably a vice-regent). Belshazzar enters the realm of spiritual conflict by contemptuously using the sacred Jewish Temple vessels for debauchery with his wives and concubines while they praise the false gods. Famously, the finger of God appears, writing on the wall – Belshazzar is fearful and the Babylonian wise men again are confounded. Daniel is summoned at the suggestion of the queen (notably absent from the debauched feast) and pronounces God's judgement. Herodotus (i 191) confirms that Babylon was indeed captured while the besieged were off their guard during a festival, and Xenophon, alluding to the capture of Babylon, states that Cyrus had heard that a feast was going forward (*Cyropædia*, viii 5, 15). Cyrus was later referred to by Jews as 'the anointed of the Lord', and he restored the Jerusalem Temple (Ezra 6:3-5) and religion. Daniel's clear prophecy that Belshazzah would be overthrown could well have demoralised the Babylonians and led to rapid victory for the forces of Cyrus and Darius. Daniel was again working with God to bring in his plans and strategy.

It is under Darius, probably a ruler under Cyrus the Great, that we read that Daniel makes thanks and supplication in thrice-daily prayers (6:10-11) and it is because of his faith that the lions are stopped from hurting him (6:23). This leads Darius to acknowledge the power of the God whose kingdom shall never be destroyed. It may also anticipate the Kingdom-day of Isaiah 11:6-9 and 65:25.

Daniel chapter 7 onwards records the various visions in prayer that Daniel had over this period. So it is as a godly and prayerful man that Daniel set himself 'to understand and to humble himself before his God' (Daniel 10:2-12, RV). His prayers were heard, but for three weeks God's messenger was prevented from reaching him by the 'prince of Persia'. Only when Michael assisted the messenger were Daniel's wrestlings in prayer answered. The angel says, however, 'I have come because of your words' (10:12) – it was because of Daniel's prayers and confession of sin (9:20) that the word of the Lord came through to them.

Who is this Michael, and who are the other spiritual combatants? Much of the book of Daniel is concerned with the history and destiny of the chosen nation Israel, and we will cover this in a lot more detail in the second part of this book, *The History of the Conflict*, starting on page 57. Through them God was to prepare for the coming of the Messiah, the anointed one, who was to be the redeemer. This was a part of what NT Wright, in his book *Justification: God's Plan and Paul's Vision*, calls 'the single-saving-plan-through-Israel-for-the-world-now-fulfilled-in-the-Messiah'.

Michael is the prince of Israel (see Daniel 10:21, 12:1 and Jude 9) and he becomes involved in spiritual conflict with the other two spiritual powers or beings: the prince of Persia and the prince of Greece (10:13,20). These two principalities may well be 'rulers of the darkness of this age' as mentioned in Ephesians. These princes seem to be powers who seek to manipulate other nations playing a part in the history of Israel. In Daniel 9 the activities of another 'prince who is to come' are predicted (v26), whose people will destroy the city soon after the anointed one is cut off. We know that Jesus is the anointed one, the Messiah, who was 'cut off' (as in Isaiah 53:8), so it seems likely that this 'prince who is to come' could represent the spiritual power of Rome, because it was the Romans under Vespasian who destroyed Jerusalem and the Temple in 70 AD.

So we discover there are spiritual battles underlying world politics, and through Israel and their Messiah, God works for the extension of his Kingdom of Light. In Daniel we see the spirit powers as combatants. We also see the important messianic figure, the one whom we know to be the Messiah, or in Greek *Christos* – the 'anointed one'.

The Saints of the Most High

Closely associated with this messianic figure is the role of the 'saints of the Most High'. In Daniel 7:13, 'one like the Son of Man' is presented to the Ancient of Days, and is given a kingdom and a dominion:

> And behold, *one* like the Son of Man, coming with the clouds of heaven! He came to the Ancient of Days, and they brought him near before him. Then to him was given dominion and glory and a kingdom, that all peoples, nations, and languages should serve him. His dominion *is* an everlasting dominion, which shall not pass away, and his kingdom *the one* which shall not be destroyed.

'Son of Man' was Jesus' favourite designation for himself, which he used 80 times. It is this 'Son of Man' who comes in verse 13, yet in verse 18 it is the 'saints of the Most High' who receive the kingdom:

> But the saints of the most high [*places?*] shall receive the kingdom, and possess the kingdom forever, even forever and ever.

Actually there is no definite article in the phrase usually rendered 'saints of the most high' and the word is a general term for 'higher', not necessary meaning God. A related word is used for 'upper chambers' (for example in Ezekiel 42:5), so the phrase here could mean 'holy ones of highest (places)'. This may point forward to the day when all believers are called saints and are seen to be 'raised up with him' and 'seated with him in the heavenly places in Christ' to take his authority in this warfare (Ephesians 1:3,20; 2:6).

Daniel says that there is war between the 'horn' and the 'saints' (v21) who eventually triumph (v23) and receive the kingdom (v27). So Daniel is not only involved in wrestling in prayer himself, but has the vision of how God's saints are involved in this spiritual warfare. It is in the 'heavenly places' where the spiritual warfare is going on, where we wrestle against principalities, powers, rulers of the darkness of this age and spiritual hosts of wickedness (Ephesians 6:12).

In Ephesians 6 Paul explains further this warfare with the saints mentioned by Daniel, and in the next chapter we will look at how the saints fight in the armour of the Messiah and the weapons that they use. The Messiah has won the victory, but in him we stand and implement it – the saints are to 'withstand and stand' (v13) and v18 makes it clear that prayer is at the centre of our warfare.

The book of Daniel, then, shows us that the war and the Kingdom belong both to the Messiah and to his saints. Through prayer Daniel himself is active in the conflict. Those who love God and are called according to his purpose are not just bystanders or victims, but combatants in the battle.

In the rest of the book Daniel receives a series of revelations concerning the heavenly battlefield to help both him and us understand the times and the movement, of the nations towards the last Battle, and giving essential revelation. For more on understanding the book of Daniel and our role in bringing in God's Kingdom, see *The Kingdom of Jesus* by Roger Forster.

Daniel's Life of Prayer

Through his life of prayer Daniel reveals and models a number of things to us about God's coming Kingdom in New Testament days. First, Daniel is known as a Spirit-filled man (5:11,14) prefiguring the Church Age where the Holy Spirit would be poured out to all believers (Acts 2:17).

Second, God's Kingdom is righteousness, peace and joy in the Holy Spirit (Romans 14:17) and Daniel anticipates this Kingdom, for example when he interprets the writing finger in chapter 5. In Luke 11:20 Jesus said 'if I cast out demons with the finger of God, surely the kingdom of God has come upon you', and if we compare this with the parallel passage in Matthew 12:28 we can see that 'the finger of God', is the same as 'the Spirit of God'. Daniel says the finger that wrote on the wall was sent from God (5:24), and so we see in both Daniel and the New Testament that the Kingdom of God operates when we cooperate with the finger/Spirit sent from God.

Finally, just as those in Christ have resurrection hope (1 Corinthians 15; 1 Peter 1:3-5) it was revealed to Daniel that he would rest and rise again at the end of the age (Daniel 12:2,13). This hope of the resurrection of the dead is more clearly revealed here than anywhere else in the Old Testament, and is as necessary for us today, as it was for him then. The key theme in all this human participation in the spiritual warfare is prayer – prayer is central for Job, for Daniel, and for the saints in the New Covenant (who are seated in Christ fighting in his armour in the heavenly places).

Prayer Changes Things

Sometimes Christians have suggested that prayer functions only to change the one praying. We have even heard it said that prayer is like bringing a ship alongside the shore: God is the shore and we as the ship need to bring ourselves alongside his will. Of course prayer does do this, and we all need to stay close to our Father and let him work through us. But the Bible seems to indicate that this is not its only function. In Daniel the veil is drawn aside and we see the spiritual battles and conflicts going on, and Daniel's prayer has activated action in these realms – even though this is not immediately apparent to him.

When God asked Job to pray for his friends, it may have also blessed Job, but God portrays it to have been for *their* benefit – it was not only to somehow bring Job alongside his will.

James brings us another righteous man, Elijah, whose prayers had effect:

> The effective, fervent prayer of a righteous man avails much. Elijah was a man with a nature like ours, and he prayed earnestly that it would not rain; and it did not rain on the land for three years and six months. And he prayed again, and the heaven gave rain, and the earth produced its fruit. (James 5:16-18)

The prayers of righteous people change not only those people themselves but world events. According to James, the prayers of Elijah did not 'avail' in just changing Elijah, but also in producing an effect in the world around him.

This and other aspects of prayer are explored in the book *Prayer: Living in the Breath of God* by Roger Forster.

3

The Church – Weapons, Methods & Banners

B elievers are combatants. In Ephesians we find out much more about *how* we fight. The letter begins with an ecstasy of praise for all that we have been given *in Christ*. In Christ we:

o   share his 'election' as the chosen one of God

o   have redemption through his blood, the forgiveness of sins

o   have an inheritance

o   have a destiny to be conformed to his image and to be used to release the created world.

None of this, of course, has been earned or deserved in any way. But the very first thing Paul mentions is that God has:

> ... blessed us with every spiritual blessing in the heavenly places in Christ. (Ephesians 1:3)

This does not mean that God has chosen us for a life of ease and pandering. Later we are told:

> Finally, my brethren, be strong in the Lord and in the power of his might. Put on the whole *armour* of God, that you may be able to stand against the wiles of the devil. For we do not wrestle against flesh and blood, but against principalities, against powers, against the rulers of the darkness of this age, against spiritual hosts of wickedness in the heavenly places. (Ephesians 6:10-12)

It is in the heavenly places that the battle rages – even though Jesus is seated there above all powers and principalities (Ephesians 1:20-21). Jesus has won the ground but we are called to *stand* and defend it.

The Armour of God

Christ is seated in the heavenly places, and we are 'in Christ' so we fight in his armour – the panoply of God. These words show that we fight in God's strength and God's armour. This reminds us of Philippians 4:13 'I can do all things through Christ who strengthens me' – only in the Lord do we have strength. Paul goes on to compare various parts of christian character with the different sections of a soldier's armour. To help us understand this 'armour of God' we should start by looking at the Old Testament inspiration of Paul's ideas on it – Isaiah 59:16-20:

> He saw that there was no man, and wondered that there was no intercessor; therefore his own arm brought salvation for him, and his own righteousness, it sustained him. For he put on righteousness as a breastplate, and a helmet of salvation on his head … 'The Redeemer will come to Zion, and to those who turn from transgression in Jacob,' Says the Lord.

This is the armour of God. It is God's armour because it is worn by the Messiah as he comes to bring redemption. By comparing Isaiah 59:16,17 and Ephesians 6:13-17 we see it is also the armour that should be worn today by the body of the Messiah on earth – the Church. In the book of Daniel we saw how the saints entered into the battle, and that when the Kingdom was given it was given both to the Messiah and to the saints. In Ephesians we find that the battles of the Messiah and the Church are the same. The Christian soldier is not fighting a lone battle against the forces of evil, but as part of the body of the Messiah, using Jesus' own armour, 'and in the power of his might'.

The actual weapons mentioned in Ephesians 6 are well known: the belt of truth, breastplate of righteousness, shoes of the preparation of the good news of peace, shield of faith, helmet of salvation and the sword of the spirit.

The Sword of the Spirit

It is particularly important to note that only one of these weapons is for attack. So, what is our sword? We know that to have a 'shield of faith' means that faith is our shield, and our 'helmet of salvation' is comprised of salvation. It seems, therefore, that to have a 'sword of the spirit' means that we use a sword comprised of spirit, or breath – the Greek word *pneuma*, like the Hebrew *ruach*, can equally be translated as spirit, breath, or wind. In Ephesians 6:17 *pneuma* is commonly taken to mean the Holy Spirit, but nothing in the Greek text necessitates this. Paul further clarifies this by adding that this 'spirit' (or 'breath') is the word of God.

The Greek word for 'which' in the phrase 'sword of the spirit *which* is the word of God' is neuter. This suggests that 'which is the word of God' refers to the 'spirit', as this word is also neuter – so the spirit is the word of God. The expression 'the word of God' here should not be confused with the title 'Word of God' given to Christ (eg John 1:1, Revelation 19:13), for Christ is called by the Greek term '*logos* of God' whereas in Ephesians the term is '*rhema* of God'. There is no distinct line between the meanings of these two Greek terms, but *rhema* usually means a saying, and is included in the more general term *logos*. *Rhema* is often used when describing spoken words, as the word itself makes a breathing sound.

So Ephesians 6:17 might be literally rendered as 'the breath which is the saying of God'. Our sword is the breath with which God speaks. This may also be the breath with which the Messiah shall slay the wicked:

> He shall strike the earth with the rod of his mouth, and with the breath of his lips he shall slay the wicked (Isaiah 11:4)

The LXX version of Isaiah 11:4 is:

> He shall smite the earth with the word (*logos*) of his mouth and with the breath (*pneumati*) through his lips he shall slay the ungodly.

This is taken up in Revelation 19:15:

> Now out of his mouth goes a sharp sword, that with it he should strike the nations. And he himself will rule them with a rod of iron. He himself treads the winepress of the fierceness and wrath of Almighty God.

The sharp sword comes out of Christ's mouth, for his weapon is the truth he speaks (also see Revelation 1:16; 2:12,16). To us Christ's words are spirit and life – the living application of Christ's revelation in our lives brings life, feeds and cleanses (John 6:63; Matthew 4:4; Ephesians 5:26). But his sword of truth is double-edged, and to the wicked it is destructive.

We have already seen how Satan used the weapon of words through the mouths of Job's comforters. Twice at the end of the book of Job the Lord judges them for their words and commends Job for his. Words are a weapon, but how does Satan use them? Earlier we looked at Jesus' words about the devil:

> He was a murderer from the beginning, and does not stand in the truth, because there is no truth in him. When he speaks a lie, he speaks from his own resources, for he is a liar and the father of it. (John 8:44)

Even at the beginning of human history the devil used a lie in the garden of Eden to seduce humankind into rebellion and death. Yet though Satan uses words of truth perversely, he is afraid to stand in the truth, which reveals him for who he is. Words of truth are like light, in that both reveal an object or person for what they are. Those whose deeds are evil are afraid to come into the light (John 3:19). Through the weapons of truth and light Christ will finally reveal evil for what it is, and in doing so will destroy it. Paul links light with words of truth in his expansion of Isaiah 11:4:

> And then shall be revealed the lawless one whom the Lord Jesus shall consume with the *spirit of his mouth* and shall destroy with the brightness of his coming. (2 Thessalonians 2:8, KJV)

Here we have used the KJV to emphasize that the word *pneuma* can mean either 'breath' or 'spirit'. The KJV renders it 'spirit of his mouth' but most others render it 'breath of his mouth'. So it seems to be the truth he speaks which consumes evil.

The 'sword of the spirit' is given to us, as well as to Christ, but how should we as ordinary Christians use it? Paul says:

> And take... the sword of the Spirit, which is the word of God; praying always with all prayer and supplication in the Spirit. (Ephesians 6:15,17)

Andrew Lincoln in the WORD commentary *Ephesians* also links this with Isaiah 11:4 cited above – through praying in the Holy Spirit we learn how to use the spiritual weapon of the sayings of God. We learn to praise, we learn to use the name of Jesus, we learn when and how to speak God's message to a person, and how to apply a verse of Scripture in our lives. There is power in the words of Scripture, but there is, of course, no virtue in quoting Scripture for the sake of the words themselves – the devil himself did this in tempting Christ (Matthew 4:6,7). It is not the words as such, but the illuminating power they have as we apply them correctly – Jesus used a verse in this way when he replied to the devil's 'proof text'. This is the power of Scripture, as the Holy Spirit applies it in our lives.

We see that in Ephesians, as in Daniel, prayer occupies a key place in the fight. It is through prayer that Christians learn to use their weapons. Through prayer we support and intercede for each other (Ephesians 6:15), but Paul makes it clear that this should be prayer 'in the Spirit'. We should let the Holy Spirit direct our prayers so that God can use us according to his overall strategy.

So now we have some insight into the weapons of warfare. But can we find out more about these and about the methods of fighting used by the forces of the Lord of Hosts?

The Lamb As Though Slain

Another book in the Bible that clearly presents the picture of these spiritual battles is Revelation. In Revelation 4 and 5 we read of a throne from which come peals of thunder and lightning, that is set right in the middle of the elders, the creatures of the earth, the angels and every created thing. Everyone is waiting for a person who would be worthy to open the scroll concerning man's destiny (5:3,4). Then John hears that the 'Lion of the tribe of Judah' has overcome and is worthy. He looks around for this 'overcoming lion', perhaps expecting something like the one in 1 Peter 5:8, only bigger! In fact, what he sees is a little lamb (*arnion* in Greek) which looks as if it has been killed. This is the symbol of God's power and armies throughout the book of Revelation, and is used in this way 28 times. Can we imagine any militant nation marching out to conquer under the banner of a dead-looking lamb? Yet this is God's emblem, and by the end of Revelation the lamb is seen to be on the same throne as the Father himself.

If this is the leader of God's armies, what can their weapons be like?

> And war broke out in heaven: Michael and his angels fought with the dragon; and the dragon and his angels fought, but they did not prevail... for the accuser of our brethren, who accused them before our God day and night, has been cast down. And they overcame him by the blood of the Lamb and by the word of their testimony, and they did not love their lives to the death. (Revelation 12:7-11)

43

Throughout history the armies of the world have used weapons of ever increasing power and violence. Swords and bows have been replaced by guns and missiles. The weapons of God – truth, martyrdom and the blood of his Lamb – are of a totally different order from any of these. They do not destroy by violence, but by revealing the depravity and ugliness of evil for what it is, thus leading to its destruction. So the blood of the martyred saints and prophets itself becomes a weapon: in drinking it the wicked become drunk for their own destruction (see Revelation 16:6; 17:6; 18:24; 14:5). Time and again in Revelation there is war between the forces of good and the forces of evil. For example:

> These will make war with the Lamb, and the Lamb will overcome them, for he is Lord of lords and King of kings; and those who are with him are called, chosen, and faithful. (Revelation 17:14)

The conquerors are the Lamb and those who are 'called' and 'chosen and faithful' – the faithful saints, called and chosen in Christ. Remember that these saints fight in the same armour as Jesus the Messiah, for they fight in the 'armour of God' and 'the strength of his might'. In chapter 4 of *Volume 2: Reconsidering Key Biblical Ideas,* we will see how their chosenness also depends on being part of the Messiah's body, for they are 'chosen in him'.

In Revelation we find two great images of evil: the Beast and the Harlot. Professor FF Bruce, gave us the suggestion that, in view of the background of the time, the Beast represents the Roman Empire in its military ruthlessness, and the Harlot is the city of Rome in its commercial prosperity persecuting the saints in the one guise or the other. We can regard the Beast as a perversion of the truly masculine, representing love of power for its own sake – a 'might is right' philosophy that is typical of monstrous dictators. The Harlot represents perversion of the truly feminine, a desire for material things, a worship of pleasure and manipulation. (For more on the nature of true masculinity and femininity see chapter 12 of *Women and the Kingdom*, by Faith & Roger Forster.)

God's answer to both the Beast and the Harlot is a slain lamb. What can this represent but innocence, suffering and death, and through them the victory.

As Christians we fight spiritual battles in prayer and worship under the banner of the slain lamb. We wear the armour of God and our weapon is the sword of the spirit – the words God speaks. As we fight, we bring the light and truth of who Jesus the Messiah really is.

4

Jesus the Messiah– God's
Glory in the Battle

This is the marvellous thing about God – God gave the name 'Jesus' to Mary for his son, and it is at the name of *Jesus* that every knee shall bow. Donald Hagner writes:

> Jesus had indeed come to save his people – the very meaning of his name in Hebrew, *Yeshua*... is '*Yahweh* is salvation'. (*Matthew 1-13*, p 19)

This is the name above every name (Philippians 2:9,10). The throne of God does not contain a roaring lion, but a slain lamb. By failing to understand this, many Christians have misunderstood what the glory of God is.

God's Glory vs Worldly Glory

Eliphaz and his friends seem to spell out the greatness and glory of God in terms of his supposed emotional detachment about human 'righteousness', coupled with his absolute sovereignty in bringing healing or sickness. Eliphaz says that God is so high and holy, and Job in comparison so wicked, that his 'righteousness' could bring God little or no pleasure. Moreover, he adds, 'for [God] bruises, but he binds up; he wounds, but his hands make whole' (Job 5:18). So, according to Eliphaz, all Job's present sufferings are the outworking of God's glorious power, and if he seeks God he will get all he wants (Job 5:8 and following). Unfortunately, such interpretations are not confined to theologians of Job's day.

Do we think that the glory of God is that he should lord it over people and exercise authority, and like to be called 'benefactor'? According to Jesus this is the type of glory sought by the kings of the Gentiles (Matthew 20:25-28; Mark 10:42-45; Luke 22:24-27). Is it possible that God himself is merely a bigger version of a heathen despot? When put like this, Christians should surely unite in condemning this notion as blasphemous rather than glorious.

There is a tragic context to these words of Jesus about the kings of the Gentiles. While he is thinking of his coming suffering and the cup he must drink (Matthew 20:22), his closest friends are arguing about which of them is greatest. Many great human leaders in his place might have said: 'You can all stop arguing because I am so incomparably greater than any of you: so you're all nothing compared with me!' But Jesus did something totally different – he explained that in the kingdom of heaven everything is upside-down, or rather right-side-up! The disciples rightly call him Master and Lord, for that is what he is (John 13:13), but in the kingdom of heaven this means that he voluntarily makes himself the greatest servant of all: Jesus came to them and knelt to wash their feet. The greatness and glory of God is precisely in that he gives himself freely to us, his creatures, who are but dust – it is not in lording it over people. Jesus was 'the brightness of [God's] glory and the express image of his person' (Hebrews 1:3). Being the express image of God's person, Jesus showed us what God is like. True Christian theology, therefore, lies in looking at Jesus' example and words, rather than following the path of Job's traditionalist comforters. We learn from Jesus what the glory of God is.

Jesus was glorified when he ascended into heaven, but he himself also seems to refer to his crucifixion as the time of his glorification:

> The hour has come that the Son of Man should be glorified. Most assuredly, I say to you, unless a grain of wheat falls into the ground and dies, it remains alone… and what shall I say? 'Father, save me from this hour'? But for this purpose I came to this hour. Father, glorify your name… And I, if I am lifted up from the earth, will draw all peoples to myself… (John 12:23-32)

> So, when he had gone out, Jesus said, 'Now the Son of Man is glorified, and God is glorified in him. If God is glorified in him, God will also glorify him in himself, and glorify him immediately…' (John 13:31-2)

The glory of the Lamb of God is that he is a 'lamb as though slain' and that he has conquered by becoming like a grain of wheat which dies to give life. We should never consider that the glory of God is anything like the worldly glory of the rulers of the Gentiles.

This should help inform our view of a recent controversy in which John Piper in *The Future of Justification* claimed that God's righteousness is a concern for his own glory, seeming to mean by this self-elevation:

> God defined 'right' in terms of himself... what is right, most ultimately, is what upholds the value and honour of God – what esteems and honours God's glory... (p 64)

In response, NT Wright wrote that he is unaware of any other scholar of any persuasion who takes the phrase 'God's righteousness', either in Greek or Hebrew, to mean this. Wright goes on to add that Piper's view of God's supposed self-concern is really at odds with the biblical God and his:

> ... overflowing, generous, creative love... concern... for the wellbeing of *everything else*. (*Justification: God's Plan and Paul's Vision*, p 51 – we quote this in full in chapter 2 of *Volume 2: Reconsidering Key Biblical Ideas*)

God is Love, God is not self-love. Paul tells us what *Love* is, for example in 1 Corinthians 13 – it is not a concern for your own self-elevation.

Another important point to note is that the two books most obviously concerned with the glory and majesty of God – Daniel and Revelation – are the two in which the battles between good and evil are seen most clearly. God does not directly determine everything that happens and his glory lies partly in the fact that he triumphs in spite of this. The forces of evil put Jesus the Messiah to death. God foreknew that it would happen (Acts 2:23; 1 Peter 1:20, see also chapter 5 of *Volume 2: Reconsidering Key Biblical Ideas*), and God delivered him up to them (Acts 2:23), knowing and intending what would happen. But they alone did the act. 'Yet it pleased the Lord to bruise him' (Isaiah 53:10) and through his sin-offering to save the world. This is typical, in a sense, of God's whole way of working with us and the human race – the righteous are not wafted away to heaven, leaving the wicked to suffer. God allows the righteous, like Job, or for that matter like Jesus himself, to stay in situations where he knows they will suffer. Yet through suffering and love the victory is achieved.

Unrighteousness vs Faith

The righteous live by faith, whereas the wicked who practise injustice are insecure and may also themselves become victims of injustice and the arbitrary use of power and violence. An example of this is found in Habakkuk, where those in Israel practising injustice would themselves become victims through the evil Chaldeans, whose motto 'might is right' (Habakkuk 1:11) was also the devil's philosophy. Habakkuk, who had complained about these evil people in Israel, did not find much consolation in their forthcoming comeuppance at the hands of the Chaldeans! So God replies:

> Behold, his soul is puffed up, it is not upright in him; but the righteous shall live by his faith. (Habakkuk 2:4, ASV and ESV)

The proud, or 'puffed up', person has a pretentious, overblown aspect, and his soul or inner being is not 'upright' or 'pleasing' (another meaning of the word used). But there are also the righteous – the just, who are living by their faith even in persecution or difficult times. Habakkuk finally understood how the righteous were to live even in times of trouble, and that the wicked would burn themselves out in judgment. This is God's way with evil – 'How unsearchable are his judgments and how inscrutable are his ways!' God does not remove the righteous from suffering, but is willing to be right there with them in the middle of it. Jesus is the perfect example of God being in the midst of human suffering. Through Jesus, God himself knows what it is to suffer as a human but to triumph through it. The righteous person lives a faith-life, secure in the knowledge that even if he or she should one day face the ultimate injustice of an unjust death, God will raise them up on the last day as he did Jesus (2 Corinthians 4:14).

Jesus, God in human form, was God's ultimate weapon, and through his life of righteousness and death on the cross he revealed the glory of God as he won the victory. As we read in John 1:

> And the Word became flesh and dwelt among us, and we beheld his glory, the glory as of the only begotten of the Father, full of grace and truth. (v14)

So God's glory is defined by Jesus, not in terms of worldly power or wealth, but in terms of grace and truth.

5

The Conflict is Real

This chapter may to some people seem a parenthesis, but here we want to briefly raise an issue which is vital to the meaning of this book. The problem arises because there are theologians whose views amount to a belief that *everything* that happens is God's direct will, and the whole spiritual conflict that we have looked at in chapters 1–4 is effectively a fraud – ie there is no battle between God and Satan. As we show in chapter 7 of *Volume 2: Reconsidering Key Biblical Ideas* this idea was invented by Augustine in the 5th century. Such views may be expressed in various ways, but the basic idea is the same: God is 'sovereign' (by which they mean that he determines everything that happens) so, while men and women are responsible for breaking God's commandments, *whatever* men and women do is God's will being enacted. So for example, one modern Augustinian says:

> … even on those occasions when the command of God is disobeyed, the disobedience is in accordance with his will, in the sense of his decree. (Paul Helm, *The Providence of God*, p 48, also p 131 and following)

Some would state specifically that there is not even any real conflict between God and Satan:

> Satan also, himself… is so completely the servant of the Most High as to act only by his command. (Calvin, *Commentary on Romans*)

Some would even go as far as to say that God deliberately ordains all the suffering and sorrow in the world. They reject the fundamental understanding (so well expressed, for example, by CS Lewis in *The Problem of Pain* and *Mere Christianity*) that suffering is the price that had to be paid for freedom and love to exist at all.

If we were able to find any support in Scripture for such teachings on God's 'sovereign will', we would have to completely rewrite this book! So we need to examine exactly what the Bible does say on these matters. Is God's will always done? If it is always done then why does Jesus tell us to pray 'Your Kingdom come, your will be done'? Is it God's will that I should have the sin that is in my life? On the other hand, if God's will is *not* always done, then does this not contradict the 'sovereignty of God'?

Understanding Language

In considering this last question, first of all we need to note that much of human language contains analogy. This applies not only in describing God, but also for example in describing unimaginable sub-atomic phenomena. An electron is not *really* a particle in the same sense as a speck of dust, it only resembles it in some of its properties. Likewise a radio wave is not *really* a wave in the sense that a water wave is, but resembles it in some of its properties. God is not *really* a father, but resembles a father, a shepherd, and a king in various ways. Sometimes, different picture analogies of something, each appropriate within their own sphere, may appear contradictory. So for example, photons in the two-slit experiment in physics can be pictured as both waves and particles. Similarly, we can picture God as both One and a Trinity.

However, we should be careful not to introduce into our thinking something which really is just a contradiction. Paul, in his letters, continually makes logical arguments; he assumes that his gospel *makes sense* and is consistent with the Old Testament which he knows to be inspired by God. Allowing blatant inconsistency in theology is not only wrong, but dangerous – it can lead to all kinds of immoral or wrong behaviour in the name of God, from sexual promiscuity to burning people to death at the stake. We need to keep all of Scripture in harmony, and if an idea doesn't fit, then it should be thrown out.

Moreover, we cannot make the language of analogy mean whatever we like, nor assume that it means nothing at all. For example, if you say you feel 'broken-hearted', this is an analogy, but it cannot be made to mean that you are happy, nor can it be made to mean nothing at all. If God is said to 'change his mind' or to 'be angry' these are, in a sense, pictures or analogies – but they cannot be reinterpreted to mean anything a theologian wants, or nothing at all.

Much of Jesus' teaching was not meant to be literal: for example 'you must be born again' or 'you are of your father the devil'. But this does not mean that we can stand the words on their heads, by for example making the last of these statements mean 'you are all good people'. But we have seen many instances where theologians take apparently straightforward passages and seem to reverse their meaning to squeeze them into some preconceived overriding philosophical principle. Paul warns us against such traditions in Colossians 2:8.

This point is important but needs to be made with care. It *is* important to be aware of literary genre, hyperbole, language convention and context in understanding what a text meant to the person who wrote it. Many books on hermeneutics emphasize this, for example *The Hermeneutical Spiral* by Grant Osborne, *Introduction to Biblical Interpretation* by Klein et al, and the popular *How to Read the Bible for All Its Worth* by Gordon Fee and Douglas Stuart. Scholarship is to be valued, especially that relating to the Jewish contemporary background in which the Bible was written. But increased understanding of a text and its background is unlikely to cause the whole general impression of it to become reversed. There is a danger of our theology dominating our interpretation of a text, rather than letting the text speak for itself.

What is the General Picture in the Bible?

So, what would be the *general* picture a person would get in reading through the Bible without any background of commentary from generations of ingenious theologians? We suggest it would be something like this:

1. God is the creator of the world which owes its continued existence to him (Genesis 1, Hebrews 1:3; 11:3).

2. He gave the human race a moral law (symbolized by the tree in Eden) but also the freedom to choose whether or not to obey it (Genesis 2:17).

3. The first humans freely chose to disobey, bringing sin into the world (Genesis 3:6).

4. God continues to act in the world with power, but also gave the Jewish people the freedom to choose whether to serve him or not (eg Joshua 24:15; Isaiah 56:4). To truly serve God isn't just about making a moral effort, but about living a faith-filled life after receiving undeserved grace (eg Habakkuk 2:4; Romans 5:1-2).

5. Often the Jewish people used their freedom of choice in ways which God did not like or want (eg Isaiah 65:12).

6. Even those who chose to follow God could slip into major sin, and require divine purging and forgiveness (eg Psalm 51:7; 1 John 1:9).

7. All humans (apart from Jesus the Messiah) have sinned (Romans 3:23) and anyone who denies this is lying to others and themselves (1 John 1:10).

8. Jesus' faithfulness in his sacrificial death made forgiveness of sin possible for all those with faith in God (Romans 3:22), and those who choose to receive him receive the free gift of forgiveness and sonship (John 1:12).

9. God wants everyone to be saved and come to a knowledge of his truth (1 Timothy 2:4), but their own rebellion and waywardness defeats his desire to gather them (as he desired to gather Israel) like chicks under his wing (Matthew 23:37).

10. God is ultimately in control and will bring in a New Heaven and New Earth (Revelation 21:1) but individuals can opt out of his plans for them (Luke 7:30) and so miss out.

We have given verses for each of these, but it is not really a matter of proof texts. The whole flow of the biblical account would give any unbiased reader this impression throughout. One of our aims in this book is to demonstrate that this impression is not mistaken, even though there may be many ideas widespread in the Church today that do not fit in with it. A detailed examination of the whole Bible, paying particular attention to its Jewish background, will confirm this impression. There is a sense in which God *is* 'sovereign', but the Bible does not picture this as ordaining everything which happens – including the sin in our lives.

God's Sovereignty, Will and Plan

So does God's 'sovereignty' imply that his will and plan are always done? We should not decide this by applying some preconceived philosophical idea of what such 'sovereignty' might mean, but rather we need to let Scripture set our understanding of God's will and plan. The New Testament uses two terms: *thelō/*

ethelō/thelēma (will) and *boulē/boulēma* (plan), and teaches that neither God's will nor God's plans are always done. In chapter 1 of *Volume 2: Reconsidering Key Biblical Ideas* we look at these terms in depth, but here we will briefly outline their meanings. (See also the summary on p 185 of this volume).

Jesus told us to pray that God's will (*thelēma*) *would* be done on earth, which seems pointless if it always happens anyway. Jesus also said that God's will (*ethelō*) was to gather Israel, but implied that it did not happen because their own will (*thelō*) was set against this happening (Matthew 23:37; Luke 13:34). If someone aligns his will (*thelō*) with God's will (*thelēma*) then he will know the truth (John 7:17) and those who do God's will are Jesus' brothers (Matthew 12:50; Mark 3:35), enter God's kingdom (Matthew 7:21) and live forever (1 John 2:17). The Early Church noted all this and concluded that God did not determine all the moral choices made by the humans he had created. So they coined the term 'freewill' to say that God allows humans freedom to go against his will for them. That this was held universally by all Christian teachers until Augustine in the 5ᵗʰ century is shown in detail in chapter 7 of *Volume 2: Reconsidering Key Biblical Ideas* (see also chapter 16 of this volume). None of them, of course, were implying that anyone (apart from Jesus) could by strength of will live a sinless life, or could live a righteous life without God's enabling. But they did all believe that God had given humans the freedom to choose to go against what he wanted them to do.

Concerning God's plans, God's actual plan (*boulōmenōs*) is that none should perish because he wants them all to repent (1 Peter 3:9). So why then isn't everyone a Christian? Well Luke 7:30 says that an individual can reject the plan (*boulē*) of God for him or herself. In rejecting God's plan for them to repent the Pharisees chose the road to destruction. No one can, of course, thwart God's overall plan for the coming Kingdom with a New Heaven and a New Earth, but they can opt out personally by refusing to repent and put their faith in God's Messiah who died for their sins.

So Scripture teaches that neither God's will nor his plan is always done. However, in the history of the Church some theologians have thought that this is not in accord with their view of God's 'sovereignty' or 'glory'. So they came up with the idea of a 'secret' or 'effectual' will or plan of God that was always done. They said that what God *says* he wants is not *really* what he wants. There is no actual evidence of this in Scripture, so these views should be regarded as highly speculative.

We explore in depth this whole idea of a 'secret' or 'effectual' will of God that is always done in chapter 1 of *Volume 2: Reconsidering Key Biblical Ideas*. Here we will just outline the two main problems with it:

The first is that it would mean God would be lying about what he wants, and God cannot lie (Titus 1:2). Some may suggest that God's command to Abraham in Genesis 22:2 to sacrifice Isaac is an example of God's 'secret' will, but God does not actually say he wants Isaac dead he just orders Abraham to sacrifice him knowing that he will intervene.

The second big problem with this idea is that God himself says that he does not always get what he wants – and the implication is that what he says he wants is what he *really* wants. One example is Jesus' great lament over Jerusalem in Matthew 23:37:

> Oh Jerusalem… How often would I have gathered you… and yet
> you would not…

Augustine, who introduced the thinking about God's will always being done, wrote about this passage:

> … despite her unwillingness, God did indeed gather together those
> children of hers whom he would. (*Enchiridion* xxiv)

Instead of a sigh and lament, Augustine makes it a kind of 'Ya boo!', crowing over them – God didn't really want to gather those who didn't come anyway.

In *Enchiridion* xxiv and xxvii: Augustine writes:

> … we must understand the Scripture, 'Who will have all men to
> be saved', as meaning that no man is saved unless God wills his
> salvation.

This makes no more sense in Greek or in Latin than in English, and is a prime example of standing a biblical text on its head (bolstered by his main argument for it that babies are saved against their will by baptising them!).

In reality, Augustine began with a philosophical idea of God's sovereignty and then manipulated Scripture to maintain it.

God's Sovereignty and Almightiness

Some Christians seem keen to emphasize the 'sovereignty of God'. Actually, in the NKJV God is nowhere described as 'sovereign' nor is the 'sovereignty' of God ever mentioned (the NASB uses it just once in Psalm 103:19). God is proclaimed to be a great king (eg in Psalm 47:2) and 'king of kings' in 1 Timothy 6:15, and Revelation 17:14 and 19:16 (though this same title is also used of Artaxerxes in Ezra 7:12 and Nebuchadnezzar in Ezekiel 26:7). The implication is that, like earthly supreme kings, God is powerful and defeats his enemies and protects his subjects – but there is certainly no implication that he always gets what he wants. Our Parliament and Queen are sovereign, but many things that happen in the United Kingdom are not what they want. It would be really dangerous to make an overriding principle from a concept like 'the sovereignty of God' that is barely in Scripture if at all.

What about God being 'almighty'? Many modern versions render the Hebrew *El Shaddai* as 'almighty'. The only reason for this, according to Van Gemeren's *Dictionary of Old Testament Theology and Exegesis,* vol 4, p 401, is that this was an 'educated guess' by the translators of the Septuagint (LXX), who translated the term as *pantokrator* in Greek (meaning 'all powerful one') – and this translation is dubious to say the least. In Hebrew, *El* is the Canaanite word for God adopted by the followers of *Yahweh*. But what of *shaddai*? The word *shad* is used many times in the Old Testament to mean a female bosom or breast (eg Isaiah 66:11) and most probably *Shaddai* relates to this. The word *dai* means 'enough' and again is common in the Old Testament (eg Exodus 36:7). So a more natural translation of *El Shaddai* would be 'The all-sufficient God' – this is reflected in Genesis 49:25 where the word rendered 'almighty' is the singular form of the plural word rendered as 'breasts' later in the verse. Therefore there is really no word 'almighty' in the Hebrew Bible. The LXX also often uses *pantokrator* to translate the Hebrew 'Lord of hosts'. This is probably behind the loose Old Testament quotation used by Paul in 2 Corinthians 6:18, which is the only time the Greek *pantokrator* is used in the New Testament other than in Revelation, where it is used 8 times. Revelation is the book where we most clearly see that God does not always get what he wants as spiritual forces battle against him. *Pantos* means 'all' and *kratos* can mean 'power' or imply 'dominion' (for example in 1 Peter 4:11 and 5:11, Jude 25 and Revelation 1:6). Dominion is ascribed to Christ and God, whose right it is to rule. God has 'all dominion' and is rightfully ruler of all, and we can cry 'Hallelujah the Lord *pantokrator* rules!' But the Bible is clear that God does not always get what he wants – even though ultimately he *will* triumph and evil *will* be destroyed.

The conflict is real

The Bible does not present God as some kind of a cosmic puppet-master, determining everything that happens in the world, including all the moral decisions of those who sin. What the New Testament teaches is that God limits Satan, and acts powerfully in the world he made, but does not always get what he wants. God wants you to live a life pleasing to him, but he neither forces you to do so nor does he have some secret will that you actually keep on sinning in your life. If you have sin in your life it is up to you to freely respond to his will for you to repent, and to ask for forgiveness and cleansing from unrighteousness through the blood and power of Jesus.

So in the first part of this book we have demonstrated that the conflict between God and the forces of evil is real, and as the body of Christ we are called to fight in this conflict. Having established this we move into the second part of this book, *The History of the Conflict*, where we explore how God's strategy has unfolded through Scripture.

Part 2

The History
of the Conflict

or 'what the Bible says about
how God's rescue plan began....
and how it will end'

6

How War Was Declared – Genesis

Beginnings

We have seen that God's will and plan are not always obeyed in this world – an opposing movement is working against them. How did this rebellion begin, and in what way was God's plan first violated? Where did evil come from?

The Bible is God's message to humanity, and it begins at the creation of the world and its human inhabitants. It seems that even before this creation Satan had arisen as a spiritual opponent to God, but little is said as to how or why Satan came to be there. We can, perhaps, imagine that God created spiritual beings to set up love-relationships with himself. Love, by its very nature, seems to require the ability to choose which is an innate part of being a person. Satan was presumably free to love or to reject God. In choosing the latter path he created his own evil where none had existed before. Capacity to love is also capacity to hate and rebel against the Lord and his anointed. The Bible tells us little about Satan and his fall, but he appears at the outset of human history as the corrupter of humankind. God's message to humanity tells us only such facts about Satan as are relevant to our own history, and we must be content with this. So the question of where evil came from must be limited to the entry of evil into our world, rather than into this universe or to reality as a whole – and God *has* told us about this.

However figuratively people take some features of Genesis 2 (for our own views see our book *Reason, Science and Faith*, chapter 14 and Paul Marston's *Understanding the Biblical Creation Passages*), it is clear that the Lord intended us to understand that the first humans faced a choice. In the idyllic situation in which they were placed, they could eat of any fruit, including that of the tree of life, but must not eat of the tree of the knowledge of good and evil. Someone would presumably be attracted by the tree of the knowledge of good and evil because of a lust for power through knowledge. He or she would have a selfish desire to set himself or herself up as a god (Genesis 3:5) and so be independent of God. This would lead to a life centred on self and not on God, who is Love. When 'the man' (*adam*) and the woman chose such a life they (in reality) chose death (Genesis 2:17). It is clear that they could not choose the way of death and also choose to eat of the tree of life. In choosing the one they lost the opportunity to eat of the other. God's command, which was surely also his purpose, was that they should eat of the tree of life. They disobeyed and rejected God's plan for them.

Nevertheless, God's ultimate plan will finally be realised, for we find various features of Genesis reappearing in Revelation 22, including the tree of life – those whose robes have been washed have a part in it (v14); it is for the healing of all, when there shall be no curse any more (v2,3, see also Revelation 15). Finally everything will be restored to the harmony with himself that God intended, and his servants will live in adoration of the self-sacrificing 'little lamb' and the Father, who are their light. Had the man and woman in Eden grasped the nature of this God of the Lamb, they could never have accepted the devil's caricature of God, which was implicit in the suggestion that a lust for knowledge and power would make anyone resemble him (Genesis 3:4,5). Ironically, God did intend humankind, both male and female, to be in his true image, and in becoming sons of God we share in him and become like him.

Nothing in the Bible hints that the wrong choice of the first humans might have been the will of God. It is true that God could have prevented their sin by removing their freedom to choose. The trouble with this would have been that a deterministic robot or computer cannot show love – only free beings with independent wills can love. If love was to be a meaningful thing, they had to be allowed some form of free choice (see also eg CS Lewis *The Problem of Pain*, John Wenham *The Enigma of Evil* and our own book *That's a Good Question*). God allowed them the freedom to choose wrongly, but nothing indicates that he wanted them to. If the serpent Satan had been doing God's will, then we might have expected him to receive congratulations and eternal life (1 John 2:17). Instead his rebellious activities brought a curse and a declaration of war (Genesis 3:14,15), for God's will was not that his human creations should fall. Of course, when they did sin, God was not taken by surprise. God knew in advance what he would do, and so we read that the divine redemption through the blood of the Lamb was:

> … foreknown before the foundation of the world, but has appeared in these last times for the sake of you. (1 Peter 1:20, NASB)

The verb here is definitely 'foreknown' (*proginosko*), and there is no linguistic reason to translate it as 'foreordained' (NKJV) or 'chosen' (NIV) for which there are perfectly good Greek words which were not used. We will look at this in depth in chapter 5 of *Volume 2: Reconsidering Key Biblical Ideas*.

In Genesis 3 God tells humanity of the bad consequences of their wrong choices, and also makes a kind of declaration of war on the serpent Satan:

> So the LORD God said to the serpent: 'Because you have done this… I will put enmity between you and the woman, and between your seed and her Seed; he shall bruise your head, and you shall bruise his heel'. (Genesis 3:14-15)

As we have already noted, the seed of the woman is the Messiah, and the 'offspring of the Devil' or 'brood of vipers' who oppose the Messiah would turn out to be religious people, though in the end the conflict would finish with the crushing of the serpent's head as Jesus Christ died on the cross.

Between Adam and Abraham

In the remainder of the period before Abraham, God interacted with righteous people like Enoch and Noah in their generations (Genesis 5:24; 6:9), yet there seems to be no sign of any coordinated plan of campaign. However, we can find some hints of God's intentions. As early as Genesis 4 the acceptable sacrifice of Abel was a lamb: God's battle emblem. In many primitive societies there are vestiges of this symbol of God's warfare, which is a warfare waged through self-sacrifice. In some places people have misunderstood or perverted its meaning as they supposed this sacrifice to be for placating the blood lust of a vindictive tyrant god or gods. Yet perhaps others between Abel and Abraham grasped a revelation from God of the significance of this symbol. Abraham did when he said:

> My son, God will provide for himself the lamb for a burnt offering.
> (Genesis 22:8)

Abraham rejoiced to see the day of the Lamb of God (John 8:56) – perhaps it was as he himself raised the knife over his son on Mount Moriah. Thousands of years later, in this same area of Mount Moriah, just outside Jerusalem, at a place called Calvary, Abraham's designation 'In the Mount of the LORD it shall be provided' (Genesis 22:14) became true in a much deeper sense. (While there seems no evidence to suggest that the exact position of Abraham's altar was Calvary, it does seem that the general area coincided. According to the Jewish tradition embodied in 2 Chronicles 3:1, the Temple itself was built on Mount Moriah. See also Douglas *The New International Dictionary of the Christian Church*.)

So the first moves in this conflict were made at the start of human history when Satan led the man and woman into rebellion against God. After the disobedience of 'the Fall', rather than giving up on humankind God instead started to reveal his rescue plan for humanity. In the next 5 chapters we look at the role that Israel played in God's strategy, leading up to the coming of Jesus the Messiah (or in Greek *Iesous Christos*).

7

Israel and God's Plan - Introduction

Israel and the Early Church

All Jews and Christians (and for that matter Muslims) recognize that Abraham and his Jewish descendants occupy a special place in God's battle strategy in history. But what exactly is it? If Israel was God's 'chosen' or 'elect' nation what did it mean? And what did it mean for the increasingly Gentile Church? This, of course, was one of the key theological issues to be worked out in the Early Church. It colours much of Paul's theology, and underlies much of the opposition he faced (sometimes violent) from Jews both inside and outside the Church. We explore some of these contemporary Jewish ideas in more depth in *Volume 2: Reconsidering Key Biblical Ideas*, but need to note here that their fundamental concerns are often unfamiliar to Christians today and need to be understood:

o   Had God's covenant with Israel been cancelled?

o   If it had, then how could God be a faithful, and *right-dealing* God?

o   If not, then how could non-Jews (ie Gentiles) join the Church without at least being circumcised as the badge of the covenant promises made to them (Romans 9:1-5; 10:1; 11:1-2)?

Jesus is the Jewish Messiah (Romans 9:5), who came indeed to fulfil the Law (Romans 8:4). So Paul, in his systematic treatise to Christians in Rome, addresses two issues fundamental in controversies between the Early Church and its Jewish opponents:

1)   What is the indication of a right-standing with God?

2)   What is the meaning of God's choice, or election, of Israel?

To most contemporary Jews these two questions were bound together. They believed the fundamental mark of being a part of the people of God in right-standing with him consisted in 'works of the Law' – particularly ordinances concerning circumcision, dietary laws and Sabbath keeping. This was not about trying to 'earn' salvation through moral 'good works', but about a capacity for expressing right-standing in serving God, arising through having received the Law (Torah) from God. They gloried not in themselves but in the Torah. As Ellison explains:

> Rabbis believed that God had so delivered himself into the hands of men by the revelation of the Law, that it was for them to decide how he was to be served, provided that the decision was consistent with the Law. (*Jesus and the Pharisees*, p 43)

Thus on one occasion even a voice from heaven was apparently insufficient to decide the meaning of a part of the Torah (see Davies *Paul and Rabbinic Judaism*, p 214-215). While this incident may be an extreme example, and may not represent the common rabbinical view in Paul's day, Paul certainly saw the indication of being part of the people of God and in God's service, *not* as doing works of the Law, but as being in a *faith-relationship* with God which *results* in 'works of righteousness' (ie acts of mercy and justice). This was Paul's view, and emphatically that of John, James and other New Testament writers. Not only does this apply to us in the Church today, but it has *always* been the basis of being declared in right-standing with God: for Abraham, David, Habakkuk and all the Old Testament people of faith. Hebrews sees being in right-standing with God by faith as also applying outside the Abrahamic covenant:

> By faith Noah, being divinely warned of things not yet seen, moved with godly fear, prepared an ark for the saving of his household, by which he condemned the world and became heir of the righteousness which is according to faith. (Hebrews 11:7)

Noah's faith led to action. For New Testament writers, this kind of faith-relationship does not depend on 'works of the Law', ie keeping the ordinances in the Torah, though it does lead to a God-orientated lifestyle.

The Election of Israel

So why did God choose Abraham, and through him the nation of Israel, to be part of his plan? Paul asserts several fundamental points:

1. God's election of Israel was a choice made purely in the strategy of God – it was not directed by any human acts nor controlled by human will.

2. Israel's election did not ensure right-standing for particular individuals within the nation. This was determined by whether they were in a faith-relationship with God.

3. God is free to use both those in right relation with him and those who reject him to demonstrate his mercy and justice. We cannot control God's strategy in this respect, either to direct or to stop his action.

The profound effects in Paul's life and thinking that were brought about by the separation of the issues of right-standing and Israel's possession of the Torah is hard to grasp for us today. What marked off Jews in their own eyes, as well as those of their contemporaries, was circumcision, their keeping of the food ordinances (eg not eating pork) and the Sabbath. The Jewish hero-martyrs recorded in the books of the Maccabees perished for refusing to break these ordinances.

Whenever Paul himself talks about his Damascus Road experience it is actually in terms of his radical call to preach to the Gentiles – as though being set apart for this from his very conception was something he had been fighting against (the goad against which he had been kicking). We read about this in Galatians 1:15, Acts 9:5,15 and 26:17 (see also Acts 13:46-47, 18:6; 22:21, Romans 11:13, Galatians 2:8, Ephesians 3:8 etc, and see James Dunn - *Jesus, Paul and the Law*). In Acts 22:22 a Jewish audience listened quietly to the Rabbi Paul's message about Jesus... until he said that God sent him to the Gentiles, at which a riot arose!

Even Christian Jews found it difficult to understand that God was no respecter of persons, but that those in every nation who feared God and did righteously were accepted by him (Acts 10:34, 35). To suggest that a person could be living in a truly right faith-relationship with God but without possessing the Torah would be like suggesting to some modern evangelicals that someone might be in a faith-relationship with God today but not have a Bible. To be in right-standing with God, they thought, required particular knowledge through scriptural revelation.

The Book of Romans

The book of Romans contains a sustained theological treatise. In the first 8 chapters Paul establishes that what indicates right-standing with God is not adherence to ceremonial works, but a faith-relationship with God. God is able to forgive sins based on the faithfulness of Jesus the Messiah in making his sacrificial death – this always was God's basis, but now as Christians we can see this clearly. We will look at this in depth in chapter 2 of *Volume 2: Reconsidering Key Biblical Ideas*. Paul also speaks of the holy life as being not through moral effort, but through recognising the freedom in Christ and the power of the Holy Spirit.

However this section of our book does not concern these issues, but God's historical battle strategy. This is what Paul takes up in Romans 9–11. He deals with the place of Jews in God's plan, addressing both the legitimate questions which Christians and Jews might ask, and also some of the more casuistic criticisms which were aimed at distorting Paul's message. He outlines a history of Israel, during which he explains three things about God's choice of them (ie about their 'election'). He shows:

1. *The basis of God's choice.* This was not because of 'works of the Law' or in fact any other kind of works, since it predated anything Israel did.

2. *Its effect on individuals.* God's choice of Israel in some way affected many individuals (both Jews and Gentiles) concerned in the nation's history.

3. *Its allegorical significance.* God's actions had various symbolical and typological meanings, which are relevant to the question of who should be saved (Paul had already mentioned these in Galatians 4).

Romans 9 therefore serves as a good framework to explore Israel's place in history. It will, however, be necessary at various points to fill in a lot of background information which was familiar at first hand to Paul's readers in the 1st century Church at Rome. It has always been our view that, as NT Wright recently put it:

> Chapter 9 has long been seen as a central New Testament Passage on 'predestination' though as we shall see the theological tradition from Augustine to Calvin (and beyond) did not grasp what Paul was actually talking about here. (*The New Interpreters Bible*, p 620)

Israel Still Chosen

Paul begins Romans chapter 9 by reiterating his own personal attachment to his people. Paul never thought of himself as anything other than a practising Jew, and thought centrally of Jesus as the Jewish Messiah or 'the Christ'. Note the present tense of his words: they *are* Israelites, to them *belong* the adoption, the glory, the covenants, the giving of the law, the service (the Greek here means 'priestly service' or 'Temple worship' [NEB]) and the promises. Theirs *are* the patriarchs and from them came the Messiah as far as earthly descent was concerned. As a nation they received sonship (Exodus 4:22), the glory (Exodus 40:34; 1 Kings 8:11), the covenants (Exodus 19:5,6; 2 Samuel 7), the Law (Deuteronomy 4:8) and the ceremonies of service (Leviticus 1–16). As a nation they paved the way for the Messiah Saviour of the world. Paul paints a central and glorious picture of his people.

But this left the big question. If all these things rightly belonged to his Jewish nation, then why have so many rejected their Messiah? Is God still faithful to them? This is what the apostle has to explain, and so he introduces the theme for the whole chapter:

> But it is not that the word of God has taken no effect. For they are not all Israel who are of Israel... (Romans 9:6)

Here Paul may be making a play on the meaning of the word 'Israel' (just as he does on the meaning of 'Jew' (praise) in Romans 2:29). The name Israel is given in Genesis 32:28:

> And he said, 'Your name shall no longer be called Jacob, but Israel; for you have struggled with God and with men, and have prevailed'.

The meaning of 'Israel' is uncertain, though the NKJV 'prince with God' seems today to have little support. The NEB, RV, RSV, ESV and NASB all give 'God strives' or 'he who strives with God', the NIV 'he who struggles with God', and the JB says: 'The probable meaning of "Israel" is "May God show his strength" but it is here explained as "He has been strong against God".'

FF Bruce writes:

> (*yiśrā'ēl* 'God strives') The new name given to Jacob after his night of wrestling at Penuel: 'Your name', said his supernatural

antagonist, 'shall no more be called Jacob, but Israel, for you have striven (*śārîtā*, from *sārā*, 'strive') with God and with men and have prevailed'... cf Hosea xii 3f, 'his manhood he strove (*sārā*) with God. He strove (*wayyāśar*, from the same verb) with the angel and prevailed' (RSV). (*The New International Dictionary of the Christian Church*)

Derek Kidner, writes:

> Israel, is a verbal name. In itself it would convey the meaning 'May God strive ('for him'),' but like other names in Genesis it takes on a new colouring from its occasion, and commemorates Jacob's side of the struggle and his character thus revealed. The key verb, strive (possibly 'persevere'), is found only here and in Hosea 12:4,5, and its meaning is not certain; but there is no support for deriving it from the noun 'a prince' as in KJV (where the whole phrase as *a prince hast thou power* represents this single word)! (*Genesis*, p 170)

An interesting early comment on the meaning of the word occurs in the *Dialogue* of Justin Martyr (c114-175 AD). He says that *Isra* is a man overcoming and *El* is power, thus Israel is a man who overcomes power –which Justin says was truly fulfilled in Christ. Evidently Paul's tendency to an occasional word-play of this type was not lost on the Early Church. Whatever the literal meaning of 'Israel', it seems clear that to the Hebrews it implied something of Jacob's own perseverance. He had received the name because he himself had striven with and prevailed over God and man – and this is how Hosea looks back at the incident. Yet it was a perseverance that turned into dependence and submission. Kidner writes:

> It was defeat and victory in one. Hosea again illuminates it: 'He strove with the angel and prevailed' – this is the language of strength; 'he wept and sought his favour' – the language of weakness. After the maiming, combativeness had turned to a dogged dependence, and Jacob emerged broken, named and blessed... The new name would attest his new standing: it was both a mark of grace, wiping out an old reproach (27:36), and an accolade to live up to. (*Genesis*, p 169)

It was just such a personal encounter and experience that Israelites in Paul's day lacked. Though they were 'of Israel' (ie his descendants), they were not 'Israel' (ie those who had persevered with God in personal encounter). For further light on this incident in Genesis 32:28 see *Bible History* by Edersheim vol i, p 135-137, and the commentaries by Derek Kidner, Walter Brueggemann and Gordon Wenham.

In other words, not all Israelites live up to their name and have prevailed until they received a blessing in a personal relationship with God as Jacob did. As Gordon Wenham says in his commentary:

> … his new name, Israel, recalled this incident in which he wrestled with God and prevailed… whenever his descendants heard this name, or used it to describe themselves, they were reminded of its origin, and its meaning… (*Genesis*, vol ii, p 297)

But why, then, did some of the nation of Israel fail to wrestle until blessed? To explain this, Paul goes back to the start of Israel's history, to the patriarch Abraham. So it makes sense for us to do the same, and return now to the story of Abraham.

8

Israel and God's Plan – Abraham and Isaac

God Speaks to Abraham

The story opens with the first recorded words of God to Abraham:

> Get out of your country, from your family and from your father's house, to a land that I will show you. I will make you a great nation; I will bless you and make your name great; and you shall be a blessing. I will bless those who bless you, and I will curse him who curses you; and in you all the families of the earth shall be blessed. (Genesis 12:1-3)

What is God's purpose here? What he is certainly *not* doing is choosing Abraham to receive personal redemption and leaving the rest to perish. For one thing it would seem that Abraham already knew God, for the Lord simply begins to speak to him without any introduction. More importantly, at that time there were other righteous men such as Lot, who were upset by the wickedness of people around them (2 Peter 2:7). One, the 'King of Righteousness' Melchizedek, seems even greater than Abraham (Hebrews 7:7) and was holy enough to be described as like the one who was truly perfect (Hebrews 7:3). The Lord is, in fact, more concerned right from the beginning with the nation than with Abraham as such. Abraham is chosen as the head of a great nation. Moreover, the purpose of the choice is not simply to give Israel a good time. The Lord makes his purpose clear: '…be a blessing… in you all the families of the earth shall be blessed'. God's design is not merely that Israel should be blessed, but that they should be a blessing to others. It is a part of God's strategy in the conflict, which is a battle to bless humankind.

In his first words to Abraham, God anticipates the time when he will justify the Gentiles through faith, for from Israel came Jesus the Messiah in whom all nations were to receive blessing (Galatians 3:8). How exactly would this blessing be achieved? God had already spoken of this in the garden of Eden, as he looked forward to a Messiah whose heel would be bruised. It would be in the cross of Christ, the focal point of history and of the battle. Centuries later, Paul saw that Christ became a curse for us:

> ... that the blessing of Abraham might come upon the Gentiles in Christ Jesus, that we might receive the promise of the Spirit through faith. (Galatians 3:14)

It is vital to our whole understanding of the special place of Israel in God's plan, that we should grasp this point right from the start. The choice of Abraham and Israel was not merely for their own benefit; it was not a guarantee that all Jews would be saved – it was so that through them God could do something for the world. Only if we grasp this will we understand Paul's explanation of why, in spite of their 'chosenness', many Israelites had been free to reject Jesus and salvation.

Abraham's Response

We have seen how God began his dealings with Abraham. How did Abraham react?

- o In Genesis 12, Abraham obeyed God's command and in faith (Hebrews 11:8) went out to the land of his inheritance.

- o In Genesis 13, the Lord made the great promise about the numbers of Abraham's descendants.

- o At the beginning of Genesis 15, the promise was repeated. When Abraham pointed out that he still did not have a son, the Lord assured him that he would have one.

- o In Genesis 15:6 Abraham believed the promise of God and it was counted to him for right-standing before the Lord.

Then, in Genesis 16 and 17, Abraham listened to the voice of his wife rather than to God. He still had no children, and God's promise had not come true, so he himself tried to make it come true. It was at that time fairly common practice to take the wife's maid as a kind of concubine or junior wife and so

Abraham did this. This union with Hagar resulted in the birth of Ishmael. This was not, however, a part of God's plan, for he intended Abraham to have a promised son as heir. Only later, in Genesis 21, did Abraham's wife Sarah give birth to Isaac, in spite of her great age and apparent loss of capacity to bear children. The birth of Isaac was a divinely wrought miracle – he was the son who fulfilled God's promise to Abraham.

The Distinction between Ishmael and Isaac

What then, is the distinction between Ishmael and Isaac? We discover that this is in keeping with what we have found about the first call of Abraham: the great distinction is that from Isaac would spring the nation whose Messiah would bring worldwide blessing. Remember that although only Abraham was chosen, individuals like Lot and Melchizedek were also right with God, even though they were not part of God's covenant with Abraham. Similarly, only Isaac was chosen, but there is every reason to believe that, as an individual as distinct from as an heir, Ishmael may also have been acceptable to God. Ishmael was the seed of Abraham (Genesis 21:12,13), and shared in the duties of a son, such as burial rites (Genesis 25:9). As Gordon Wenham points out:

> 'God heard the voice of the boy' is repeated by both the narrator and the angel. (*Genesis*, vol ii, p84)

As far as his personal life was concerned, the Scripture clearly tells us that God was with the lad (Genesis 21:20). Not only was God present in his life, but his destiny was assured; the angel of the covenant who stayed Abraham's hand and made promises about Abraham's descendants also appeared to Hagar and made similar promises about Ishmael (see Genesis 16:10 compare 22:17-18). Hagar even addressed the angel in terms similar to Abraham (Genesis 16:13; 22:14, LXX – 'A God of Seeing'). Gordon Wenham again points out that:

> ... although separated from her husband, Abraham, we find Hagar acting in the best tradition of his faith and practice. (p 86)

The great difference was, of course, that it was only through Isaac that the Messiah would come to bring blessing to all nations. God made this point explicit to Abraham in the words:

> In Isaac your seed shall be called. Yet I will also make a nation of the son of the bondwoman, because he *is* your seed. (Genesis 21:12,13)

The NKJV renders the Hebrew *zera* (LXX *sperma*) consistently as 'seed', in Genesis 21:12-13, and *sperma* also in Romans 9:6-7. The ESV is also consistent but uses the more modern word 'offspring':

> But God said to Abraham, 'Be not displeased because of the boy and because of your slave woman. Whatever Sarah says to you, do as she tells you, for through Isaac shall your offspring be named. And I will make a nation of the son of the slave woman also, because he is your offspring'. (Genesis 21:12-13, ESV)

> But it is not as though the word of God has failed. For not all who are descended from Israel belong to Israel, and not all are children of Abraham because they are his offspring, but 'Through Isaac shall your offspring be named'. (Romans 9:6-7, ESV)

The NASB consistently uses 'descendant(s)', which again reflects the ambiguity as to whether the term is singular or plural. The NIV is inconsistent in Romans 9:6-7 using 'descendants' and 'offspring' for the same word.

Both Ishmael and Isaac were Abraham's seed/offspring, but 'in Isaac shall a seed/offspring to you be named' (this is the literal translation of the LXX and Romans 9:7). Paul makes it clear in Galatians 3:14-16 that the seed/offspring named to Abraham was Jesus the Messiah, and the blessing which came through Abraham to the nations was in Christ. This is the great difference between Ishmael and Isaac: from Isaac sprang the nation into which Jesus was born. This also explains the climax of Paul's list in Romans 9:4-5 of the distinctive characteristics of Israel:

> ... of whom *are* the fathers and from whom, according to the flesh, Christ [Messiah] *came*, who is over all, *the* eternally blessed God. Amen.

We find, therefore, that God's choice of Isaac rather than Ishmael related to his place in God's battle strategy – there was something that God wanted to do through Israel for the world. Their chosenness did not automatically save them and damn all others. As Cranfield remarks in his commentary on Romans:

> We must not read into Paul's argument any suggestion that Ishmael, because he is not chosen to play a positive part in the accomplishment of God's special purpose, is therefore excluded from the embrace of God's mercy. (vol ii, p 475)

The Allegory of Ishmael and Isaac

Before we return to look explicitly at Romans 9, we can learn an important allegorical lesson from the story of Isaac and Ishmael, which Paul refers to in Galatians 4:21-31. God had made a great promise to Abraham, which had no apparent likelihood of being fulfilled. Abraham went ahead without God's guidance and tried to fulfil the promise by a device of his own, the result of which was Ishmael. Ishmael, therefore, represented Abraham's 'works' in an effort to produce by his own initiative what God had promised. In this sense Ishmael was a child 'according to the flesh' (Galatians 4:23,29). When it came to Isaac, Abraham could only consider the womb of Sarah which was then as good as dead, and yet have faith that God would work a miracle (Romans 4:19,20). Isaac, therefore, was a child of the 'promise', a result purely of God's power and Abraham's faith (Galatians 4:23).

God has also made a great promise to us, a promise of eternal life. If we go ahead in our own strength and try to earn it or make it come true, then this too would be 'works' of a kind comparable with those of Abraham. If we did this, we might (like the Galatians) become enslaved to a series of petty regulations, producing in us a slavish character rather than a holy one. Paul compares this to the son of a slave, the son that Abraham produced in his own strength and 'works'. If, on the other hand, we have the faith that God will work the miracle of rebirth and continue to bring eternal life to us, we become children of the promise. Paul sees both Abraham's situation and our own as involving a choice between two different pathways to follow:

1. Promise → works → slavery as a child of the flesh.
2. Promise → faith → God's power brings life as a child of the promise.

This allegorical meaning teaches that faith-relationship and not works is God's method. This parallel was not meant to be taken too far. For one thing the promise concerning Isaac was made to Abraham, whereas the promise concerning us is made to ourselves. Second, the promise to Abraham implied nothing about anyone's individual eternal destination; the promise to us certainly does have such implications. As with Paul's other analogies (eg Romans 7:1-14), this allegory is helpful only if not pressed to extreme detail. Within the context intended, Paul uses it in Galatians to warn us that living a holy life and fulfilling God's purposes for us is not done through legalistic self-effort, but by faith in cooperation with the God who is working in us.

Paul Relates this to Israel

Paul uses three trains of thought:

1. The basis of God's choice of Israel.
2. Its effects on individuals.
3. Its allegorical significance.

Looking back to Romans 9, we remember how Paul stated that they are not all 'Israel' just because they are physically descended from the one who was called 'Israel'. He then goes back to the start of Israel's history:

> Nor are they all children because they are the seed of Abraham; but, 'In Isaac your seed shall be called'. That is, those who are the children of the flesh, these are not the children of God; but the children of the promise are counted as the seed. For this is the word of promise: 'At this time I will come and Sarah shall have a son'. (Romans 9:7-9)

He is, remember, not at all concerned here with the individual destinies of Isaac or Ishmael, but he draws out the allegorical meaning very strongly. The line chosen to be the path to the Messiah (v7) was that of Isaac, the child of the promise (v8). Paul makes it quite clear what promise he is talking about here: it is the promise that Sarah should have a son (v9). To us, today, his meaning may seem obscure, but as a thrust at some of his expert pharisaic Jewish opponents it is masterful. Can they not see that God, even in his original choice of their nation, was implicitly repudiating the 'justification by works of the law' principle which they teach? This is really ironic: God chose Isaac, and the Pharisees laid claim to a share in this chosenness because they were his descendants. Yet many of these same Pharisees accepted a principle of works, which was completely contrary to the whole basis of God's choice of Isaac. The birth and choice of Isaac were a result of faith in a promise and in God's power, not of works. The Pharisees thought that God's choice of Isaac marked out their nation to receive in the Law a unique means to please God through ordinances. If they had understood the true reason for God's strategy in choosing Isaac, they might also have understood the allegory it contained, which taught that God's principle was faith, without which the ordinances are empty.

9

Israel and God's Plan – Jacob and Esau

God Chose a Nation in Embryo

In the next part of Romans 9 the apostle Paul passes on to the next point in the history of Israel:

> … and not only this, but when Rebecca also had conceived by one man, even by our father Isaac (for *the children* not yet being born, nor having done any good or evil, that the purpose of God according to election might stand, not of works but of him who calls), it was said to her, 'The older shall serve the younger'. As it is written, 'Jacob I have loved, but Esau I have hated'. (Romans 9:10-13)

People often fail to understand that in this whole passage Paul is talking about nations and not about individuals. This is understandable given that some translations obscure the argument by putting in words not in the original Greek text – for example, 'the children' (italicized) in the NKJV, 'twins' (italicized) in the NASB and 'the twins' (unitalicized) in the NIV, make it seem that Paul is talking about children, rather than nations.

Wesley made this point in *Predestination Calmly Considered* and it has been emphatically reiterated in many commentaries of undisputed scholarship and authority, such as Allen Barnes, FF Bruce, Emil Brunner, Philip Doddridge, JR Dummelow, HL Ellison, Alfred Garvie, EH Gifford, Charles Gore, WH Griffith-Thomas, HA Ironside, Leon Morris, and W Sanday & AC Headlam. Even a scholar more sympathetic to the Augustinian tradition can write: 'It is, in fact, with the election of community that Paul is concerned in Romans 9-11' (Cranfield, *Romans*, vol ii, p 450).

Turning to the passage quoted by Paul we read:

> And the LORD said to her: 'Two nations *are* in your womb... And the older shall serve the younger'. (Genesis 25:23)

Esau the individual never did serve Jacob; in fact it was, if anything, the other way around. Jacob bowed himself down to the ground before Esau (Genesis 33:3), addressing him as 'my Lord' (Genesis 33:8,13) and calling himself Esau's servant (Genesis 33:5) – Jacob begged Esau to accept his gifts (Genesis 33:11) for Esau's face seemed like the face of God to him (Genesis 33:10). Esau the individual certainly did *not* serve Jacob, it was the nation Esau (or Edom) which served the nation Jacob (or Israel). Paul's point is that God's choice of Israel was made when both nations were still in the womb, and neither had done good or evil (Romans 9:11, quoting Genesis 25:23). The choice of the nation was not a reward for merit, but part of a God-determined strategy. Again, Cranfield rightly remarks:

> It is important to stress that neither as they occur in Genesis, nor as they are used by Paul do these words refer to the eternal destinies either of the two persons or of the individual members of the nations in history. What is here in question is not eschatological salvation or damnation but the historical functions of those concerned and their relations to the development of the salvation-history. (*Romans*, vol ii, p 479)

In other words, Paul is talking about Jacob and Esau in relation to what we call 'God's strategy in human history'.

God Loved Jacob but Hated Esau

Paul's next quotation: 'Jacob I have loved but Esau I have hated' also concerns issues of their place in God's strategy, not individual destiny. Thus again Cranfield insists in his commentary:

> But again it must be stressed, as in the case of Ishmael, so also with Esau, the rejected one is still, according to the testimony of Scripture, an object of God's merciful care. (p 480)

Commentators from Moule to Cranfield have noted that the quote actually comes from Malachi 1:2-3, written a millennium later, and again (in FF

Bruce's words) 'the context indicates it is the nations of Israel and Edom, rather than their individual ancestors Jacob and Esau, that are in view'.

So we read that the Lord *loved* the nation of Israel but *hated* the nation of Edom. Since God has used these words 'love' and 'hate' in this way, we must ask whether he indicates anywhere what he means by them. Does the God of love really *hate* Edom? The first clue comes within the history of Jacob himself:

> And he went in also unto Rachel, and he loved also Rachel more than Leah, and served with him yet seven other years. And Jehovah saw that Leah was hated, and he opened her womb. But Rachel was barren. (Genesis 29:30-31, ASV)

The text itself seems to indicate that 'hated' here means 'loved less than'. Indeed, the NIV and NKJV here put 'not loved' and 'unloved' (though inconsistently render the same Hebrew word as 'hated' in Malachi 1:2-3!)

The two Hebrew words for love and hate (*aheb* and *sane*) are the same in Genesis 29:30-1 as in Malachi 1:2-3 and Proverbs 13:24. The Septuagint also used the same Greek words (*agapaō* and *meseō*) in all three of these passages. The New Testament uses the same two Greek words (*agapaō* and *meseō*) in all the verses which contain this form of comparison (ie Matthew 6:24, Luke 14:26, 16:13 and Romans 9:13). There can be little doubt, therefore, that this form of comparison would have been well known to the Jews as an idiom – both in the Hebrew and in the Greek.

Barnes, in *Notes on the New Testament: Romans*, says:

> It was common among the Hebrews to use the terms love and hatred in this comparative sense, where the former implied strong positive attachment and the latter, not positive hatred, but merely a less love, or the withholding of expressions of affection. (See also WH Griffith Thomas, *St Paul's Epistle to the Romans*, and others.)

In *Everyday Life in the Holy Land* James Neil (1885) remarked on a similar semitic figure of speech:

> In ever so many places the negative 'not' followed by 'but' does not deny at all; and 'not this but that' stands for 'rather that than this'. Thus God says to Samuel, of the children of Israel, 'They rejected not thee, but they rejected me', which must mean, 'They rejected

me rather than thee'. For they did very definitely reject Samuel, on the ground that he was old and his sons were not walking in his ways. When Joseph magnanimously said, to comfort his brothers, 'It was not you that sent me here, but God', his words could only mean 'It was rather God than you', etc.

Jesus himself speaks to the Jews using their own language conventions, when he says:

If anyone comes to me and does not hate his father and mother, wife and children, brothers and sisters, yes, and his own life also, he cannot be my disciple. (Luke 14:26)

He who loves father or mother more than me is not worthy of me. And he who loves son or daughter more than me is not worthy of me. (Matthew 10:37-38)

The parallel text of Matthew 10:37 shows us that again the word hate in Luke is not literal, but implies 'love less than' (see also Proverbs 13:24 and Matthew 6:24 for other uses of love-hate in such comparisons). We may see, therefore, that when the Bible uses the word 'hate' as a contrast to 'love', it intends us to understand it to mean 'love less than'. This is its meaning in all other references, and we must suppose it to be so in Malachi 1:2-3. The verse does not mean that in a literal hatred of Esau and his descendants God has condemned every one of them to hell. It simply refers to the higher position of the Hebrew race in the strategy of God. Sanday & Headlam, in their commentary on Romans wrote:

The absolute election of Jacob – the 'loving' of Jacob and the 'hating' of Esau – has reference simply to the election of one to higher privileges as head of the chosen race, than the other. It has nothing to do with the eternal salvation. Moreover, in the original to which St Paul is referring, Esau is simply a synonym for Edom. (In this instance they were quoting Charles Gore in *Studia Biblica* vol iii, p 44.)

The context of Malachi 1:2-3 is also important for our understanding of the meaning of Paul's quotation. God said that he had shown special favour to Israel (Malachi 1:2) and when they asked in what way this was so, the prophet pointed out how severely the Lord dealt with the nation of Edom compared with Israel (v2-3). Yet the Israelites, the prophet complained, were behaving very sinfully even in spite of this special privilege (v6-14). Paul may well have had this context in mind when he put the quotation into Romans 9:13. It is, he notes, in the passage where the chosenness of Israel is stated in the strongest terms, that the prophet also berates Israel for their evil deeds. This makes it obvious that God's choice of Israel could not be a result of their merits or works – remember that Paul has in mind at this point those of his opponents who believed that 'works of the law' were involved in God's choice of Israel, and the way to holiness. His introduction of the quotation from Malachi 1:2-3 is therefore very relevant here, and he uses it as he develops his theme that it is God's strategy, and not Israel's ceremonial observance, which has caused God to choose them, and to maintain that choice.

In summary, then, God's 'love' of Jacob but 'hatred' of Esau means this: God has chosen to give to the nation of Israel a special place and privileged position. This is not because of their works, because the passage Paul quotes not only affirms God's choice of Israel, but also proclaims their sinfulness. Rather, God's choice is purely a result of his own strategy.

10

Israel and God's Plan – Moses

Paul's Starting Point

Paul has been arguing that God's original choice of Jacob, and in him the nation of Israel, was not determined by anything they did. But was this *fair*? Jews were well familiar with Abraham's question to God: 'Shall not the judge of all the earth do right?' (Genesis 18:25). The 'Righteousness of God' meant fair dealing, so the thought of him giving privilege on any basis but merit might provoke a reaction: 'Is there unrighteousness with God?' (Romans 9:14). Paul answers the opponents 'Certainly not!', but what kind of reasoning does he give?

Some commentators seem to think Paul's answer amounts to: 'God acts arbitrarily – he does whatever he wants, and anyone who argues against this will be put down because they are guilty anyway'. But as we will see, this isn't what Paul is saying – rather, he begins by going back to Moses, the founder of the nation, to demonstrate to his audience of Jewish Christians and also of opponents that God does act righteously in his decisions.

Moses and God's Strategy

Paul starts off with a quotation from Exodus 33:

> For he [God] says to Moses, 'I will have mercy on whomever I will have mercy, and I will have compassion on whomever I will have compassion'. So then it is not of him who wills, nor of him who runs, but of God who shows mercy. (Romans 9:15-16)

This quotation that Paul uses is central to a key passage in Exodus where God is relating to Moses. Earlier, God had said to Israel:

> Now therefore, if you will indeed obey my voice and keep my covenant, then you shall be a special treasure to me above all people; for all the earth *is* mine. And you shall be to me a kingdom of priests and a holy nation. (Exodus 19:5)

Moses told the people that they did not have to do any great feats to keep the commandments in God's covenant:

> But the word is very near you, in your mouth and in your heart, that you may do it. See, I have set before you today life and good, death and evil, in that I command you today to love the Lord your God, to walk in his ways, and to keep his commandments, his statutes, and his judgments ... I have set before you life and death, blessing and cursing; therefore choose life, that both you and your descendants may live; that you may love the LORD your God, that you may obey his voice, and that you may cling to him, for he is your life... (Deuteronomy 30:14-20)

God did not give the Law as some kind of impossible task to prove the point that no one could get to heaven by living an ethically perfect life. Through Moses, God clearly said that they *could* keep God's commandments, statutes and judgements. Moses was not, of course, suggesting that they could 'live a sinless life'. As we have already seen, this was not the meaning of being 'righteous'. The whole point of the Law was that it contained atoning sacrifices for the remission of sin (see Hebrews 9:22), which pointed forward to their true fulfilment in the Messiah (see Hebrews 10:1,4;9:12). Moses said they could keep the Law, but not by independent effort – his assumption was that it was meant to be done by living out a loving, intimate, faith-relationship with God. As Paul later said, they did not achieve the right-standing God intended through the Law: 'because they did not seek it by faith, but as it were, by the works of the law'. He later adds that specifically *Christian* faith applies just the same principles, but now with an increased understanding of the Christ-centred basis on which the faith-relationship can occur (Romans 9:31; 10:6).

If God intended that their holiness should arise out of relationship, a part of this was a hope to dwell among them:

> I will dwell among the children of Israel and will be their God…
> (Exodus 29:45)

Righteousness is fundamentally about living *in faith-relationship* with God. Reading this whole passage of Exodus, the first thing which seems pretty plain is that God really does want a *relationship* with them, but is unable even to go among them because of their 'stiffneckedness' and sinful self-will. So what happens while God is giving Moses instructions about the Tabernacle, a fitting symbol of his presence among the people, and what John Durham in his Exodus commentary calls 'guiding principles' about holiness? Well meantime, the people are constructing their own symbol for *Yahweh* – a young bull – which HL Ellison and Alan Coles in their commentaries on *Exodus* suggest may be an ancient Canaanite god. The people follow this with revelry and debauchery. Real worship in faith-relationship (such as Moses in 34:8) leads to awe (34:8), care for others (34:9) and a lifestyle which shines forth with the awesome love of God (34:29). Moses had it, they did not.

This point about Moses is reiterated throughout the passage. Unlike the Israelites, Moses is in faith-relationship with God:

> So the LORD spoke to Moses face to face, as a man speaks to his friend. (Exodus 33:11)

Moses says:

> Yet you have said, 'I know you by name, and you have also found grace in my sight'. Now therefore, I pray, if I have found grace in your sight, show me now your way, that I may know you and that I may find grace in your sight. And consider that this nation is your people. (Exodus 33:12-13)

Moses' desire is to know God more personally, to develop that faith-relationship yet further. But his desire shows two fundamental principles: 'Love God with everything – love your neighbour as yourself'. In Mark 12:28-34, Jesus commends the rabbi who asked him the question for recognising that these two principles were 'more than all the whole burnt offerings and sacrifices' – ie more than any 'works of the Law'. These two, which Jesus presented as the two greatest commandments *in the Law* (from Deuteronomy 6:5 and Leviticus 19:18) were engraved on Moses' heart. He didn't really need the two tablets with the ten commandments on them!

Moses Prays and God Changes His Mind

So what of the Israelites? God's first thought (32:9) is that they are irredeemable, and he suggests he destroy them and make a nation out of Moses. It is hard to say how serious God is – whether this really is a possibility or whether he is testing Moses as he had once tested Abraham. Moses intercedes for Israel, but he does not do so on any basis of supposed works, merits, or even potential works. He simply reminds God that:

o   God himself brought them out of Egypt.

o   The Egyptians will gloat if the Israelites are destroyed now.

o   God made promises to the patriarchs about them.

All these points relate not to their merits or works, but to God's own plan, strategy and promises.

Exodus 32:14 says that at this point God 'changed his mind' (NASB) or 'relented' (NKJV and NIV). There has been no shortage of theologians who claim that it doesn't really mean that, but rather means that God now indicated his real intention had always been something different. We look at such ideas in detail in chapter 1 of *Volume 2: Reconsidering Key Biblical Ideas*. Note, however, that in Jeremiah 18 God clearly tells us that he *does* change his mind to either punish or do good to people depending on their reactions. This is not because he is capricious or whimsical, but because he is a personal God and personal relationships imply reacting to each other's choices. Thus in the *New International Dictionary of Old Testament Theology & Exegesis* it states:

> a) The word [*nḥm*] is used to express two apparently contrasting sentiments in 1 Samuel 15, where God says, 'I am grieved (*nḥm*) that I have made Saul king' (iv 11; cf v 35), but where Samuel also announces that 'the Glory of Israel does not lie or change his mind (*nḥm*), for he is not a man, that he should change his mind (*nḥm*)' (v29). The explanation seems to be that God does not capriciously change his intentions or ways of acting. It is the change in Saul's behaviour that leads to this expression of regret. The reference is notable as being one of the rare occasions when God is said to repent or change his mind concerning something intended as good (cf Genesis 6:6).
>
> b) In many cases the Lord's 'changing' of his mind is a gracious

response to human factors. Thus in Jeremiah we often read that repentance on the part of people (usually *šwb* but *nḥm* in Jeremiah 8:6 and 31:19) will make it possible for God to repent, change his mind (*nḥm*): 18:8,10; 20:16; 26:3,13,19 cf 42:10. Note also God's response to Amos' pleas on behalf of Israel (Amos 7:3,6). (vol 5, p 82)

The term (*nḥm*) certainly does mean to change one's mind, and the principle was also recognized by Jonah (3:10;4:2) and applied by God, for example in Ezekiel 12:3 and Isaiah 38:1-5. It is also the most natural way to read 1 Kings 21:1-35, 2 Kings 20:2-5, 2 Chronicles 32:24-26, Isaiah 38:1-6 and 39:1-8. God is unchanging and does not change his mind because he is capricious, but in response to how we choose to behave.

This whole passage, then, is certainly not about some implacable, unchanging, emotionless God who determines everything that happens. It is about a *personal* God who talks things over with his friend Moses, and *reacts* to both sin and intercession. Moses, having seen for himself the depths of the people's sin, can only go back and plead for mercy with God (v32). He identifies with them, asking that if they are 'blotted out' of the book of blessing then he may be treated likewise (v33). God tells Moses that it doesn't work like that – *sin* is the reason for being blotted out. We can only imagine Moses' utter incredulity were he ever to meet an Augustinian or Reformed theologian who told him that the Israelites were unrepentant because God 'sovereignly' chose not to make them repent! In reality it was no more use for Moses to pray that God would blot him out of the book of life if Israel were condemned, than it was for Paul to wish to be accursed to save his brethren (Exodus 32:32; Romans 9:3). Nevertheless, God promised Moses that his judgment on Israel would be partial and postponed (v34).

Moses' intercession reminds us of an incident earlier in the life of Abraham. When God was intending to destroy Sodom he told his servant Abraham about it (Genesis 18:20,21). In a moving passage, Abraham is shown pleading with the Lord, who finally agreed that for the sake of ten righteous men he would spare the city. Maybe God already knew that Lot was the only righteous one in Sodom, or maybe the angelic visit was to see if some would repent in response to Lot's continuing witness. But in any event in this episode Abraham showed that he was a person after God's own heart.

Indeed, in Ezekiel God says:

> Say to them, 'As surely as I live', declares the Sovereign LORD, 'I take no pleasure in the death of the wicked, but rather that they turn from their ways and live. Turn! Turn from your evil ways! Why will you die, people of Israel?' (Ezekiel 33:11, see also 18:23)

Abraham may not have understood the war strategy as the Lord did, but his motives were right and God loved him for it. Moses shows a similar attitude, and shows that he too has a heart like God's own when he pleads with God to spare Israel.

Moses, having obtained some stay of judgment, focuses on pleading with God to go in and among his people (33:15-16; 34:9). Throughout these passages the Lord offers to go with Moses, but Moses wants him to go with the whole nation. The Lord is well disposed towards Moses, and Moses' heart is in tune with God's own. But if God were to do what Moses asked, then his purity of love would consume them (see Exodus 33:5 – note that in verses 7-11 it is specified that the tent and pillar of cloud were 'outside the camp' - only Moses and Joshua went there). Moses linked the requests 'Show me your glory' and 'Go up with the people'. God responds:

> I will also do this thing of which you have spoken; for you have found favour in my sight and I have known you by name… I myself will make all my goodness pass before you, and will proclaim the name of the Lord before you; and I will be gracious to whom I will be gracious, and will show compassion on whom I will show compassion. (Exodus 33:17-19)

The whole context of these words, then, is not one of some despotic puppeteer, who predetermines everything and applies 'might is right' principles. It is of a loving personal God, interacting with and answering the prayer of a person in faith-relationship with him, but reminding the person that God knows best how and to whom to distribute blessing. God *would* use Moses as his particular agent for blessing, and *would* go within Moses rather than within Israel at large. Yet, in a sense, Moses' prayer *was* answered – for when Moses came down the mountain the Lord did indeed go into their midst, for the face of Moses himself shone and the glory of God was *in him* (Exodus 34:29-35). It was good that God did not merely grant Abraham's plea (to spare Sodom if ten righteous men could be found there but otherwise destroy it) for in this case righteous Lot would also have perished. Instead, God answered the desires of Abraham's heart, and did not 'sweep away the righteous with the wicked' (Genesis 18:23). Thus Lot was saved. It was good that the Lord did not grant Moses' plea to go up in the midst of the Israelites, for then they would have been consumed. God *did* grant what he could of what was in Moses' heart (which reflected his own heart), but in doing so he reiterated the principle that it is *God* and not Moses who decides how best to order his favours.

Points to Note

None of this is about individual eternal destinies. It is about the way God operates in distributing his special favours, and whom he chooses to use as his agent. It is not, Paul says in Romans 9:16, about human 'willing' (desires) or 'running' (effort). Of course, there is nothing wrong with setting value on being God's chosen vessel to bring in blessing, or wishing to see it bestowed in a particular way. Jacob (unlike Esau) valued and wanted this blessing for his descendants, and Moses wished it to be maintained on his protégés. Neither is there anything wrong in human efforts – 'running' is a favoured Pauline metaphor for a Christian life of discipleship and service (see 1 Corinthians 9:24,26; Galatians 2:2; 5:7; Philippians 2:16). Paul's point is simply that God's strategy is not determined by these. James Dunn writes:

> Paul does not disparage 'willing' and 'running'; willing and running are, of course, part of the human response to God... But they are not factors in election, neither in the initial choice nor in its maintenance. Paul's concern is not to debate the issues of predestination and freewill... but to clarify what the covenant means for Israel. (*Romans 9-16*, p 553)

It would be wrong to suppose that God's strategy would be dictated by human will and exertion. But this does not mean that when God does something we did not expect or pray for, there are no reasons for his actions. God's actions never compromise his justice and love.

Today, when we take part in the battle through prayer, we may perhaps 'not know how to pray as we should' because of our 'weakness' or our lack of understanding of God's strategy. Yet if we, like Abraham and Moses, lay open our hearts before the Spirit of God, then he will answer the groanings of our hearts which cannot be uttered, rather than the mistaken petitions of our minds. The Spirit knows the plan of God and his strategy in the battle, and so can transform our prayers (in spite of our preconceived ideas) as long as our hearts are pure before him (see Romans 8:26-28).

In none of this are we to suppose that God's acts are *arbitrary*. This is certainly not Paul's meaning, and would hardly have been a satisfactory answer to the issue at hand. What Paul is concerned to show, using Moses as an example, is that God's strategy is not determined by human volition or effort – God reacts and responds to human choice, but cannot be dictated to.

11

Israel and God's Plan – Pharaoh

Moses and Pharaoh – Two Key Figures

At the time of the birth of Israel as a nation there were *two* great figures: Moses and Pharaoh. Paul continues his outline of key points in God's strategy in Israel's history by taking a brief look at the case of Pharaoh. Moses' heart was in tune with the heart of his God, and God used this beyond his understanding. Pharaoh made his heart resistant to God's purpose and God used this also, beyond the feeble understanding of that 'might is right' monarch. Paul presents this as a contrast to Moses:

> For the Scripture says to Pharaoh, 'For this very purpose I have raised you up, to demonstrate my power in you, and that my name might be proclaimed throughout the whole earth'. So then he has mercy on whom he desires, and he hardens whom he desires. (Romans 9:17-8, NASB)

The first part of this is taken from Exodus 9:

> For at this time I will send all my plagues to your very heart, and on your servants and on your people, that you may know that *there is* none like me in all the earth. Now if I had stretched out my hand and struck you and your people with pestilence, then you would have been cut off from the earth. But indeed for this *purpose* I have raised you up, that I may show my power in you, and that my name may be declared in all the earth. (Exodus 9:14-16)

The Hebrew rendered here as 'raised you up' could also mean 'allowed to stand', and the Septuagint (LXX) translates it like this. Sanday & Headlam point out, however, that Paul purposely changed the LXX word to another which is sometimes used for God raising up men and nations on the stage of history (as LXX Habakkuk 1:6; Jeremiah 23:41). The NKJV therefore translates Exodus in this sense. God could simply have wiped him out, but has raised him on the stage of history by allowing him to stand. NT Wright writes:

> As with Israel after the golden calf, Pharaoh is guilty; God could have punished him at once. God has instead 'made him to stand', 'raised him up' in this sense, rather than cutting him off instantly. The reason is so that God's power might be displayed in him, and that God's name might be made known in all the world. (*The New Interpreter's Bible*, p 639)

The 'hardening of Pharaoh's heart' has sometimes been a source of puzzlement and even distress to people who believe in a God who loves everyone and has compassion wherever possible. How could our loving God and Father apparently deliberately enforce unrepentance and moral guilt on Pharaoh just to show off? However, these confusions are based on a misunderstanding of the text. God's actions on Pharaoh stimulated not so much impenitence as foolhardiness. The end effect was not about eternal destiny, but a place in God's strategy in his plans on this earth. Paul's rapid-fire treatment of the incident reflects this, and forms part of his carefully laid case. A summary of this appears in chapter 16 of this volume (p 196) and a more detailed treatment of the whole issue of hardening is given in chapter 6 of *Volume 2: Reconsidering Key Biblical Ideas*. But we will briefly outline a basic answer here. As we will see, God does not interfere with Pharaoh's basic moral alignment and choice to make him bad. Pharaoh had chosen his path of rebellion and oppression before any action of God on him.

Stubbornness and Hardening

Three distinct Hebrew words are used in Exodus in connection with the 'hardening' of Pharaoh's heart:

1) *Qashah:* stubborn

   God says he will harden (*qashah*) Pharaoh's heart in Exodus 7:3, and Exodus 13:15 says Pharaoh is *qashah*. *Qashah* as opposed to *kabed* and *chazaq*, which we cover below, seems to refer to the overall process of hardening, not to any specific instance.

2) *Kabed:* heavy/immovable/stubborn

Pharaoh makes his heart *kabed* in Exodus 8:15; 8:32; 9:34; 1 Samuel 6:6, and God says he has made Pharaoh's heart *kabed* in Exodus 10:1 (see also Exodus 7:14; 9:7). *Kabed* refers first to Pharaoh's obduracy in hardening his heart and later to God confirming Pharaoh's choice.

3) *Chazaq:* strengthen/make firm

Pharaoh's heart is *chazaq* in Exodus 7:13; 7:22; 8:19; 9:35 God strengthens Pharaoh's resolve in Exodus 4:21; 9:12; 10:20; 10:27; 11:10; 14:4; 14:8; 14:17; Joshua 11:20. *Chazaq* refers to Pharaoh being made firm in his resolve and having courage to follow his inclinations.

Strength of resolve (*chazaq*) is either just there in a person, or God acts to provide it. However, obduracy and refusal to change (*kabed*) is something over which someone has a moral choice – and in general it is Pharaoh who makes his own heart hard, with God acting on it in a kind of confirmatory judgment only at the end of the process (10:1). It is as if the Lord says: 'Very well, if he is determined to be hard and unrepentant then I will make his heart hard, just as he wishes'. This is the only place where *kabed* is used with God as the subject. From this point onward, though, we read again and again that the Lord strengthened (*chazaq*) Pharaoh's heart to carry out his own wicked desires – even though his guilt became increasingly apparent.

Even before the Lord began to deal with him, Pharaoh had adopted a contemptuous attitude toward God. Exodus 4:21 and 7:3 are predictions, but in the actual process it is Pharaoh who throughout chapters 7:13–9:11 makes his heart immovable (*kabed*) and has firm resolve (*chazaq*), breaking his word in 8:28. God's first act is in 9:12 – a strengthening of Pharaoh's resolve. This is not about moral repentance, but about foolhardy courage to defy a powerful God.

What happened is that, when any normal person would have given in because of fear or prudence, Pharaoh received supernatural strength to continue with his evil path of rebellion.

God wanted to demonstrate his power and judgement to the nations, but there is no indication that God's motives were to somehow increase Pharaoh's guilt – the wicked desire was already in Pharaoh; the Lord's action simply gave him courage to carry it out. As Jesus implied on the sermon on the mount, an evil design and intention is itself sin – irrespective of the opportunity to fulfil it. God's motives in this hardening are actually stated:

o That Israel should clearly understand who had delivered them (Exodus 6:6-7; 10:2; 13:14-5).

o That they should carry possessions with them away from Egypt (Exodus 3:21-2).

o That God might multiply his signs and bring them forth in great acts, so that the Egyptians should know that he was the true God (Exodus 7:3-4; 11:9; 14:4,17-8)

o That his name might be declared not only in Egypt but in the whole earth (Exodus 9:14-18; Joshua 2:10-11; 1 Samuel 8:8; Exodus 15:13).

As NT Wright summarises:

> What God has done to Pharaoh is not arbitrary. Pharaoh has already enslaved God's people and refused to set them free. (*The New Interpreter's Bible*, p 639)

Israel's Place and God's Emblems

In Romans 9:14-18, the apostle Paul brings together God's dealings with Pharaoh and the special favour shown to Moses. Neither of these acts of God concerns the destinies of the individuals as such, and Paul is not concerned with such questions here. Indeed, James Dunn states in his commentary *Romans* it is 'unlikely' that Paul is talking about:

> ... eternal reprobation... since the talk of Pharaoh's hardening evidently prepares for the later talk of Israel's hardening... which Paul sees as a partial and temporary phase of God's purpose (11:26-31). (p 555)

Paul cites that first point of God's action, to give Pharaoh courage to stand – referring to the overall process as 'hardening' (as Exodus 4:21?). Neither Moses' nor Pharaoh's eternal destiny is in question. It is the impact of Moses and Pharaoh on the earthly function and destiny of the nation of Israel that is at issue. While God's actions do affect the two individuals concerned, they do not alter their eternal and personal destinies – this is not what the passage is concerned with.

Paul is interested in the way in which God is intervening in earthly history to shape the course of the chosen nation of Israel: here God shows special mercy to their leader, and through him to the nation; there he causes someone to have the courage to stand and carry out rebellious designs... and so God's plan for Israel was being worked out. God is working out his plans by acting in the world of human affairs, but he does so without overruling the moral choices of those involved. He neither forces good people to do evil nor forces evil people to repent.

It seems to have been God's intention that Israel should go straight into the Promised Land (Numbers 13–14). The episode with Pharaoh had so frightened the Canaanites (Exodus 15:15) that Rahab remembered it fearfully over forty years later (Joshua 2:9-10). This meant that *if Israel had been obedient* they could have easily conquered Canaan. This should have enabled the nations around about to recognize that the true God was with Israel. Then, when the Temple was built, they could indeed have been ready to look toward it for the true God (as Solomon hinted in 1 Kings 8) and to admit that 'the services' belong to Israel (Romans 9:4).

The Lord moves in history, strengthening resolve or showing special self-revelation (Romans 9:18), and Paul explains the purpose of it all is the strategy of development of the nation of Israel. This is in turn the preparation for that Seed of Abraham who was to come to redeem the world.

So going back to the question posed by Paul's critic that we looked at in chapter 10 above: 'Is there unrighteousness with God?' (v14), we can now see this is senseless. It would be wrong to expect that man could direct God's strategy in history by his own efforts. Righteousness and unrighteousness simply do not enter into the question, for it could only conceivably be *unfair* if through study and works a man could become as well able to direct God's actions as God himself! But it is obvious that God alone knows the best way for him to intervene in the affairs of humankind as he seeks to extend his plan of salvation. The origin of Israel, God's election of them in Jacob, and the events surrounding their emergence as a nation: these all demonstrate this principle of God-determined strategy – there is no trace of a principle of 'works'.

In Exodus it is also exciting to see the emblems of God's warfare that appear again at the time of Israel's birth as a nation. In the final and conclusive plague, any house (Israelite or Egyptian) that marked itself with the blood of God's symbol of the slain lamb escaped the wrath. At this, the emergence of the nation, the Lord was looking forward to that greater victory and the method of its achievement in Christ the Passover lamb.

Pharaoh and his hosts were overcome by the Red Sea. The nation of Israel was 'baptised into Moses' as they passed *through* the same Red Sea (1 Corinthians 10:1-2). Here God was showing that the way of deliverance from the forces of evil is through baptism – which we know represents the path of suffering, death and resurrection (Romans 6). The suffering and atoning death of Christ, and the suffering and death of the martyrs, will finally be too much for the forces of evil. The horse and his rider will be thrown into this 'sea'. The emblems Christ left for his Church were the Lord's supper (ie communion) and Christian baptism. These are reminders for us, just as there were reminders for Israel, of the methods by which God works.

God's strategy today is similar to then. In the Church he is teaching us (like Moses) to stand, that we may see the salvation of our God (Exodus 14:13). The Church is moving toward the 'evil day' in the battle of the Lord. In this day we must withstand, and having done all must stand (Ephesians 6:13) – as though trapped between Pharaoh and the Red Sea. Through this will come the final overthrow and exhaustion of Satan and his power, in which the knowledge of God will fill the universe as the waters cover the sea (Isaiah 11:9; Habakkuk 2:14).

12

Objectors and Vessels

Paul Deals with a Casuistic Heckler

We have been looking at how Paul deals with the subject of God's choice of Abraham, Isaac and Jacob, and with the patriarchal age. He imagines the question being thrown up at him: 'Is there unrighteousness with God?' He answers 'Certainly not!' for God explained to Moses that he knew best the way in which his special self-revelation and presence should be distributed. If he had answered Moses' request to go up with the people, the nation would have been consumed. Similarly the story of Pharaoh shows that it is not man's will but God's strategy that ultimately shapes history, and in this instance the Bible even clarifies for us the Lord's motives and purposes in his actions.

Paul's allusions here, however, although full of meaning, would hardly silence the critic who earlier in Romans 3:8 was casuistic enough (ie using deceitful and specious arguments) to suggest that Paul's message was: 'Let us do evil, that good may come' (Romans 3:8). The same sort of critic could be relied upon here to throw up the objection: 'Why does he [God] still find fault? For who has resisted his will?' (Romans 9:19). (Interestingly, the word here for 'will' or more properly 'plan' (*boulēma*) is used by Josephus (who shared Paul's pharisaic background) when he says that Pharaoh was disobedient to the *plan* of God to have the Israelites go (*Antiquities* 2:304).)

It is important for us to realise the nature of the question and questioner at this point. The sincere questionings of God's ways that come from a person like Habakkuk (Habakkuk 1:2; 2:1), do not provoke a command from God to keep quiet. The Lord replies to Habakkuk (Habakkuk 2:2), who breaks into a hymn of praise (Habakkuk 3) as he realizes something of God's strategy. Similarly the Lord commends what Job has said in his sincere bewilderment at what he thought were God's actions. It is never the Lord's way to condemn or knock down the questions or objections of a sincere person wanting to be real with him. The apostle Paul is always reasonable in his replies to honest questioners. The whole of Romans 9–11 is, in fact, a serious treatment of a serious question about Israel's place.

But who is Paul aiming his comments at here? First, the objector is obviously Hebrew, as Paul's blunt reply uses Scripture as an authority. If the question had come from someone who doubted God's existence or Scripture's authority, we may be sure that Paul would have followed his usual practice of beginning his discussion from what the person *did* believe (see for example Acts 14:15-17 or 17:22-31). There was Jewish opposition to Paul from within the Church (for example Galatians 1–3), but more probably as he dictates his letter he is dealing with imagined non-Christian hecklers like those in Acts 13:45,50 and 14:2. He must often have had questions like 'Do we make void the Law through faith?' (3:31), 'Shall we continue in sin that grace may abound?' (6:1), 'Shall we sin because we are not under law but under grace?' (6:15).

There are some striking parallels between two passages that feature the questions of this heckler – Romans 3:3-8 and Romans 9:14-9:

1 i)   3:5-6 – Is God unjust who inflicts wrath?... Certainly not! For then how will God judge the world?
   ii) 9:14-5 – Is there unrighteousness with God? Certainly not! For he says to Moses...

2 i)   3:7-8 – Why am I also still judged as a sinner? And why not say...
   ii) 9:19 – Why does he still find fault? For who has resisted his will?'

3 i)   Romans 3:5 – I speak as a man.
      Romans 3:8 – As some affirm that we say.
   ii) Romans 9:19 – You will say to me then...

It seems clear that it is the same critic who appears in both Romans 3 and 9. The idea that no one can resist God's will is no more a part of Paul's teaching than the idea that we should do evil so that good may come. The first is an unjustifiable deduction from Paul's teaching that God's strategy is not under man's control, and the second is an unjustifiable deduction from Paul's teaching that God's faithfulness is shown all the more by man's lack of it.

In Romans 3 Paul simply gives a crushing retort to the critic ('Their condemnation is just!'), not bothering to answer the charge in detail. Of course, this was not because Paul had no answer – his whole theology shows the absurdity of the suggestion – it was simply because he didn't wish to break the flow of his argument in order to answer what was either a foolish or wilful misrepresentation.

So what of the same critic in Romans 9? First, Paul pictures God as moving in history: 'He has mercy on whom he wills, and whom he wills he hardens' (v18). Yet Paul does not say here (or anywhere else) that God's eternal plan for an individual is irresistible. Paul uses the same Greek root word here for 'will' or 'plan' (*boulē*) as Luke uses in 7:30, which refers to the Pharisees and lawyers (or rabbis) who rejected the will of God for themselves, clearly showing that God's will can be resisted. In Romans 9 it might be just such a person who demands of Paul: 'Why does he still find fault, for who has resisted his will (*boulēma*)?' On a human level, Luke was Paul's friend and travelling companion and would have used similar terminology, so when they use the same words, Paul and Luke mean the same things by them. Paul's most voluble critics, therefore, were themselves living proofs that their objection was spurious.

We have seen that the Exodus story to which Paul alludes is far from implying any 'irresistible will', as the people reject God's plan for them and God also changes his mind. It is true that God will ultimately achieve his plan for the world in spite of those who resist it, but every individual still has his or her own moral choice of whether or not to reject God's plan for themselves. Just as Paul dismissed the misrepresentation in Romans 3 without detailed refutation, here in Romans 9:19, the equally untrue misrepresentation of what he has said is likewise dismissed. HL Ellison says of the heckler:

> Like most controversialists, he distorted his opponent's arguments
> – Paul is not inventing him; he must have met him often enough.
> (*The Mystery of Israel*, p 52)

Yet Paul's abrupt reply: 'But indeed, O man, who are you to reply against God?' (v20) itself demonstrates the weakness of such a misrepresentation.

How could the man reply against God if, as he supposed, he could not resist God's will? Paul's response implies 'You can, for one, for you are doing so now!' Here Paul applies to a specific case what Luke said of the group who resisted God's will for themselves.

The critic is a living demonstration that his criticism is nonsense! But Paul is not content merely to couch his remark as a statement but throws it in as a question, thus also forcing the critic to see where the critic is putting himself (compare similar ironic questions in Romans 2:17, etc). Then the apostle proceeds to the point at issue, the reason behind the critic's emotional resistance to God's revelation:

> Will the thing formed say to him who formed it, 'Why have you made me like this?' Does not the potter have power over the clay...
> (Romans 9:20-21)

The real question underlying the accusations and misrepresentations was whether man had the right or authority to control God's strategy. Paul's critic may have been indignant because God was using his nation of Israel without any reference to the merits or guaranteed position he supposed it to have. This sentiment was not new, and Paul goes back to a previous instance – the prophet Isaiah had a similar vision of God using some specially chosen figure in the shaping of Israel's history. Cyrus, a heathen king, was anointed as God's shepherd (Isaiah 44:28; 45:1) for the sake of God's chosen servant Israel (Isaiah 45:4). At that time, just as in Paul's day, someone objected to God controlling such temporal features of his creation and using his anointed Cyrus and servant Jacob in these ways. Again, God's strategy did not, predetermine the eternal destiny of either Cyrus or the Israelites. Isaiah in chapters 44–45, like Paul in Romans 9, was concerned with God's movements in history and not with the final destiny of individuals involved. Isaiah attacked such people who thought themselves wiser than God:

> Woe to him who strives with his maker! ... Shall the clay say to him who forms it, 'What are you making?', or shall your handiwork say, 'He has no hands'? [handles]. (Isaiah 45:9)

Just as a potter decides on the special features of a pot (for example, having handles) so special features like the election of a nation are decided by God alone, for he knows the best strategy. It would be ridiculous for a mere creature to set itself up as knowing better.

The Potter and the Clay

God is using his chosen nation Israel to demonstrate his truths to the world. He has fully revealed his will to show two things in particular through them: one part of the nation he will shape into a 'vessel for honour', and the other part into a 'vessel for dishonour' (or 'no-honour') (Romans 9:21).

It is regrettable that the fatalistic image brought to our Western minds by this metaphor of the potter is almost the reverse of what would occur to a Hebrew mind knowing the background of the Old Testament. To us we may think that the potter has total control over the clay, and it will do exactly what he wants it to. Paul's words, however, are coloured by the parable of the potter in Jeremiah 18. Through Jeremiah the Lord says: 'O house of Israel, can I not do with you as this potter?' (18:6). Israel is in his hands like a potter's clay. If the Lord promises 'to pluck up, to pull down, and to destroy' a kingdom (v7), and if after this they repent, then he will repent of the evil he would have done to them. If he promises to build up a nation and then they turn away from him, he will destroy them. The basic lump that forms a nation will either be built up or broken down by the Lord, *depending on their own moral response*. If a nation does repent and God builds them up, then it is for him alone to decide how the finished vessel will fit into his plan and whether or not it will have handles! God alone determines the special features/privileges/responsibilities of a particular nation. Nevertheless it is the actions of the nation itself that determine whether it shall be built up into some type of 'vessel for honour', or broken down and destroyed.

Paul's adversary in Romans 9:19 is, as we have observed, a Hebrew. As such he would accept the prophet's picture of God building up or breaking down the lump of clay forming a nation. Therefore, in Romans 9:21 Paul asks:

> Does not the potter have power over the clay, from the same lump to make one vessel for honour and another for dishonour?

God obviously has the right to make from the nation of Israel *two* vessels rather than *one*, just as a potter can divide one lump and make two pots. This is, in fact, what God has done. The unrepentant portion of Israel has become a 'vessel for dishonour', and the faithful part a 'vessel for honour'. This faithful section of Israel are like the natural branches of an olive tree and the Christian Gentiles like wild branches that have been grafted into it (see

Romans 11:17). Paul alludes to this teaching when he adds in verse 24 that the 'vessel for honour' is made up not only of some Jews but of some Gentiles as well. Mark Nanos in *The Mystery of Romans*, (p 259) sees this division into two parts as the 'mystery' of Romans 11:25 – the new unexpected factor.

Vessels for Honour and No-honour

We must pause briefly here to explain why we believe it is preferable to accept Ellison's translation of 'no-honour', which he adopts in his book *The Mystery of Israel* (p 53), rather than the more common one of 'dishonour'.

First, it is not the vessel that gets the honour, but the owner. Paul uses exactly the same phrase in 2 Timothy 2:20-21, and is surely not exhorting Timothy to cleanse himself with a selfish motive of increasing his own honour. Gold and silver vessels did not bring honour to themselves, but rather to the master of the house. We are to cleanse ourselves in order to become vessels bringing honour to our master, ready for him to use us as a great man would utilize his expensive vessels. For the purpose of bringing honour, vessels of wood and earth are of no use whatever; this is the meaning of Paul's imagery here. The individual faces a choice, and Paul urges Timothy to cleanse himself and become a vessel bringing glory to God. The use of the same phrases 'vessels for honour' and 'vessels for no-honour' in Romans 9:21 seems to indicate a similar meaning. The two vessels made from the nation of Israel bring honour or no-honour primarily to God, rather than to themselves.

In addition, Paul's use of prepositions is important. When he talks about the vessels of wrath and of mercy in v22-23 Paul uses the preposition *eis* with the genitive case (meaning '*of*'), however for the vessels of honour and no-honour he deliberately uses *eis* with the accusative (meaning '*for*'). Someone to whom God has shown mercy is called a 'vessel of mercy' and someone to whom God has shown wrath is called a 'vessel of wrath'. If God were to give honour to someone, it would seem natural to call him a 'vessel *of* honour' but, in fact, Paul deliberately uses a different preposition and says 'vessel *for* honour' and 'vessel *for* no-honour'.

So it seems fairly certain that the honour or no-honour is brought by the vessel *for* God. Israel is known to be God's special people entrusted with his oracles, covenants, law etc (Romans 3:2; 9:4,5). When people see the repentant section of Israel, living in harmony with God's will and exhibiting the fruits of his Spirit (Galatians 5:22-23) it will be just like looking at a beautiful gold vase. Glory and honour will then be brought to the master of the house. When, however, anyone looks at that section of God's people who are in rebellion against him, then no-honour is likely to be given to God. Perhaps it could even bring dishonour, as the name of God may be blasphemed among the Gentiles because of them (Romans 2:24).

Vessels of Wrath and Vessels of Mercy

The vessel for honour is made up of vessels of mercy, that is, of individuals to whom God has shown mercy. Upon them God wishes to make known the riches of his glory (Romans 9:23). As we have already seen, the glory of God as revealed by Jesus is in his giving of himself to us, his creatures. What better way to make this glory known than for he himself to pay the price of showing mercy to undeserving, but repentant sinners? God's continual love and mercy to his unworthy servants is a tremendous revelation of his glory.

The vessel for no-honour is made up of vessels of wrath. Those Israelites who rejected God's plan for them and refused to repent, had the wrath 'come upon them to the uttermost' (1 Thessalonians 2:16). Soon after this time the physical Temple was destroyed. Those of the nation who had rejected Jesus, who was the true Temple, were scattered among the Gentiles. As the Lord had promised, if they would not obey him, he would scatter them among the nations (Leviticus 26:27-33). If they did evil in the sight of God to provoke him to anger, he would scatter them among the peoples (Deuteronomy 4:25-27). Yet if from there anyone should seek God with all his heart he would find him (Deuteronomy 4:29). Any individual Israelite who (like Paul himself) repented and sought the Lord, would become a vessel of mercy. He would then become part of the vessel for honour, and God's glory would be made known upon him. We must not imagine that God ever drew hard and unchangeable lines between the vessel for honour and that for no-honour. Many Jews who were under the wrath of God did, in fact, repent. Others missed the obvious teachings about Jesus in their own Scriptures because 'a veil lies on their heart' (2 Corinthians 3:15). Yet if their heart 'turns to the Lord, the veil is taken away' (v16). As the light of God begins to shine in their hearts he will make known his glory on them as they are 'transformed into' the image of Jesus (2 Corinthians 3:14–4:6).

A vessel of wrath could turn to the Lord and so become a vessel of mercy, upon whom God would show his glory.

Why does God endure with much longsuffering the vessels of wrath which are fit only for destruction (Romans 9:22,23)? He himself gives as his reasons:

o   to show his wrath, which means righteous anger,

o   to make his power known,

o   and in order that he might make known the riches of his glory upon vessels of mercy.

We can see some similarities between the situation of Israel in Paul's time and the situation under Pharaoh we looked at above in chapter 11.

Firstly, we could regard Pharaoh as a *vessel of wrath*, for God certainly showed his wrath on Pharaoh. Further, God could have easily destroyed the Egyptians with an immediate plague (Exodus 9:15), but instead (using the language of Romans 9:22) he endured them with much longsuffering in their rebellion against him.

Secondly, God's purpose at that time was *to make his power known* on Pharaoh, just as he would make it known on the vessels of wrath in Paul's day. But God's purpose never seems to be merely to exhibit power. In the case of Pharaoh, God wanted to show the Hebrews, the Egyptians and the surrounding nations that he was the true God and that Israel was his people.

Thirdly, God did this two-lumps of clay thing *in order that he might make known his riches on the vessels of mercy*. Those of God's special people who rebel against him are allowed to live, but he shows his power and wrath in the dispersion of the nation. He intends that some should be led by this to repent. Paul might ask them:

> Or do you despise the riches of his goodness, forbearance, and longsuffering, not knowing that the goodness of God leads you to repentance? But in accordance with your hardness and your impenitent heart you are treasuring up for yourself wrath in the day of wrath… (Romans 2:4-5)

These words, Paul says, apply even more to the Jew than to anyone else (v9). The wrath of God is revealed from heaven against those who in unrighteousness ignore the truth (Romans 1:18), yet his longsuffering in not destroying them immediately is meant to lead them to repentance.

God's strategy is perfect – it is for him to choose the shape of a vessel for honour or the shape of a vessel for no-honour. Pharaoh chose to rebel, and God decided to use him as a special demonstration of his wrath. In this way someone like Rahab could be encouraged to repent and, through faith, receive right-standing with God (Joshua 2:9-10, Hebrews 11:31 and James 2:25). In this way God 'will be honoured through Pharaoh' even though Pharaoh in himself is bringing him no honour (Exodus 14:4, NASB). Similarly God could use even that part of Israel which rebelled against him. He used them to demonstrate his wrath, and so their disobedience led indirectly to the extension of the gospel among the Gentiles (Romans 11:30).

Gentiles may also Become Vessels of Mercy

In Romans 9:1-23 Paul has been dealing with the Jewish question. At this juncture he breaks off to point out that Gentiles can also have a place. The vessels of mercy whom God has called include people 'not from among Jews only, but also from among Gentiles'. In verse 24 the Greek word *kaleo* can mean either 'called' or 'named' – the latter sense is obviously the one intended here because of Paul's reference in v25-6 to the principle of renaming previously outlined by Hosea (see also chapter 4 in *Volume 2: Reconsidering Key Biblical Ideas*). In Hosea God had called Israel 'Not-my-people' because of their sin (Hosea 1:9). Yet he promised that when they repented he would rename them as his people (2:23). We must realise the importance of names to the Hebrew mind – to rename a person or a group had great significance. For example, Abraham, Sarah, Israel and Peter were all renamed. RA Stewart in his book *Rabbinic Theology* says:

> Knowledge of a proper name was supposed to give a certain measure of power over its bearer... (p 43)

To have authority to rename a person would be even more significant (see also James Neil's, *Everyday Life in the Holy Land* (p 126-34) and WN Carter's, *The People of the Book and Their Land* (p 28-32)).

The principle in Hosea is this: God might, if he considers it necessary, remove or bestow a privileged name and position as he sees fit. Paul considered the same principle to be involved in God's actions in his own age. Those who have been 'named' (Romans 9:26, the name being 'sons of the living God') include some who – as Gentiles – formerly did not have a name as people of God. What, through Hosea, God said he could do for rejected Israel, in the time of Paul he has done for repentant Gentiles.

Gentiles, then, as well as Jews, are called sons of the living God. He has shown them mercy. They are known to be his and are part of the vessel for his honour.

The Election of Grace

Paul spends much of the remaining part of Romans 9–11 demonstrating that the principles upon which God is working are not new. Paul points out that on various previous occasions God had to judge his people Israel when they were rebellious. Yet there was always a section of them who were the chosen of God on a basis of faith and grace (Romans 11:5). There is, we must realize, more than one context and meaning for the word 'chosen' in Paul's writing (see also *Volume 2: Reconsidering Key Biblical Ideas* chapter 4, and the summary on page 192 of this volume). In one sense, the whole nation of Israel was undoubtedly *chosen* by God. In another sense only those who had individually accepted God's grace were really his *choice* people. Some Israelites, although in the chosen nation, had rejected God's grace and were therefore not in the 'election of grace'.

Why was this? Paul explains at least part of the answer. A number of Israelites, such as the Pharisees, were almost obsessed with the idea of being shown to be in a right-standing as the people of God according to his Law (Romans 9:31, compare 10:20). What they did not grasp was that the way to 'righteousness' (see also chapter 2 in *Volume 2: Reconsidering Key Biblical Ideas*) was through faith, and not through meritorious acts and strict conformity to ceremonial law (Romans 9:30-3). Moses had made it clear from the beginning that simple trust in what God had done was more necessary than any deed of great prowess (Romans 10:5-8). How ironic that some Gentiles, who had never been so obsessed with being right before God's bar of judgment, had obtained just such a declaration of right-standing because they understood and applied all the more readily the principle of faith and grace. Paul is careful to point out that the idea of Gentiles being right before God is not a new one. The Old Testament says that *whoever* shall call on the name of the Lord shall be saved, which includes Gentiles as well as Jews (Romans 10:12).

The Church and Israel

Paul has progressed from discussing the historical position of Israel into discussing the 1st century position. Many of the Israelites had rejected God and were under God's wrath, but some had accepted Christ and (together with believing Gentiles) became the Church. Paul nevertheless made it clear that the believing Gentiles should not exult over those Israelites who did not believe (Romans 11:13-24). The believing Gentiles had received great benefit from God's strategy involving Israel, leading to Jesus the Messiah. It is as though the Gentiles were wild olive branches grafted into the olive tree of the messianic program, and some of its natural branches have been cut out. Commentators on this text have interpreted the 'root' in verse 16 in different ways. Some regard it as Abraham, others as Christ, and others as the first Christians. Whichever of these we accept, Paul's meaning is obviously that Gentile Christians benefit from the heritage of God's messianic program in Israel – as Jesus said in John 4:22, 'Salvation is of the Jews'. Gentiles must not, therefore, exult. Moreover, if any of the unbelieving Israel repent, they can all the more easily be grafted back by God into his plan and program. The Gentile believers must themselves be careful, for it is only by their faith that they have become part of God's path to victory. If they cease to exercise daily faith they will no longer be of use in it.

God had said to Israel:

> ... if you will indeed obey my voice and keep my covenant, then you shall be a special treasure to me above all people; for all the earth is mine. And you shall be to me *a royal priesthood and a holy nation*. (Exodus 19:5-6 in the LXX)

Israel was not only chosen to receive the land, but also, as the people of God, to represent God on earth and act as a light in the world. Peter applies exactly the same phrase to the Church:

> But you are a chosen generation, *a royal priesthood, a holy nation*, his own special people, that you may proclaim the praises of him who called you out of darkness into his marvellous light; who once were not a people but are now the people of God, who had not obtained mercy but now have obtained mercy. (1 Peter 2:9-10)

Clearly, the 'people of God' who have this priestly, holy, function is now the

Church – both Jews and Gentiles. This function cannot be done by those who have not accepted the Messiah, but Israel as a nation is still significant since 'Salvation is from the Jews'.

Paul further explains in Romans the position of unbelieving Israel by picturing the two different feelings of God toward them in a typically Hebrew exaggerated contrast (just like God saying he 'loves' Jacob, but 'hates' Esau – as we looked at in chapter 9 above). They are the chosen nation and their descent and heritage from the patriarchs give them a special place before God, ie they are 'beloved for the sake of the fathers'. Yet, as far as their opposition to the gospel is concerned, they are 'enemies' of God (Romans 11:28). Paul's words are that 'they are enemies for your sake' – God has used the disobedience of some Israelites to show his wrath and thus to lead some Gentiles along the path of repentance to receive mercy (v30). God's wrath is not for its own sake. He does not want Gentiles to exult over Israel because of the wrath. His intention is that Christians should be vessels on which he may so pour out his mercy, that those Jews who disbelieve are provoked to repentance.

How utterly contrary to God's will it is that some calling themselves Christians have persecuted Jews. Elements in the Catholic, Orthodox and Reformed traditions have all done this. It is especially tragic that in 1543 Martin Luther, having moved from his earlier tolerance, wrote *On the Jews and Their Lies*, an extreme, virulently anti-Semitic book that could be seen as a foundation to later German anti-Semitism. God's wrath did come upon the bulk of the nation at the time of Paul, but his intention was that the grace shown in the Church would provoke them to repentance. God's wrath was not for its own sake. God's aim in drawing out the lessons of obedience and disobedience was to have mercy on all (v32), and eventually the whole of Israel would come in.

Past Principles Guide Present Understanding

Certain principles emerge from God's treatment of Israel and these may help our understanding of God's methods in the present. The same God is at work today, in the Church (Jews and Gentiles) phase of the conflict. We can draw out these principles as follows:

God's sovereignty

God's choice of Abraham rather than of Lot or Melchizedek was not because of his deeds, nor even, necessarily, because of his faith. It was because God knew the best strategy. God alone decides what part he will assign to us in his great plan for humankind. He used his sovereign choice again in deciding that Isaac rather than Ishmael should be in the line of descent to the Messiah. Paul shows us that his choice was not made without reason – but nonetheless he alone made the choice. We are not explicitly told the reasons for God's choice of Jacob rather than Esau, but perhaps hints are given in the later history of the individuals and their descendants.

Today also, God assigns his servants to different positions and functions. It is not our business to question this, but to seek to fulfil, to his glory, the role with which he has privileged us. To put this bluntly: when God puts a particular task before us, it is our responsibility to run well and finish the course (1 Corinthians 9:24; Hebrews 12:1; 2 Timothy 4:7). But as to what course God shall set us, that is not a matter determined by our willing or running (Romans 9:16), but by God's strategy and mercy. Failure to accept gladly the position that God has assigned to us in the body of Christ is one great source of spiritual sterility and failure.

God's foreknowledge

God's sovereign and strategic assignment of positions is made in the full light of his foreknowledge. For one thing, God knows the hearts of men and how they will react to what he says. Before Moses ever began his task, God knew that the Israelites would listen to his voice (Exodus 3:18). In the same passage he also told Moses 'I am sure that the king of Egypt will not let you go' (v19). The Lord assigns positions in the full knowledge of the man, for 'the Lord looks at the heart' (1 Samuel 16:7).

God also foreknows aspects of the distant future. This is seen in his prophecy to Abraham that all nations shall be blessed by his messianic seed. Another example is seen in the prophecy at the birth of Jacob and Esau that one nation would serve the other. God may send us somewhere or inspire us to do something today for reasons we do not understand. Yet when he does this we may be sure that he can foresee repercussions of our actions – even far into the future.

God manoeuvres good and evil

God was able to use the faith and obedience of his servants Abraham and Moses, but he was also able to encompass even the hard heart of Pharaoh into his plan. Moses chose to follow God's way and was used beyond his intellectual understanding of God's strategy. Pharaoh chose the path of rebellion and God manoeuvred him into a position where the consequences of an evil heart were made clear to all, and it was shown that *Yahweh* was the true and living God. Such a demonstration could be used by God to bring repentance and life to many. Similarly, when part of Israel rejected the Messiah and rebelled against God they were used as vessels to demonstrate his wrath. Again he utilized this to stimulate repentance and to bring life.

God will not manoeuvre people by forcing them to remain unrepentant, because he is not willing that any should perish but that all should come to repentance. However, he is the Lord of all and we believe that he can operate to overrule on events and decisions that do not affect the individual's chosen moral alignment.

So we see that God can use even the evil in the world to bring in blessing. This is not to say that he wills evil himself, but such is his greatness that he can use it for good. When the enemy brings some disaster or failure into our lives we must remember this. For example, at first Moses seemed only to have made matters worse with Pharaoh (Exodus 5:21-2). He was disheartened, but he took his disappointment to the Lord who directed him how he should continue in order to obtain eventual blessing. It may not be God's will that it should happen – any more than it was God's will that Pharaoh should rebel against him – yet nevertheless God is able to overcome and utilize it for his own ends. We know that 'in all things God works together with those who love him to bring about what is good' (Romans 8:28, NIV margin, see above in chapter 1). Whenever disaster or failure strikes, we know that God will be there, wanting us to cooperate with him to bring good from it. What seemed to be the greatest disaster ever, Christ's crucifixion, was in fact used by God to bring untold blessing to humankind.

> Oh, the depth of the riches both of the wisdom and knowledge of God! How unsearchable are his judgments and his ways past finding out! (Romans 11:33)

13

The Effects of the Cross

To Christians the sacrificial death of Jesus the Messiah on the cross is central to our faith. Jesus was the Lamb of God who takes away the sin of the world (John 1:29). No one can come to God the Father except through Jesus (John 14:6). But how does this work for the Old Testament saints who had never heard of Jesus? Could it work for any Old Testament-period Gentiles who had likewise never heard of Jesus? For many Christians this kind of question hangs in the air. If someone has to 'believe in Jesus' to be saved, how can it be answered? Some have even seen the whole Jewish thing as having the Law in order that none of them could keep it and virtually everyone before Jesus would be damned. Yet the Old Testament is full of references to the contemporary 'righteous', whose lifestyle was distinct from 'sinners'.

Does Paul answer these questions for us? Actually he does, but unfortunately the interpretations that commentators have tried to read into Romans 1–4 have disguised it. The traditional interpretation of these passages is:

o   From Romans 1:18 onwards it is about God's wrath against universally sinful humanity.

o   Romans 2 shows that all Jews and Gentiles are equally condemned.

o   Romans 3:9-19 quotes the Old Testament to prove that 'none is righteous', ie no one is ethically perfect.

o   Romans 3:22-3 says that the only true righteousness is given through faith in Jesus Christ. There is no difference between Jew and Gentile, for all have sinned and fall short of the glory of God. So only Christians (Jew or Gentile) can be saved.

o Romans 4 says that Abraham was made righteous through faith (so presumably he was a Christian?).

When we first started to study Romans intensively in the late 1960s we were puzzled by the number of commentaries which took this kind of line, because it makes neither contextual nor cultural sense of what Paul actually wrote. There are three major problems with it:

1. 'Righteous' does not mean sinless, and Paul did not need to *prove* that no one was sinless because none of his critics doubted this.

2. 'Righteous' means living in right-standing with God, so to take 'none is righteous' literally is absurd because the Old Testament and New Testament are full of references to the righteous – even in the Psalm 14 that Paul quotes in Romans 3:10.

3. If only those with *faith in Jesus* can be saved, then what about Old Testament saints? Paul will have failed to tell us on what basis God accepted them.

So what does Paul *really* say? In summary it is this:

o From Romans 1:16 onwards Paul is comparing two streams of humanity: the righteous (who live by faith in God) and the wicked (who suppress the truth in unrighteousness).

o In chapter 2 he asserts that historically (to him this was pre-1st century) God's kindness was meant to lead Gentiles to repentance. On judgement day God will give eternal life to those who seek 'glory, honour and immortality' because what they are seeking is the Christ who enlightens every man who comes into the world, and is the man crowned with glory and honour and incorruption.

o In chapter 3:9-19 he notes that for the Jews to have the explicit 'oracles of God' was a definite advantage, but that nevertheless taken as a whole Jewish society did not do any better than Gentile.

o In 3:21-5 he notes that the reason God can count faith as right-standing is the faithfulness of Jesus the Messiah in his sacrificial death. *This* explains how God could 'pass over' sins of faithful Jews and Gentiles throughout history.

o In chapter 4 he insists that active faith *in God* and not ritual works is the basis on which the righteous can be recognised – ie they are 'justified' or shown to be in right relationship with God.

o   Christian faith (ie faith in Jesus) is not specifically mentioned until the beginning of chapter 5.

Paul begins his train of thought like this in Romans 1:14-8 (which we give in a slightly adapted version of the NKJV):

> [14]I am a debtor both to Greeks and to barbarians, both to wise and to unwise. [15]So, as much as is in me, I am ready to preach the gospel to you who are in Rome also.
>
> [16]*For* I am not ashamed of the gospel of Christ, for it is the power of God to salvation for everyone who believes, for the Jew first and also for the Greek.
>
> [17]*For* in it the righteousness of God is revealed from faith(fullness) to faith; as it is written, 'The righteous shall live by faith'.
>
> [18]*For* the wrath of God is (being) revealed from heaven against all ungodliness and unrighteousness of men, who suppress the truth in unrighteousness.

The verse he quotes from Habakkuk makes a fundamental comparison between the righteous who live by faith and the unrighteous who are empty and crooked. Habakkuk 2:4 is not speaking about 'universal sinfulness', and neither is Paul here. He intends, like Habakkuk, to contrast two streams of humanity: those living by faith in God and those who suppress the truth in unrighteousness. So the wrath of God is revealed against those who suppress the truth – and Paul then describes graphically what the effects are of putting creation above the creator – a word for our times where the morality, of for example gay relationships, is deduced from biology rather than revelation!

Romans 2:1-4 refers to the general trait of humankind to make moral judgements – and yet often then excuse themselves. But Paul then implies that sometimes those who make moral judgements do not recognise the God-dimension:

> And do you think this, O man, you who judge those practicing such things, and doing the same, that you will escape the judgment of God? Or do you despise the riches of his goodness, forbearance, and longsuffering, not knowing that the goodness of God leads you to repentance? (Romans 2:3-4)

Surely this must refer to those in general who make moral judgements? It cannot just mean those who repent when they hear about Jesus, because it is the general goodness of God that leads them to repentance. Paul goes on:

> But in accordance with your hardness and your impenitent heart you are treasuring up for yourself wrath in the day of wrath and revelation of the righteous judgment of God, who 'will render to each one according to his deeds' [Psalm 62:12]: eternal life to those who by patient continuance in doing good seek for glory, honour and immortality; but to those who are self-seeking and do not obey the truth, but obey unrighteousness – indignation and wrath, tribulation and anguish, on every soul of man who does evil, of the Jew first and also of the Greek; but glory, honour and peace to everyone who works what is good, to the Jew first and also to the Greek. For there is no partiality with God. For as many as have sinned without law will also perish without law, and as many as have sinned in the law will be judged by the law (for not the hearers of the law are just in the sight of God, but the doers of the law will be justified; for when Gentiles, who do not have the law, by nature do the things in the law, these, although not having the law, are a law to themselves, who show the work of the law written in their hearts, their conscience also bearing witness, and between themselves their thoughts accusing or else excusing them) in the day when God will judge the secrets of men by Jesus Christ, according to my gospel. (Romans 2:5-16)

He identifies those who seek 'glory, honour and immortality' who will receive eternal life, and says that they 'do not have the law, by nature do the things in the law… show the work of the law written in their hearts – their conscience bearing witness'. But who are these people?

NT Wright, one of the greatest modern New Testament scholars, identifies three possibilities in *The New Interpreters Bible* (p 441):

a) 'This is a purely hypothetical category. Paul is indicating that when God judges the secrets of all hearts, *if* there should be any who succeeded in doing good, they would indeed reap the appropriate reward; but he is holding up a mirage that will disappear when the argument is complete. There may, in other words, be Gentiles who fulfil part of the Law, but this will count for nothing'.

b) 'Others have… seen 2.1 as evidence that Paul does not hold, after all that all humans are sinners. He is aware, they say, that in both the Jewish and pagan world there are some humans who really do that which God intends, who avoid vice and practice virtue, and who will be suitably rewarded at the end'.

c) The people in question are *Christian* Gentiles.

The first option a), doesn't seem to make sense. Why talk about hypothetical non-existent people – who would it convince anyway? Paul is holding up these Gentiles to the Jews in 2:17f to make his point – what weight would hypothetical non-existent Gentiles carry in such a context? Surely they must be real ones!

The second option b), is ambiguous and Wright does not really clarify what he means. As we saw in chapter 1, both Old and New Testaments consistently contrast 'the righteous' and 'sinners'. If it means 'sinners' in the biblical sense then plainly not all humans *are* sinners. But how then, as Wright goes on to claim, could it be that this option 'falls foul of Paul's emphasis on the universality of human sin'? Paul (like everyone else) knows that everyone has sinned, but nowhere says that all humans are 'sinners' in the biblical sense of this term. In *Romans for Everyone* (p 41) Wright seems to identify this option as 'any Gentile who happens to make a special moral effort'. But the Bible doesn't define a *righteous person* as someone 'who makes a special moral effort' – faith is always the basis of being righteous. In summary, therefore, if b) means people who have never sinned, then this is the same as option a) – and doesn't make sense. If it means Gentiles who 'make a special moral effort', then there is no indication anywhere that this is a basis of being in right relationship with God. So in either case option b) cannot be who Paul is talking about.

Wright himself goes for his option c), but there are two major problems with this (which we expand on in *Volume 2: Reconsidering Key Biblical Ideas*, chapter 1):

1. Firstly, why would Gentile Christians have to rely on nature and conscience to know what is right? They have access not only to the Old Testament Jewish Scriptures but also to the sayings of Jesus conveyed to them by his followers.

2. Secondly, these people lack the Christian certainty of God's forgiveness.

Paul characterizes them: '(... their conscience also bearing witness, and between themselves their thoughts accusing or else excusing them) in the day when God will judge the secrets of men by Jesus Christ'.

This contrasts with the ringing confidence later in Romans with which Paul assures Gentile Christians that they have been declared righteous 'by faith' (5:1), 'have peace with God through our Lord Jesus the Messiah' (5:1), 'have died with Christ' and been buried in baptism and risen anew with him (6:2-5) and there is 'now therefore no condemnation for those who are in Jesus the Messiah' (8:1). So, with all this, am I, as a Gentile Christian, just to kind of hope that my thoughts might accuse or maybe even excuse me on the day of judgement? Whoever these people are in Romans 2:15-16, surely they *cannot* be us Gentile *Christians*? Wright suggests that for Gentile Christians 'being outside the Torah and yet fulfilling it from the heart, leaves them with questions that may produce a moment of panic in even the most settled believer' (p 442). This seems totally unrealistic. We do not personally know any Christians, either alive today or who have died in peace, for whom not having fulfilled Torah gave them moments of panic. It all seems wildly improbable. Paul is not talking about people who sound anything like Gentile Christians.

So these people appear to be *none* of the three groups Wright suggests. Rather, they are Gentiles who have faith in God because his goodness in creation has led them to repentance and to seek glory and honour and incorruption through their faith. They are not sinless, but are 'righteous', like Habakkuk, though faith in God. The basis on which this can happen is given later in Romans 3, as we shall see. But it is important to note that the traditional understanding of these passages actually *contradicts* what Paul is trying to prove. According to the traditional understanding no pre-christian Gentile could be saved before Jesus came, only Jewish people could be saved before Jesus, because only they had the revelation of Scripture.

Paul did not need to 'prove' to his Jewish critics that everyone has sinned – no one denied it. What he did need to show was that in general Jewish society was little if any better than Gentile society. This is what he does in Romans 3:9-19. He has said that the Jews have an *advantage* because they have the 'oracles of God' – yet in practice (as his Old Testament quotes show) both Jewish and Gentile Societies were castigated (even though in the same passages there is usually reference to the righteous – a remnant as Paul will later argue). The Jewish feelings of superiority referred to in 2:17 and following verses are misplaced.

As already noted, in 3:19-20 Paul says that it is 'works of the Torah' that Jews take as distinctive, but these cannot in themselves be enough, because actually through the Law comes knowledge of sin, and we all know that we are guilty. So he goes on to explain how now it has been 'revealed' what was not clear before, that the basis on which God can 'overlook' past sin and declare faith to be counted as righteousness is the *faithfulness of Jesus the Messiah*. In pre-Christian times this was unknown to the righteous Gentiles and only dimly perceived if at all by most faithful Jews.

It is so sad that most translations render this key phrase wrongly. It was surely Paul's greatest 'Ah ha!' experience when he saw that it was the faithfulness of Jesus the Messiah in dying sacrificially, that had enabled God to forgive the sins of all who had faith in God in any era of human history. The key recognition is that the Greek *pisteus Iesou Christou* (both here and in all the other times it is used in the New Testament) means the '*faithfulness of* Jesus the Messiah'. The rendering in the NIV and other translations as 'faith in Christ' is unnatural and very unlikely. We argued this in 1973, and increasingly scholars have recognised the 'faithfulness' translation as correct (see *Volume 2: Reconsidering Key Biblical Ideas* chapter 3). The key passage of Romans 3:21-26 is well translated by NT Wright:

> But now God's righteousness has been revealed apart from the law – though the law and the prophets bear witness to it: it is God's righteousness through the faithfulness of Jesus the Messiah to those who believe. For there is no distinction, for all sinned, and came short of the glory of God, and they are justified freely, by his grace through the redemption which is in the Messiah Jesus. God put him forth as a means of atonement, through faithfulness, by means of his blood; this was to demonstrate God's righteousness because in his forbearance he had passed over previous sins. It was to demonstrate his righteousness in the present time – that he himself might be in the right and might justify people by Jesus' faithfulness. (*What St Paul Really Said*, p 128)

Ah ha! This is how throughout history God could be just/righteous himself and yet accept and forgive people of faith. The faithfulness of Jesus the Messiah operates to 'those who believe' or 'those who have faith'. But this is faith *in God* – it is not specifically *Christian* faith, or even necessarily faith in the Abrahamic covenant. How was Noah declared righteous? Presumably through the faithfulness of Jesus the Messiah to all who have faith. How about Lot? Or Melchizedek? Or Epimenides (to whom Paul refers in Acts 17:28 and Titus 1:12)? It would be hard to say that the Samaritans were in the Abrahamic covenant, and in John 4:22 Jesus says to the woman at the well:

> You worship what you do not know; we know what we worship, for salvation is of the Jews.

He goes on, however, to identify himself as the Samaritan Messiah (v26)! So could there be other societies where their religious faith is really looking for a Messiah who is in fact Jesus? In Chinese Bibles today it is the *Word*, the *dao*, who is the light who 'enlightens every man who comes into the world' (John 1:9). In the 6th century BC, Lao Tzu spoke of those in harmony with the *dao* doing good spontaneously, and a recent book *Lao Tzu and the Bible*, Yuan Zhiming argues that this original message of Lao Tzu was later subverted into mere legalism in the systems of Confucianism and Daoism.

Of course a central point here is that the declaration that it is 'counted as righteousness' is based on faith rather than on ritual observances, but surely the faith is in *God* not in the Abrahamic covenant? Is God restricted to speaking only to Jews and Christians? Surely not. The *logos* of God enlightens *every man who comes into the world* (John 1:9).

Romans 3:21-26 also refers to those sins that were 'left... beforehand unpunished' (NIV)? Is this *only* the sins of those Old Testament-period Jews in the Abrahamic covenant? Well if there is really no 'partiality with God' then surely it refers also to some Old Testament-period Gentiles not in the Abrahamic covenant? Paul does not say 'Well God used to be partial throughout most of history but now he has become more egalitarian'.

God may have spoken to other groups post-Jesus who never heard of him. In *Eternity in Their Hearts* Don Richardson mentions the Karen Tribe who worshipped *Y'wa*, the Lahu who worshipped *Gui'Sha*, the Wa worshipped *Siyeh* and various other tribal groups who worshipped a high God who led them to accept Christ when eventually missionaries reached them.

This, then, is God's strategy for dealing with human sin. The faithfulness of Jesus the Messiah is the focal point in his whole plan of action for humankind. It is the only basis on which sin can be forgiven, No one can come to the father except through Jesus. And the basis on which he declares people righteous (or in right-standing with him) is *faith*. For us this can be specifically *Christian* faith. But the sacrificial death of Jesus the Messiah on the cross operates for all, throughout history, who had or have genuine faith *in God*. This is certainly *not* saying that any religion is as good as any other. Religious practice is not any indication of a true faith, but God knows those who have genuinely fulfilled Romans 2 with a real faith in him.

The Cross in History and Eternity

We can discern two main fields of operation in which the cross is effectual. First, it enabled sinful humans to be put into a right relationship with God, to be righteous rather than sinners, and so enter the spiritual battle. Second, it had direct effect on the spiritual forces themselves. These two aspects are brought out well in Colossians 2:14-15:

> … having wiped out the handwriting of requirements that was against us, which was contrary to us. And he has taken it out of the way, having nailed it to the cross. Having disarmed principalities and powers, he made a public spectacle of them, triumphing over them in it.

So there are two aspects of the work of the cross: the atonement for man and the victory over Satan. Both should be borne in mind as we look now at the setting of the cross in time and in eternity. The blood of Christ, symbolizing his life given up, similarly has a dual function – see for example Hebrews 9:14 and Revelation 12:11.

God's relationship to time is mysterious. He may experience sequence, especially in relationships, but is eternal. It seems, moreover, that the atonement which Christ brought between God and the human race operated in an eternal or multi-time framework rather than working in a specific time frame. In other words, believers in Old Testament times, no less than those in New Testament times, were redeemed through the life given up by Jesus on the cross (John 14:6). As such the atoning effects of the cross reach backward as well as forward from the date of the crucifixion.

But, although this is true, we must beware of treating the cross as a wholly isolated or self-contained event. It is also God's key move in his activity throughout a whole chain of events in human history. Right from the beginning, God looked onward to the coming One through whom the serpent's head would be crushed (Genesis 3:15). His action in choosing Abraham and the nation of Israel was, as we have seen, with the purpose of preparing the way for Jesus the Messiah (Genesis 12:3; and see chapter 9). Throughout history God's actions prepare for the cross, and at key times his symbol of the slain lamb appears. It comes in the story of Abel at the beginning of history (Genesis 4:4). It appears at the start of Hebrew history, in the words of Abraham (Genesis 22:8). And it appears in the Passover ceremony at the time of Israel's birth as a nation (Exodus 12:4). God always points onward to the cross.

After the crucifixion had occurred, what then? God continued his action in human affairs as the power and message of the cross began to be applied in human lives. Christ's chosen apostles were intended to carry this message to the ends of the earth (Matthew 28:19-20; Acts 1:8). There is then, a sense in which throughout the period before the crucifixion God is preparing for it, and in the period after the crucifixion is working to apply its power in human lives.

So we can compare the eternal and temporal aspects of the cross for humanity. On the one hand the death of Christ was effective in bringing atonement to anyone at any time who has faith in God. On the other hand, the cross has a place as one link, albeit the vital one, in a whole coordinated plan of God as he intervenes in human history according to his own strategy.

What are the effects of the cross on Satan's forces? The cross has enabled men to be used as God's agents. This is important since the revelation of those believers conformed to the image of Christ will contribute to the destruction of Satan's power. The cross is obviously basic to this part of God's plan.

But there is also, as we have said, a direct effect of the cross on Satan's forces. The historical date of the crucifixion did not, of course, mark the time of Satan's final overthrow and destruction – for we know that he is still very active today. This is why we are told to resist him in James 4:7 and Ephesians 6:11-12, and presumably the war in Revelation 12:7 arises after the cross, showing just how active Satan is. What the cross did was to provide Christ and his followers with powerful weapons against Satan, and also ensure his eventual overthrow. It is like the key move in a game of chess – the move that finally seals the fate of an opponent. Scripture teaches that a new increase in Christ's power was marked by his death and resurrection (Luke 12:50; Romans 1:4). Christ's servants also, who fight in his armour, know the power of the blood and name of Jesus in their lives (this is especially true of Christians who have dealt with evil spirits). When Satan's forces make war in heaven (Revelation 12:7) they are overcome by the blood of the Lamb and the revealing power of truth spoken by martyrs. It is as the Lamb that Christ himself is pictured as fighting the satanic forces in Revelation – it is because he was slain as an innocent sacrifice that the sight of him is so terrible to the evil forces. It is, in other words, through the cross that eventually the final overthrow of Satan will be made.

This completes, then, this brief outline of the setting of the cross in God's strategy, both in time and eternity. These ideas should be borne in mind as we continue to look both at the present conflict and at its final future culmination and completion.

God's Instrument Today – The Church in Christ

Whatever the Church is, or possesses, is 'in Christ'. The battles of the 'saints of the most high' are, as we have already noted in chapter 2, the battles of Jesus the Messiah. We are his body and wear his armour – the armour of God. We fight in the strength of his might. Our whole life and battle are in him.

This incorporation in Christ is brought out vividly in Ephesians. The grace of God was bestowed on us in *Christ* and it is 'in him we have redemption through his blood' (Ephesians 1:7). It is because we are *in him* that we have boldness and confidence to approach God (Ephesians 3:12). Furthermore, since Christ has been raised from the dead and seated in the heavenly places at God's right hand, God has also 'raised us up together, and made us sit together in the heavenly places in Christ Jesus' (Ephesians 1:20; 2:6). We have therefore been blessed 'with every spiritual blessing in the heavenly places in Christ' (Ephesians 1:3). This then, is the Lord's chosen position for the Church in Christ: to be in the heavenly places at God's right hand. God has blessed us with every spiritual blessing:

> ... just as he chose us in him before the foundation of the world, that we should be holy and without blame before him in love. (Ephesians 1:4)

We share in both the *position of* Christ beside God and the *chosenness of* Christ by God. God said of Jesus:

> Then a voice came out of the cloud, saying, 'This is my Son, my *Chosen One*; listen to him!' (Luke 9:35, NASB. This follows the best Greek manuscripts as do most modern versions).

Elsewhere Christ is said to be the servant whom God has chosen (Matthew 12:18). The chosenness of Christ has nothing to do with going to heaven or to hell. He is not chosen to go to heaven, but is chosen to be God's servant – God's 'suffering servant' for the redemption of the peoples. The fact that he is chosen affects his function in God's plan, but does not mean that he is given an easy time while others suffer. Rather, he himself is in the thick of the battle.

It wasn't that there were a great number of others whom God could equally well have chosen to fulfil the office of suffering servant – Jesus was unique. Jesus was also the chosen or choice one of God in the sense of being closest to the heart of the Father (see *Volume 2: Reconsidering Key Biblical Ideas* chapter 4 for the connection between 'belovedness' and 'election').

We are chosen in Christ. This does not mean that we were chosen to *be put into* Christ. It does not mean that God chose to make us repent but left others unrepentant! It means that as we repented and were born again into the body of Christ, we share in his chosenness. He is chosen, and we are chosen in him. This was planned by God in his foreknowledge even before the world began – see for example 1 Peter 1:2.

God decided that the Church in Christ should be holy and blameless before him and should (also in Christ) be seated in the heavenly places. Yet these heavenly places are not, as some have imagined, a haven of rest. Rather, we must wrestle there against the 'spiritual hosts of wickedness in the heavenly places' (Ephesians 6:12). Our chosenness in Christ is not merely a privilege but also a call to a task. In God's workings, privilege inevitably implies responsibility. It was, for example, a great privilege to be an Israelite, for the whole nation was chosen by God. Yet only some Israelites were faithful in fulfilling the purpose that God intended for them. There were, as we have seen, the 'elect according to grace' – those who had the inner experience for which the nation had so many outward symbols. Other Israelites were also part of the chosen nation, but tried to claim the privileges without accepting the responsibilities. This would not, and could not, work.

For us today it is an even greater privilege to be chosen in Christ, to be seated in him before God's throne in the heavenly places. Yet this also gives us the responsibility of (in Christ) fighting the spiritual hosts of wickedness. Thus Peter calls on us to fulfil God's purpose for us, to 'make your calling and election sure' (2 Peter 1:10). This is our calling or vocation, and it is what we were chosen in Christ to do.

Peter is not telling us to make sure that we don't go to hell, for the calling and election are not primarily concerned with this. He is concerned that our personal characteristics are such that we are neither barren nor unfruitful in our knowledge of Jesus, that we are fully prepared to enter richly into the Lord Jesus' eternal reign which is to come. And so we find that the present runs on into the future, for there is to be an end to the present warfare in the heavenly places. One day Satan's power in the universe will be destroyed, and the Church is destined to play a part in this. The final purpose of God, and the role in this of the Church in Christ, are the subjects of the next chapter.

14

God's Great Project and the Final Battle

God's Purpose for Christ

God has seen fit to reveal to us his eternal purpose to:

> ... gather together in one all things in Christ, both which are in heaven and which are on earth. (Ephesians 1:10)

God will, through Christ, finally reconcile to himself all things in heaven and on the earth and all the works of evil will be destroyed (Colossians 1:20). Christ will have pre-eminence in all things, and to him every knee shall bow (Colossians 1:18; Philippians 2:10). Christ has been appointed as heir over all things (Hebrews 1:2). It is against this appointment that Satan is in rebellion.

As we looked at in chapter 1, there have been those who have suggested that 'Satan' or 'the devil' is simply some kind of personification or symbolism of evil, but both Scripture and experience indicate that non-physical (ie spiritual) personal beings exist. To many of us, the mysterious features scientists find and speculate about in our physical world actually make it easier to accept realities in dimensions other than our own. We are not told much about such beings, or about the origins of Satan the leader of opposition to God, but Christianity is not dualistic (ie we do not believe that good and evil eternally coexist), so we presume Satan is a created being. Isaiah 14:12-13 refers to an evil Babylonian king as the 'Day Star' and 'Son of Morning' who sought to exalt himself above God, and was cast down. Commentators believe, however, that there is some intended reference beyond the human king in the word *Helel* = Lucifer/Day-Star/Shining One (see for example the commentary by John Watts). Traditionally many have taken this also to apply to the spiritual force behind the human king – the one known in the New Testament as Satan or the devil.

So what more does the Old Testament say about Satan? In 1 Chronicles 21:1 we find Satan moving David to hold a census (though, paradoxically, God seems to be behind it in 2 Samuel 24:1). In Job 'the Satan' is shown in his role of 'accuser' in accusing Job. In Zechariah 3:1 'the Satan' again stands as the accuser, before the Lord himself declares that Joshua the priest is cleansed and forgiven.

In the New Testament, Satan/the devil tempts Jesus with doubts about God's declaration that he is the chosen and beloved son, and offers to give Christ all earthly kingdoms if in return he might receive the authority and worship for which he lusts (Matthew 4:9 etc). Satan hates it that Christ, and not himself, should have pre-eminence. He hates God for determining that it should be so. He hates the Church because it will both share in Christ's reign and be used by God to establish that reign. He hates the Church because of the great destiny that God intends for it. This seems to be the motivation behind Satan's warfare with God.

What, we might ask, is the greatest possible destiny that God could have conceived for those who believe in him at the end of all this warfare? Surely it is that they should become like him, for nothing is greater than God. And this is, in fact, what God has ordained – this is the great project of God for man, against which Satan will fight to the end. Yet Satan will finally fail, for even before time began God foresaw the achievement of his chosen destiny for humankind.

Predestination

In chapter 5 of *Volume 2: Reconsidering Key Biblical Ideas* we explore the meaning of 'foreknowledge', and how it is linked to 'predestination'. However, because correctly understanding predestination is so important to making sense of God's strategy, we will briefly look at what it means here. (See also the summary in chapter 16 of this volume).

The traditionalist view of 'predestination' in Augustinian/Reformed theology is that if God determines everything that happens, then he has also chosen, or 'predestined', who will and who will not become Christians and be saved. However, as we have clearly demonstrated, while God does determine certain aspects of the future, humans have freewill to choose to accept or reject God's will for themselves, and so choose to accept or reject salvation. 'Predestination' cannot therefore be talking about God deciding the eternal destiny of individuals. So what *does* it mean?

The word 'predestine' or 'foreordain' is made up of two Greek words: *pro* (= in advance) and *horizō* (= boundary/designate). 'Predestination' or 'predestined' is the word used in the KJV, NKJV, NASB, NIV and ESV; the RV uses 'foreordained'; the RSV uses 'predestined' or 'destined and appointed'.

The term *horizō* is used in the LXX to mean 'mark off boundaries' (see *A Manual Greek Lexicon of the New Testament*, Abbot-Smith, p 323) and from it we get our word 'horizon'. It means to set out or mark off, and can be used with a human subject without connotations of inevitability (see for example Acts 11:29). The combined word *prohorizō* is used only of God in the New Testament, so to find out what exactly the New Testament writers meant by it we must look at the immediate context of how they used it, as well as at the teaching of Early Church leaders who stood closest to them in language and culture.

In any event, the most important point to grasp about predestination is that it concerns man's future destiny. It does *not* concern who should, or should not, *become* Christians, but rather their destiny *as* Christians. The word is used altogether six times in the New Testament.

The first use is in Acts 4 where, after Peter and John are released, their companions praise together:

> For truly against your holy Servant Jesus, whom you anointed, both Herod and Pontius Pilate, with the Gentiles and the people of Israel, were gathered together to do whatever your hand and your purpose (*boulē*) determined before (*pro-horizen*) to be done. (Acts 4:27-8)

Earlier, in Acts 2 after Pentecost the apostles said:

> Men of Israel, hear these words: Jesus of Nazareth, a man attested by God to you by miracles, wonders, and signs which God did through him in your midst, as you yourselves also know – him,

being delivered by the determined (*horizmene*) purpose (*boulē*) and foreknowledge of God, you have taken by lawless hands, have crucified, and put to death. (Acts 2:22-3)

God is the master strategist. Though he does not determine how people will use their freewill to choose their moral paths, he knows all the possible outcomes and plans accordingly. God planned a horizon for a suffering and dying Messiah and delivered Jesus up for this purpose, knowing what the people would do.

The other five uses of *pro-horizō* concern the future of the Church. The first is:

But we speak God's wisdom in a mystery, the hidden wisdom which God predestined (*pro-horizen*) before the ages to our glory... all that God has prepared for those who love him. (1 Corinthians 2:7-9, NASB)

'Our glory', and the horizon God has set out for those 'in Christ', is our destiny to rescue creation:

For I consider that the sufferings of this present time are not worthy to be compared with the glory which shall be revealed in us. For the earnest expectation of the creation eagerly waits for the revealing of the sons of God. (Romans 8:18-19)

1 Corinthians 2:7-9, and the other four times *pro-horizō* is used, all concern the future destiny and tasks of the Church, *not* how anyone *came to be* a Christian. We will now look at these passages in more detail.

The Origin of Predestination

Predestination was not a result of some arbitrary fiat. Its origin is in the essentially personal being of God. Way back before the foundation of the earth, before time began, God could look ahead. He foreknew that there would be those who would repent in response to his Holy Spirit and would put their hope for the future in Christ (see also chapter 5 in *Volume 2: Reconsidering Key Biblical Ideas*). God had to decide what the destiny of such people should be – they could have been condemned for their sins, for by repenting they did not 'earn' anything. Yet the essential being of God is Light

(1 John 1:5) and Love (1 John 4:8,16), or as John Blanchard puts it in *Right With God*:

> It is not just that God possesses love as one of his qualities, or that love is one of the things God exercises, but rather his very essence is love. God is love, and love governs his every activity. (p 47)

God's decision, therefore, reflected his essential nature. His decision was made 'in love' (Ephesians 1:4-5).

Scripture reflects this pattern of God's decision. First, God foreknew that there would be those who put their hope in his Messiah:

> For whom he foreknew, he also predestined... (Romans 8:29)

His decision concerned 'we who first trusted in Christ' (Ephesians 1:11-2), or as most versions have it 'we who were the first to put our hope in Christ (Messiah)', (see the NIV, NASB, ESV).

God's motive in the setting of this destiny was love:

> In love he predestined us to adoption as sons through Jesus Christ to himself, according to the kind intention of his will (Ephesians 1:5, NASB)

The NKJV links the 'in love' here to the previous sentence about being presented without spot or blemish, but this latter idea is complete in itself (see also Ephesians 5:27 and Colossians 1:22). The 'in love' seems more likely to be linked to the predestination as it is taken to be by the NASB, NIV, ESV etc.

In this way the subjects of God's decision and his motives for it are made clear. It is those who are bound up in Christ who, because God *is Love*, were given a glorious future destiny.

Predestined to Sonship

A central point is that predestination does *not* concern who should be converted – it concerns our future destiny. It is not that we are predestined *to be* Christians, it is rather that as Christians we receive a glorious future destiny:

> For whom he foreknew, he also predestined *to be conformed to the image of his Son* (Romans 8:29)

> Blessed *be* the God and Father of our Lord Jesus Christ, who has blessed us with every spiritual blessing in the heavenly *places* in Christ, just as he chose us in him before the foundation of the world, that we would be holy and blameless before him. In love he predestined us *to adoption as sons* through Jesus Christ to himself, according to the kind intention of his will, to the praise of his grace, which he freely bestowed on us in the Beloved. (Ephesians 1:3-6, NASB)

The adoption as sons is a future event when we will be fully conformed to the image of the Son (who will be firstborn of many brothers and sisters), that is, we shall be like Christ. We have the 'spirit of adoption' now (Romans 8:15), but:

> ... we also who have the firstfruits of the Spirit, even we ourselves groan within ourselves, eagerly waiting for the adoption, the redemption of our body. (Romans 8:23)

Our 'adoption as sons' is the future event when we will be fully conformed to the image of Christ and used by God in the redemption of the created world. Christ-likeness is our destiny – the 'horizon' set for us by God. It is a part of what we have received when we were put 'into Messiah'. It is 'in Messiah' that we receive all kinds of blessings in Ephesians 1, including sharing in his 'chosenness'.

It is important to point out here that while are talking about being 'sons' this refers to our position and character before God, as being Christ-like, not to our gender – both men and women can be 'sons'. There is no gender division in the Church:

> For you are all sons of God through faith in Christ Jesus. For as many of you as were baptized into Christ have put on Christ. There is neither Jew nor Greek, there is neither slave nor free, there is neither male nor female; for you are all one in Christ Jesus. (Galatians 3:26-28)

When Paul accepted the Gentile business woman Lydia as a true believer he saw her as a 'Son of God' and made her home his first mission base in Europe! Roger and Faith Forster's book *Women and the Kingdom*, and Paul Marston's book *Women in Church Leadership and in Marriage* look at some of the issues of gender in the Church.

Our Predestined Task

Christ is the heir of all things (Hebrews 1:2) and in becoming conformed to his image we become 'joint heirs with Christ' (Romans 8:17). When all things are summed up in Christ it will be seen that we also have an inheritance in him (Ephesians 1:11). It is as sons of God that we enter into the cosmic inheritance, and it will be our task to deliver it from its present bondage of corruption (Romans 8:21). Creation waits in earnest expectation for the day when the sons of God will be revealed and it will share the freedom of their glory (Romans 8:19-21).

This day of the revelation of the sons of God is also termed their 'adoption'. This word which our versions render as 'adoption' literally means 'son-placing' or 'placing-as-sons'. It is an important distinction that this does not refer to our *entry* into God's family, for we were *born* into that – 'adoption' is not an adequate translation. According to the New Testament, our adoption is still in the future and we groan within ourselves as we wait for it. The time of our placing-as-sons will be at the resurrection, when God will reveal us in our redeemed bodies. The Lord Jesus was the firstborn from the dead, and by his resurrection was 'declared' or 'designated' to be the Son of God in power (Colossians 1:18; Romans 1:4, which actually uses the Greek *horizon* – in a sense it was setting a new horizon as Son of God in power, though the root should not be pressed too much). God intends that Christ should be the 'firstborn among many brethren' (Romans 8:29) and so our resurrection will also be the time when we are designated sons of God, ie when we are placed-as-sons.

The universe will be delivered from its bondage and corruption through the revealing of men and women who are the 'sons of God', conformed to the image of the Messiah who is the firstborn from the dead. What was the nature of this Messiah to whom we shall be conformed? Above all things Christ was a servant – and a suffering servant at that. He came not to be served but to serve and to give his life (Matthew 20:28; Mark 10:45). He said that the greatest in his kingdom would be the one who was the servant of all, and demonstrated this by washing the disciples' feet (Luke 22:25,26; John 13). This is (as we saw in chapter 4), the 'glory' of Christ. The 'glorious liberty' (Romans 8:21) of those conformed to his image must be similar. We are to deliver the universe by becoming servant-like. Only a self-sacrificing attitude like that of Christ will meet the needs of the universe.

The Glory of Predestination

We were, as we have seen 'predestined... that we... should be to the praise of his glory' (Ephesians 1:11,12; also 1:5,6). We have been 'sealed... until the redemption of the purchased possession, to the praise of his glory' (Ephesians 1:13,14). Our predestination to be revealed and placed-as-sons in our redeemed bodies is for the praise of God's glory. What could be more glorifying to God than to have many sons who reflect his glorious nature? Christ will bring many sons to glory (Hebrews 2:10) and Paul considers that 'the sufferings of this present time are not worthy to be compared with the glory which shall be revealed in us' (Romans 8:18). Yet this glory is glory as taught to us by Christ (as we saw above in chapter 4). It is the type of glory that enhances both giver and receiver. It is to God's glory that we become glorified, for then we shall become Christ-like and self-sacrificing in love.

Paul places the whole process right outside of our time in Romans 8:30. God conceived his great project for humankind before time began. He then 'calls' or 'names' us – that is, he gives us a position before him. As he has named us, so he justifies us (that is, declares that we are right with him). Finally, he glorifies us. Christians, past and present, are at different stages in this whole divine process, so Paul puts it all in the past tense. This also indicates that to him it is certain, whether it is in the past, the present or the future:

> For whom he foreknew, he also predestined... whom he predestined, these he also called; whom he called, these he also justified; and whom he justified, these he also glorified. (Romans 8:29-30)

Early Church Teaching and Predestination

Our own understanding of predestination was arrived at through careful study of Scripture. But since the term is so little used in the Bible, it is useful to see how Early Church writers understood the term as they stood closest to the New Testament writers in time and in language. It is actually used little by early Christian writers, though they did use other means to refer to our future destiny. One key early mainstream Christian leader, whose language was the Greek of the New Testament, was Clement of Alexandria (c155-220 AD) – a great missionary, apologist, defender of the faith and scholar. In *The Spreading Flame*, FF Bruce explains the background of Clement's key anti-Gnostic work *Stromata*:

The influence of Gnosticism on the Church was partly good and partly bad. It was good in so far as it stimulated intellectual activity in the Church and made the orthodox leaders, like the writers already mentioned (Irenaeus and Clement), present reasoned statements of their faith. Clement of Alexandria went so far as to present what he called the true Christian *gnosis* by contrast with the false; one might be an orthodox Gnostic, he held, by contrast with the heretical Gnostics. (p 250)

MA Smith in *From Christ to Constantine* adds:

To his mind, the Christian was the only person with the right to be called 'Gnostic' (the Knowing One), because only the orthodox Christian had access to the true knowledge of God. (p 112)

Stromata, Ilk vi, chapter 9 may be strictly rendered:

For it were no longer seemly that the friend of God, whom 'God has foreordained before the foundation of the world' to be enrolled in the highest 'adoption', should fall into pleasures or fears, and be occupied in the repression of the passions. For I venture to assert that as he is predestinated through what he shall do and what he shall obtain, so also he has predestinated himself by reason of whom he knew and whom he loved. Not having the future indistinct, as the multitude live conjecturing it, but having grasped by [true Christian] knowing faith what is hidden from others.

(This is from *The Ante-Nicene Christian Fathers* (Roberts and Donaldson, vol 2, p 497). Their rendering 'gnostic faith' has been amended to '[true Christian] knowing faith' for clarity.)

Clement is saying that since before Creation, God's plan for us is that through loving and following Christ, the 'friend of God' will get such a clear vision of their glorious future destiny in adoption that they will not 'fall into pleasures or fears' or be occupied with 'repression of the passions'.

There are a couple of things to note:

a) Clement links predestination with 'adoption', which concerns what a 'friend of God... *shall* do and what he *shall* obtain'. Clement sees both the adoption and predestiny of Christians as future events – he certainly does not take predestination to concern who becomes a Christian.

b) Clement is making a play on the Greek word *dia*, which is first used with the genitive (rendered 'through') and second used with the accusative (rendered 'by reason of'). The first gives the immediate cause of a person's predestiny as that he or she has a God-given task to do and a God-given heritage. When the Sons of God are revealed in the day of their adoption then there is something they will do (liberate the creation) and something which they will obtain (their heritage as co-heirs with Christ). But, on the other hand, Clement 'ventures to assert' that in one sense the Christian has received this predestiny *by reason of* whom he knows and whom he loves. Clement himself gives a further clue to his meaning here when (earlier in the section) he refers to the Christian:

> … now that he associates through love with the Beloved One, to whom he is allied by free choice.

Clement would not, of course, have suggested that someone could receive this destiny through clocking up good deeds – for that would be 'works'. His view is rather that a person's link in a love relationship with Christ is the basis on which they have received this destiny. This, perhaps, echoes Romans 8:28-29 which links predestination to 'those who love God'.

This passage is interesting in that it shows that the earliest Christian teaching on predestination certainly did not regard it as an unalterable decree as to who should be converted. It was seen, quite biblically, to concern the future 'adoption' and task of Christians, not how they *came to be* Christians. The passage also shows that it was the view of at least one important early Christian that a person came to have this destiny through his free choice to accept and have a love for Christ. In chapter 4 of *Reconsidering Key Biblical Ideas* we look at parallel indications on 'election' in writings of the earlier Clement, Clement of Rome.

For us, like the two Clements, election and predestination are sound and exciting elements in our theology. We believe in and emphasize both concepts. Our problem with the Augustinian/Reformed approach is not that they *emphasize* these concepts but that they *misinterpret* them to refer to a supposed arbitrary selection of who to force to become Christians. As in so many other areas, Augustine introduced a novel biblical interpretation not previously known. This is not the truth, nor is it 'one side to the truth', it is simply wrong exegesis.

A Foretaste and a Training Program

God has given us a foretaste of our inheritance. The Holy Spirit has been given us as a kind of down payment or guarantee of our future inheritance:

> In him you also *trusted*, after you heard the word of truth, the gospel of your salvation; in whom also, having believed, you were sealed with the Holy Spirit of promise, who is the guarantee of our inheritance until the redemption of the purchased possession, to the praise of his glory. (Ephesians 1:13-14)

The Holy Spirit is he in whom 'you were sealed for the day of redemption' (Ephesians 4:30). The Spirit is also termed the 'firstfruits' – a foretaste of the great harvest to come:

> We also who have the firstfruits of the Spirit, even we ourselves groan within ourselves, eagerly waiting for the adoption, the redemption of our body. (Romans 8:23)

The Holy Spirit is the 'earnest' or 'firstfruits' of our inheritance. Having received this promise, we wait for the time when we shall come into that inheritance, ie the day of redemption when we shall be placed-as-sons (adopted). The Holy Spirit, therefore, is also called the 'Spirit of son-placing'. Paul says:

> ... but you received the Spirit of adoption by whom we cry out, 'Abba, Father'. The Spirit himself bears witness with our spirit that we are children of God, and if children, then heirs – heirs of God and joint heirs with Christ, if indeed we suffer with him, that we may also be glorified together. (Romans 8:15-17)

Our adoption is not past but future, and the Holy Spirit is called the 'Spirit of adoption' because he is the 'guarantee' of it. Paul explains this elsewhere, comparing it to the development of a son in the everyday life of those times. First, a baby boy was born into a wealthy family. For the first few months he was not conscious at all, either of being a son or having any relationship with the family. Gradually he learned to say Dad (in Hebrew *Abba*) and became conscious of his position as a son in the family. He was taken to school by a special slave, called a 'child-conductor' (*paidagogos*). At school he began to learn more fully of his position in the household, the duties he had and the roles he must play. He was now conscious of his inheritance as the son of his father, but he had not yet come into that inheritance. He was no longer a baby, and he could fulfil some of the functions of a son. Nevertheless, until he came of age he did not have any real authority over his inheritance; he was not treated as an adult. Although he was already living in and enjoying his father's house, his *bar mitzvah* or 'coming of age' as we would call it, was the time when he really came into his inheritance.

It has sometimes been a puzzle to people that the Old Testament says little about the afterlife and related subjects. Paul's metaphor of family and sonship goes at least some way toward explaining this. Before Christ came, the Jews were 'children' in God's family, but not yet fully conscious sons (Galatians 4:3). They knew God, and they were his children, but they did not fully understand what sonship meant. They knew little about their inheritance as fellow heirs with Christ, and little of the future day of coming of age, or son-placing, when they would enter into that inheritance. A young child in God's family is an heir, and has a loving relationship with the Father, but is under guardians and stewards, and is not conscious of his position as a son.

Just like the child-conductor who took children to school, the Law was intended to conduct God's children to Christ (Galatians 3:24) The words 'tutor' (NASB, NEB, NKJV, RV) and 'school-master' (KJV) are misleading for they do not convey the meaning of the Greek, the RSV translates it better as 'custodian', the ESV has 'guardian', the NIV has 'put in charge' and Young gives its real meaning as 'child-conductor', and commentaries like the excellent one by Richard Longenecker expand on this. In his *Lysis* dialogue, Plato explores the paradox that a freeborn son is controlled by slaves. The boy Lysis says that, although he is a free person, because he is a child he is controlled by a slave, his *paidagogus*, who takes him to his teacher (*didaskalon*).

With the coming of 'the faith' of the New Covenant, believers were past the stage of being little children (Galatians 3:25). Now, Paul says to them, 'you are all sons of God through faith in Christ Jesus' (Galatians 3:26). Now that they are in Christ they realize their inheritance and have become fully conscious sons. Part of Christ's mission was to enable them to be put in line for this inheritance. Christ was sent so that they might one day receive the placing-as-sons, ie the redemption of their bodies (Galatians 4:5; Romans 8:23). If Christ had not come, there could never have been a day when the sons of God would be revealed. Those who believe in Christ, both men and women are sons. Moreover, because we are sons:

> God has sent forth the Spirit of his Son into your hearts, crying out, 'Abba, Father!' Therefore you are no longer a slave but a son, and if a son, then an heir of God through Christ. (Galatians 4:6-7)

We should not press the metaphorical language Paul is using too far (for there were some awesome people of faith in the Old Testament as Hebrews 11 reminds us), but Paul tells his Jewish readers that they have left the child stage – the Law has conducted them to Christ. A new era in humankind's education has arrived. Christ will be their teacher while, as sons, they are training for the time when one day they will be placed-as-sons. We are sons, and should be training for what we might call our coming of age as sons. Such training is partly the purpose of this present age. God intends that we should begin to reflect the glory of the Lord and be 'transformed into the same image from glory to glory', even as 'from the Spirit of the Lord' (2 Corinthians 3:18). Our transformation into the image of Christ has already begun, by the indwelling Spirit of adoption. The day of the revealing of the sons of God will be the culmination of a process of training. God leads and trains in different ways each one of the many sons who shall be brought to glory. Yet we have as the captain of our salvation one who was made complete and perfect through sufferings (Hebrews 2:10). We who are being conformed to his image may therefore expect to undergo a training with some resemblance to his. Paul says he longs:

> ... that I may know him and the power of his resurrection, and the fellowship of his sufferings, being conformed to his death, if, by any means, I may attain to the resurrection from the dead. Not that I have already attained, or am already perfected; but I press on, that I may lay hold of that for which Christ Jesus has also laid hold of me. Brethren, I do not count myself to have apprehended; but one thing I do, forgetting those things which are behind and reaching forward to those things which are ahead, I press toward the goal for the prize of the upward call of God in Christ Jesus. (Philippians 3:10-14)

Paul is glad of his experiences because they are part of his training for that day when at last he will attain the high calling given him in Christ. He hopes to attain the resurrection in the day of glory, the day of the revealing of the sons of God. Of course his sufferings do serve some purpose in the present, and he says:

> I now rejoice in my sufferings for you, and fill up in my flesh what is lacking in the afflictions of Christ, for the sake of his body, which is the Church. (Colossians 1:24)

But part of Paul's consolation, something that helps him to rejoice even despite his sufferings, is the knowledge that he is being inwardly built up for the coming glory:

> Therefore we do not lose heart. Even though our outward man is perishing, yet the inward man is being renewed day by day. For our light affliction, which is but for a moment, is working for us a far more exceeding and eternal weight of glory, while we do not look at the things which are seen, but at the things which are not seen. For the things which are seen are temporary, but the things which are not seen are eternal. (2 Corinthians 4:16-18)

We may find difficulties and trials in doing the will of God in this life. Yet our day by day problems are part of the larger battle between God and Satan. They are helping to build our characters for the day when we shall be placed as sons, and in this we may rejoice:

> … we rejoice in our sufferings, knowing that suffering produces endurance, and endurance produces character, and character produces hope… (Romans 5:3-4, RSV, ESV)

> For I am persuaded that neither death nor life, nor angels nor principalities nor powers, nor things present nor things to come, nor height nor depth, nor any other created thing, shall be able to separate us from the love of God which is in Christ Jesus our Lord. (Romans 8:38-39)

The Last Battle

So we can see how the future destiny of humankind – predestination – is vitally connected with the subject of God's strategy in history. The final overthrow of evil and release of the universe will come when God's sons (both men and women who have a status in inheritance), are revealed and they fulfil their destiny. God's strategy now, and his training of us through suffering, look forward to that great day of release.

How does Satan react to this project of God? We have already mentioned that Satan hates the Church because of what it is becoming. The nearer the great project comes to fulfilment, the more furious he becomes (Revelation 12:12). Before that day of adoption he will throw all his forces into a last desperate battle. This will be a final showdown between God and Satan, good and evil, love and hate, self-sacrifice and powerlust. Satan's hatred of God and his Son is heightened by the thought of the universe being overrun by the divine image in man.

Throughout the book of the Revelation we see the battle raging. Again and again there is 'war in the heavenly places' (for example 12:7). The battle intensifies. Satan gives all his authority to the Beast, who personifies dehumanized masculinity, and the Beast makes war on the saints. Perverted femininity is personified in the Harlot, who rides the Beast. Insatiable in her lust for pleasure, the Harlot drinks the blood of the martyrs of Jesus, thus administering her own intoxicating destruction. Associated with the concept of the Harlot is that great city of commerce called Babylon. This seeks to exploit and eliminate the Church through economic pressures. The Beast, the Harlot and Babylon are symbols of the forces of Satan. They represent lust for power, lust for pleasure and greed. They are, in a sense, Satan's perverted counterfeit for Christ the Lamb, God's people the Bride and the heavenly city of the New Jerusalem. We might, similarly, think of Satan, the Beast and the false prophet as a diabolical counterfeit of the Father, Son and Holy Spirit. Yet God's way is self-sacrifice. The forces of good give glory to one another and build each other up (as we can see for example in John 7:18; 8:50; 17:22; 13:32; 14:13; 16:14; 17:1). The forces of evil carry the seeds of their own destruction, and so the Beast consumes the Harlot which is the City (Revelation 17:16). Finally, Christ and the Bride are attacked by the Beast and the false prophet with their army.

What weapons does the Lord use in this conflict? We can only suppose that they are the weapons we looked at above in chapter 3, which destroy evil by revealing its nature. The sword coming from Christ's mouth (Revelation 1:16; 2:12; 19:15-21) represents his word of truth which reveals evil in all its horror. The light and brightness of his presence illuminate it. His blood witnesses to the depths of its ugliness. In the face of such revelation, evil can only shrivel into itself and die. The Lord is not simply meeting force with greater force. The weapon he wields is different in kind from the brutal and depraved weapons of evil. It is as though God finally allowed the tremendous beauty and love of the Lamb of God to stand forth in all its glory and the 'sons of God' who are conformed to Christ's image are also to be 'revealed', and their brightness will add to his (Romans 8:19, 29), and this light will spread through all the universe, and evil will simply shrivel and die.

The assault on Christ and the Bride will be defeated by the revelation of what he is. Satan's forces will be overthrown. Satan's final assault on the saints and the beloved city will be overthrown by the fire from God himself. To the ancient world a light would have been a flame, and so fire and light are equivalents. So we can consider verses such as 1 Corinthians 3:10-15, 2 Thessalonians 2:8, 1 John 1:5 and Revelation 20:9-10, 21:23 to be linked. The light, the truth, the fire – all refer to God's self-revelation which destroys evil.

Isaiah 11:1-9 also brings many of these ideas together – verse 4 refers to the weapon of truthful words coming from Christ's mouth, verses 6-9 describe the idyllic peace which is to come, and verse 9 explains more how this will be achieved:

> They shall not hurt nor destroy in all my holy mountain,
> For the earth shall be full of the knowledge of the Lord
> As the waters cover the sea.

The knowledge of the beauty of Christ will spread out through the universe, revealing evil and destroying it.

God's final purpose will be accomplished.

Evil is destroyed and a New Heaven and a New Earth appear (Revelation 21:1). Then God's sons will live in the light of him.

15

Eternity

In chapters 1-14 we have looked at how God is bringing in his purposes for humankind from the start of history to the end of time. But what about after that? In the age to come, what happens to humanity (both the righteous and the unrighteous) is a key part of God's strategy. In this chapter, we investigate what the Bible actually says about eternity, death, heaven, hell and the ultimate destiny of every human.

Most Christians realise that the current popular culture views of 'heaven' and 'hell' (based sometimes on Dante or South Park!) have no foundation in Scripture. Nowhere do we see people floating straight up to heaven to waft around on clouds with angels playing harps. Neither do we see a hell as an inferno with the devil and his demons prodding depraved humans with pitchforks forever.

So what is the overall picture that the Bible gives about what happens after death? We suggest the following as a general overview of the key events:

1) The first death (when the individual physically dies) (Hebrews 9:27)

2) Intermediate state in the Grave (*Sheol/Hades*) predominantly described in both Old and New Testaments as 'sleep', probably unconscious and possibly dreaming (Acts 2:31; 1 Kings 2:10; John 11:11; Psalm 6:5)

3) Jesus comes again (1 Corinthians 15:23; 1 Thessalonians 4:16-17)

4) Resurrection (Acts 24:15)

5) Judgement (Romans 2:5; 2 Corinthians 5:10; Hebrews 9:27)

6) Eternity – the righteous in resurrection bodies enter into 'eternal life' in the New Heaven and New Earth, and the unrighteous into 'eternal punishment' (the second death) (Matthew 25:46; 2 Thessalonians 1:7-9; Revelation 20:13-15).

But what exactly do all of these things mean? What will it look like, how does it work? As we approach these issues, we need to recognise our human limitations – concepts like time and eternity will always have elements beyond our understanding, so we need to accept that we may never have the answers to all these questions in this life – and even if we did we may not be able to understand them! While the Bible does say certain things about eternity and life after death, it doesn't give us loads of detail, so on many topics we cannot be dogmatic and make definitive statements about exactly what everything means (just as the psalmists themselves ask many questions), and we must be content to embrace a healthy tension of different possibilities, while not embracing wrong ideas or contradictions – we must remember that it is Jesus who brings to light 'life and immortality' (2 Timothy 1:10).

Eternity

Jesus says that as Christians we will inherit 'eternal life', but also that there is 'eternal punishment' for the unrighteous, and 'eternal fire', but what exactly does he mean by 'eternal'? What can we know about eternity – the conditions in which the New Heaven and New Earth will exist?

Time and God

The Bible seems ambivalent on the relationship of God to time. The devout 1st century Jewish thinker Philo first clearly said that time was created with space and *Yahweh* was outside time – an idea derived from Plato rather than his Hebrew heritage. Two versions of this timeless God developed:

o Augustine (354-430 AD) believed God was outside time but also ordained *everything* that happened in time. Human freewill in any real sense was an illusion.

o Boethius (c480-524 AD) held that God was outside time and could see all things in his eternal present – 'Without doubt, then, all things that God foreknows do come to pass, but certain of them proceed from human freewill'. (This emphasis on freewill followed the views of all theologians before Augustine.)

Einstein changed our understanding of time itself – it slows down and speeds up in different frames of reference depending on how fast observers are moving. This brought real new questions about how God might relate to it. Does God have sequence but not time? Is he omni-timal? Is he timeless outside creation but time-based within it?

The limits of our human minds and the lack of clear Scriptural indication make it unlikely that we will be able to clearly see how God relates to time. But two things *are* quite explicit in Scripture:

i)   God does not always get what he wants (see chapter 5 above).

ii) If God says he will treat people in a particular way and they change their behaviour, then God will *change his mind* (see chapter 10).

For this reason both Open and Relational Theologians hold that God has voluntarily entered into the time he created. He is omniscient and knows *everything that can be known*, but not all the future is yet determined. He knows that there will be a New Heaven and a New Earth because he knows that is what he is going to do – but does not know which future individuals will accept and which will reject his plan for them (Luke 7:30), which is to accept the undeserved forgiveness offered through the cross. Like a myriad-dimensional chess grandmaster God can work out all the possible moves all his creatures may make and is prepared for all of them, even though he may not know in advance how they will exercise their moral choices. In one place God even expresses surprise at the people's unrepentance:

> I said, 'Surely you will fear me, You will receive instruction' – so that her dwelling would not be cut off, despite everything for which I punished her. But they rose early and corrupted all their deeds. (Zephaniah 3:7)

But God is never unprepared. Whatever happens he wants to be there to bring good out of the situation by working with those who love him and are called according to his purpose (Romans 8:28, as explained above in chapter 1).

Biblical Terms for 'Eternity'

The Hebrew term *'ôlām*, often translated as 'eternity' or 'forever', means a long time, a lifetime, or an age. Van Gemeren's *New International Dictionary of Old Testament Theology & Exegesis* says:

> … It does not seem to mean eternity in the philosophical sense of the word (ie neither unbounded time not eternal timelessness) although there are a few vv where the meaning… is very much like the idea of eternity. (vol 3, p 346)

When *'ôlām* is used of the future 'It can refer to a future of limited duration' (p 347). For example, a slave could choose to remain with his master *'ôlām*. In 1 Samuel 1:22 Hannah vows that her child will remain in the house of God at Shiloh *'ad 'ôlām,* meaning for the rest of his life. This is how we might use the English word 'permanently'. Likewise, the Earth is established 'forever' (Ecclesiastes 1:4), and Solomon hopes that God will dwell in his Temple 'forever' (1 Kings 8:13).

Famously Psalm 41:13 and 90:2 say God is *mē 'ôlām 'ad 'ôlām* – often rendered 'from everlasting to everlasting'. Yet the hills are also said to be 'everlasting' (Deuteronomy 33:15) so maybe 'from age to age' is also a possible rendering.

Sometimes, especially in prophecies regarding the Kingdom rule of the Messiah, *'ôlām* does have connotations beyond the present age. Passages like Isaiah 9:7 and Daniel 7:13 specifically refer to the messianic age where 'his dominion is an everlasting (*'ôlām*) dominion'. In a manner common in Hebrew prophecy some verses have a double fulfilment: immediate and ultimate. So in 2 Samuel 7:12-16 God's promises to David relate both immediately to Solomon but also prophetically into the messianic age as Jesus is the 'son of David'. Psalm 110 is clearly also messianic (see Matthew 22:44, Acts 2:34-5, Hebrews 1:13 and 7:15-24), and prophesies a coming Messiah who is to be a priest forever (*'ôlām*) according to the order of Melchizedek (v4).

So does *'ôlām* sometimes mean literally time-without-end? There is a danger here in asking philosophical questions that the Hebrews were not asking about their language – if they didn't really have concept of unending time, then it is wrong to read that into the text. It is more helpful to think about *'ôlām* in terms of permanence or durability, which can relate to this present age or prophetically to the age to come. Only the context can tell us what *'ôlām* means in each case, and even then it is not always clear.

The LXX usually translates *'ôlām* with the Greek word *aiōn*. The base meaning of this is an 'age', and in some cases it means in a lifetime (for example Deuteronomy 15:17, Exodus 21:6 and 1 Chronicles 28:4). The adjective *aionios* is often translated 'eternal'. However, some things relating to the Old Covenant are said to be *'ôlām (aionios)* (Exodus 12:14; 29:9; Numbers 10:8; 15:15;1 Chronicles 23:13) yet in Hebrews, where it speaks of the Old Covenant and its priesthood, it says:

> In that he says, 'A new covenant', he has made the first obsolete.
> Now what is becoming obsolete and growing old is ready to vanish
> away. (Hebrews 8:13)

So some things in the Old Testament said to be *ôlām (aionios)* are actually
ready to vanish away in the age of the New Covenant – so here *aionios* cannot
mean 'eternal' in the sense of existing forever. This probably colours the New
Testament use of *aiōn*, and it should also make us cautious in understanding
the terms in a Greek or Western sense rather than a Hebrew one.

In the New Testament *aiōn* is often translated as the 'present age' or 'present
world' (for example 1 Timothy 6:17; Titus 2:12; Matthew 13:32; Mark 4:19;
Luke 16:8; 1 Corinthians 1:20), and to the 'end of the age' (see Matthew
13:49; 28:20). 'This age' is compared to 'the age to come', for example where
followers making sacrifices for Jesus will receive:

> ... a hundredfold now in this age (*aiōn*) – houses and brothers
> and sisters and mothers and children and lands, with persecutions
> – and in the age (*aiōn*) to come, eternal (*aionios*) life (Mark 10:30;
> see also Matthew 12:32)

So in some cases *aionios* clearly means that which relates to the 'age to come'.
In the New Testament *aionios* is usually translated 'eternal', but in Romans
16:25 the phrase *chronos aionios* is rendered 'in long ages past' by the NIV and
'long ages' by the RSV.

Eternal Life

So what is 'eternal life'? When the young man asked Jesus 'What shall I do
to inherit eternal life?' (Matthew 19:16), was he asking how to live forever,
or how to have a life in the age that all Jews thought was to come? The latter
seems to more likely.

John's gospel and letters contain some general things about life:

> In him was life, and the life was the light of men. (John 1:4)

> I have come that they may have life, and that they may have it
> more abundantly. (John 10:10-11)

This seems to be talking about a quality of life. John also uses the phrase
'eternal life':

> And I give them eternal life, and they shall never perish; neither shall anyone snatch them out of my hand. (John 10:28)

Jesus came to give us eternal life, but is himself that life:

> Word of life – the life was manifested, and we have seen, and bear witness, and declare to you that eternal life. (1 John 1:1-2)

So is 'eternal life' a life which is for unlimited time, or is it primarily a quality of life which will continue into the age to come? If 'time' itself is bound to the present creation, is unlimited time even a meaningful concept?

Immortality

Some Greek philosophies taught that all people had an 'immortal soul'. This is really not the Hebrew concept. Adam/humanity *'became* a living soul/being' (*nephesh*) (Genesis 2:7) – he didn't *get* a soul. In the New Testament *psyche* likewise means 'being' or 'self' or 'life'. We are never said to *have* an immortal soul, rather Paul says:

> ... the dead shall be raised incorruptible, and we shall be changed. For this corruptible must put on incorruption, and this mortal must put on immortality. So when this corruptible shall have put on incorruption, and this mortal shall have put on immortality, then shall be brought to pass the saying that is written, 'Death is swallowed up in victory'. (1 Corinthians 15:52-54)

Only God is immortal as it is he:

> ... who alone has immortality, dwelling in unapproachable light. (1 Timothy 6:16)

Human beings have to seek it, because it is not inherent in them (Romans 2:7). When people argue that although immortality is admittedly never ascribed to us in Scripture it is somehow 'implied' (for example Petersen in *Two Views of Hell*) – this seems to ignore this clear message in 1 Timothy 6. Interestingly, we *have* eternal life both now and in the age to come, but will only be *given* immortality at the time of our resurrection.

So we see that 'eternity' and 'immortality' refer to 'the age to come'. But what will happen to us in this age to come? Before we look at this, we first need to look at what the Bible says about what happens after death.

What happens when we die?

As we look at what the Bible says about the afterlife, in particular in the Old Testament we must remember that death itself was portrayed from the beginning to be a negative thing and outside of God's intentions for mankind (Genesis 2:16-7). As such we need to read the following sections with this in mind.

Old Testament – The Grave/Sheol

What happens when we die? The Old Testament refers to the death of key figures like Abraham, Isaac, Jacob, Moses, Aaron and Josiah as being 'gathered to their people' (Genesis 25:8,17; 35:29; 49:33; Deuteronomy 32:50; 2 Kings 22:20). Also death is described as being like sleep, and we are told for example that David 'slept with his fathers' (1 Kings 2:10, NASB – ie in *Sheol/Hades* see Acts 13:34-7), a phrase used 36 times in the books of Kings and Chronicles. This implies that when we die we enter a sleep-like unconscious state.

The Old Testament also describes where people go after they die as *Sheol,* 'the grave'. It is often expressed as a place of darkness and gloom, a pit with a mouth that swallows up the dead (Job 10:21, 26:5; Proverbs 1:12; 27:20; Isaiah 5:14; 38:18). It is very negative.

Some verses suggest that in death there is no hope and no proclamation or praise of God (Psalm 6:5, 30:9, 88:11, 115:17; Isaiah 38:18), indicating that *Sheol* is a place where there is no consciousness. God is, of course, everywhere – even in sheol (Psalm 139:8), but:

> For in death there is no remembrance of you; in *Sheol* who will give you thanks? (Psalm 6:5)

> For *Sheol* cannot thank you, death cannot praise you. Those who go down to the pit cannot hope for your faithfulness. (Isaiah 38:18)

> The dead do not praise the Lord, nor do any who go down into silence. But as for us, we will bless the Lord from this time forth and forever. (Psalm 115:17)

These verses describe the experience that is *expected* in *Sheol* but we need to take this with caution, for deriving doctrine from Psalms isn't straightforward as some of them record questions, feelings or personal experiences (eg Psalm 137:9!).

There are a couple of places where *Sheol* or the grave is used figuratively. Psalm 88 addresses depression, and the psalmist feels as though he is dead, forgotten and cut off from God's hand (v5). In this context the psalmist asks:

> Shall your lovingkindness be declared in the grave?… Shall your wonders be known in the dark? And your righteousness in the land of forgetfulness? (Psalm 88:11-12)

These enigmatic questions are really addressing his own situation – he feels as cut off and in the dark as if he were dead, but can God raise him up? Could this indicate that actually the dead, like a man in depression, have some kind of consciousness? A similar question arises with Jonah who says: 'Out of the belly of *Sheol* I cried, And you heard my voice' (2:2). In the belly of the fish Jonah had some kind of consciousness, so might those in *Sheol* have a similar experience? This could be argued, but we need to note that the implication in both passages is that the experience is very unpleasant, and it may be stretching references that are meant more figuratively.

In Ezekiel 31–32 *Sheol* is used to refer to the collective fate of Assyria, and in 32:21 it says:

> The strong among the mighty shall speak to him out of the midst of *Sheol*... but their iniquities shall be upon their bones.

However, like Abel's blood crying out in Genesis 4:10, this is clearly figurative, given the surrounding verses, and the same is true for Isaiah 14:8-9.

We will mention one final Old Testament incident where, in 1 Samuel 28:9-19, Samuel was raised from the dead by the witch (or really rather God caused a real coming back of Samuel). Samuel says: 'Why have you disturbed me by bringing me up?' We may note several things about this:

1) Samuel's continued existence is taken for granted by the writers, and if he has been 'disturbed' it presumably was not from a bad experience.

2) Samuel promises Saul – whom he proclaims to be an enemy of God – that he will 'be with me tomorrow'. Whatever *Sheol* is, he pictures the righteous and unrighteousness in it together.

3) This unique event tells us nothing about the general condition of the dead, or whether Samuel had simply been unconscious awaiting the resurrection or had been experiencing some level of consciousness in *Sheol*.

Overall, then, Old Testament references to *Sheol* indicate negativity and lack of any conscious awareness. But does this lack of consciousness mean that those in Sheol have no hope, as King Hezekiah suggests in Isaiah 38:18?

15 | Eternity

Did Old Testament righteous people have hope beyond death?

In general in the Old Testament it does not seem that the faithful feared death as the end. To picture death as 'sleep' does not make it sound like a final cessation of existence, for that is not what sleep is to us. People who go to sleep expect to wake up again.

Genesis 3 describes how 'sin entered the world, and death through sin' (Romans 5:12). However, immediately after the fall God offers hope in that Satan, who brought in death, would be crushed (presumably also crushing the power of death) by the Seed of the woman (Genesis 3:15). Maybe this is why Adam names the woman 'Eve' – the mother of all living, *not* of all dying.

This hope of life is built upon in the Old Testament. For example, Job says:

> For I know that my Redeemer lives... and after my skin is destroyed, this I know, that in my flesh I shall see God, whom I shall see for myself, and my eyes shall behold. (Job 19:25-27)

Psalm 15:17 builds on this hope of resurrection:

> As for me, I shall behold your face in righteousness; I will be satisfied with your likeness when I awake. (NASB)

Peter C Craigie in his commentary says the Psalm provides:

> ... both hope for the immediate crisis as for the psalmist of old, but beyond that a deeper hope for the ultimate deliverance from a more dangerous and insidious enemy, a hope that reaches beyond the sleep of death itself. (*Psalms 1-50*, p 165)

Again in Psalm 16, David rejoices:

> Therefore my heart is glad, and my glory rejoices; my flesh also will rest in hope. For you will not leave my soul in *Sheol*, nor will you allow your Holy One to see corruption. You will show me the path of life. (Psalm 16:9-11)

David is prophetically linking his personal resurrection to that of the 'Holy One', and Peter picks this up in Acts 2:27, applying it to Jesus the Messiah: 'His soul was not left in Hades [see below], nor did his flesh see corruption' (Acts 2:31). Paul in Acts 13:25 also applies this psalm:

> For David, after he had served his own generation by the will of

149

God, fell asleep, was buried with his fathers, and saw corruption; but he whom God raised up saw no corruption.

Ezekiel's famous vision of the Valley of dry bones pictures the hope of a regathering of exiled, scattered Israel as a nation, but also refers to a resurrection so that 'all Israel would have a part in the age to come' (Ezekiel 37:11-14).

Isaiah, contains a powerful vision of the coming chosen one, the Messiah:

> Your dead will live; their corpses will rise. You who lie in the dust, awake and shout for joy, for your dew is as the dew of the dawn, and the earth will give birth to the departed spirits. (26:19, NASB)

Paul's renowned teacher the rabbi Gamaliel saw this as an indication of a resurrection (Sanhedrin 90b), and such a resurrection was a standard part of Pharisaic belief for Paul (Acts 23:6). At the end of the famous messianic passage in Isaiah 53, after his death is described we read that he divides spoils and intercedes for transgressors, indicating the suffering servant will arise victorious on the far side of death.

In Daniel 12:2 we get the clearest Old Testament visions of what the Messiah and the saints will bring:

> ... many of those who sleep in the dust of the earth shall awake, Some to everlasting life, Some to shame and everlasting contempt.

Jesus himself taught the resurrection of the dead from Exodus 3:6:

> ... have you not read what was spoken to you by God, saying, 'I am the God of Abraham, the God of Isaac, and the God of Jacob'? God is not the God of the dead, but of the living. (Matthew 22:29-32)

Jesus shows death was not cessation of being – the Patriarchs who are asleep will rise again. The writer to the Hebrews extols the faith of the Old Testament saints, saying: 'These all died in faith, not having received the promises, but having seen them afar off were assured of them' (Hebrews 11:13-16).

At the time of Jesus's ministry (c30 AD) most Jewish people (except the Sadducees) believed in a resurrection that would herald the 'age to come'. Martha (John 11:21-7) expresses the general Jewish view that her brother 'will rise again in the resurrection at the last day', and Jesus identifies himself as 'the resurrection' (John 11:25-6).

So, resurrection was a part of Jewish belief, which is also reflected in 2 Maccabees 7:8,13 (written c40-120 BC) and in some fragments of the Dead Sea Scrolls of the Qumran community (4Q521 and 4Q385).

We see here the full flowering of the indications in the earlier part of the Old Testament that the hopelessness in the grave is not the final story – there is continuing existence and hope of resurrection in the Messianic age.

God is the God of the living, and to Jesus this indication given as early as Exodus meant that a resurrection would happen. The Jewish expectation of something to hope for beyond the grave counterbalanced the apparently generally negative view of *Sheol* itself as a place where there is no remembrance or praise of God, which could indicate those awaiting the resurrection are simply unconscious. If so then the negative view of *Sheol* is just incomplete, looking at the lack of consciousness in the grave rather than beyond it to a resurrection. On the other hand, since death is pictured as 'sleep', some might wonder whether a dream-like experience might accompany this 'sleep' of death. This could be different from the hope and praise of this life, but imply some kind of awareness.

New Testament – Hades

The New Testament (and the LXX) uses the Greek word *Hades* as an equivalent to *Sheol*, and as a direct translation in quotations from the Old Testament.

Christians have taken three views of the state of people in *Sheol/Hades*:

1) People are unconscious, as though they did not exist.

2) People are 'asleep' but might have some kind of dream-like experience.

3) People are conscious.

The New Testament, like the Old, routinely refers to death as falling asleep, and is used by Jesus to describe Lazarus and Jairus' daughter, as well as by Luke, John, Paul and Peter (see Matthew 27:52; Luke 8:52; Acts 7:6, 13:36; 1 Corinthians 15:18, 15:20; 1 Thessalonians 4:13; 4:15; 2 Peter 3:4). John 11:11-13 illustrates that there is a word for 'death' that is different from that for 'sleep'. This seems to preclude the third option, ie that people are conscious in *Sheol/Hades*. Based on these references, Martin Luther developed his concept of 'soul sleep', where after death everyone's souls enter an unconscious sleep state, until the resurrection, when they are awakened together.

Where was Jesus in the three days between death and resurrection? His body did not rot, but what about his being or soul? The words 'not left in *Hades*' (Acts 2:27) imply this was the where Jesus' being was – and being 'raised up' (v32) is seen as a victory over Hades and death (v24).

Paul likewise in Acts 13 preaches that the resurrection was a victory over decay and corruption. Actually, the event of Jesus' death was so remarkable that the bodies of some of the saints who had 'fallen asleep' were raised and seen by many (Matthew 27:52-53) – presumably temporarily because in Corinthians 15 Paul links the resurrection of Christ with the saints own *future* resurrection. Christ is the firstfruits from the dead and believers who have 'fallen asleep' have not simply 'perished' or ceased to exit (v18), but will be resurrected as immortal (v52-4). 'Death is swallowed up in victory', 'O Death, where is your sting? O Hades, where is your victory?' (v54-5). The gates of Hades will not prevail against the Church (Matthew 16:18).

The idea of victory over death and *Hades* is also taken up in Revelation where they are personified together. Jesus has the keys to them (1:18), they are destructive forces (6:8) but they have to give up the dead in them. Finally, Death and *Hades* will be destroyed in the lake of fire (20:14), so that there will be 'no more death, nor sorrow, nor crying' (21:4).

Two-part Sheol/Hades

By the 1st century, some Jewish thinking had moved from seeing *Sheol/Hades* as a place of nothingness, to a place having two sections – for the righteous and unrighteous. Jesus refers to this in the story of the Rich Man and Lazarus. There is much debate over this passage: is it a parable, or is Jesus giving us a glimpse of what the afterlife is like? The story is unique in that unlike other parables, one of the characters, Lazarus, is named and for a parable it contains a remarkable amount of detail, leading some to suggest that Jesus is giving a historical account. However, even though the story of the Rich Man and Lazarus is not introduced as a parable, neither are the parables of the Unjust Steward or the Prodigal Son that come just before:

A certain man had two sons... (Luke 15:11)

There was a certain rich man who had a steward... (Luke 16:1)

There was a certain rich man... (Luke 16:19)

The context and structure of the passage, and the fact that the description of a split place of the dead is unlike anything else in Scripture indicate that it is most likely a parable. So rather than getting distracted by the details of the story, first of all we need to look for what the point of it is. What truth was Jesus trying to get across?

Was it to teach us about the nature of *Sheol/Hades*? Not really. The whole point is that the Pharisees should be listening to the law and the prophets, and that their lives should therefore be lives full of love and compassion (unlike the Rich Man). The sting is in the point that if they do not repent because of Moses and the prophets, they will not repent even if someone rises from the dead. Jesus is saying that nothing changes after death – the righteous are still righteous, and the unrighteous are still unrighteous. David Powys, in *'Hell': A Hard Look at a Hard Question*, suggests that this passage differs so radically from teaching elsewhere in the synoptics because it is a thrust at the Pharisees using their own imagery. Just before this Luke 16:14 says that the Pharisees were lovers of money, and Matthew 23 bemoans their lack of compassion. In their eyes and theology the Pharisees were the ones off to the Bosom of Abraham – so Jesus tells a parable set in their two-part *Sheol*, but the rich uncaring Pharisee and the smelly scabby beggar actually go the opposite ways from what they expect. Powerful imagery.

So are we to imagine that there *really* are righteous people being comforted in Abraham's Bosom, and there *really* are unrighteous people suffering and at the same time pleading to be able to help their loved ones? Or was Jesus using contemporary popular imagery in this parable to make his point, but without necessarily intending to imply it was literally true? The second is more likely – especially as this idea of a split *Sheol/Hades* only appears in this parable, which was told to the Pharisees to make a quite different point.

However, it is true that when Jesus tells a parable he sets it in a scene that is familiar to his listeners, but which is also based on real things, like lost coins, wedding feasts and agriculture (even if some of the details like the two denarii in the good Samaritan have no particular meaning). So did Jesus intend to imply some element of reality to the situation in this parable?

First we need to note that the 'flame' the Rich Man was suffering was not eternal conscious torment in the 'Lake of Fire' which comes after judgment (see below) – so was it somehow the pain of regret, that the religious but self-centred lifestyle he thought was pleasing to God, was in fact an abomination? Could Jesus be implying that, even if some of the details are parabolic, the dead have some kind of limited maybe dream-like consciousness?

Whichever view we take, we need to make it fit with the indication in both the Old and New Testaments that death is like falling asleep – so while David may be right to say that in *Sheol/Hades* there is no remembrance of God, what David did not know was that the resurrection of the body from that place, ie an awakening from that sleep, would come through Jesus the Messiah defeating death. This will be his next conscious experience.

The Dangers of Over-interpretation

We have seen that pressing meanings other than the main point that Jesus is trying to make can be dangerous – this is true for the Rich Man and Lazarus, and is also true for some of Jesus' other enigmatic Kingdom parables.

For example, in the parable of the Great Supper in Luke 14, Augustine took the phrase 'compel them to come in' (v23) to mean that God *forces* people into the Kingdom (see chapter 7 of *Volume 2: Reconsidering Key Biblical Ideas,* see also chapter 16 of this volume). Yet the parallel passage in Matthew (22:8-9) uses *kaleo* (call or invite) both for the original guests and for the later riff raff – Augustine does not explain why God did not therefore 'compel' the original guests and save face. Yet, based on his bizarre interpretation of Luke, Augustine and centuries of his Roman Catholic, Lutheran and Reformed followers imprisoned and tortured nonconformists to 'compel them' to change churches. Later in this same parable in Matthew 22, the King finds a man there without a wedding garment and has him thrown out. So are we really to take it that, in the Kingdom, as God walks around, he will spot the odd one who has slipped in past the angelic guards, maybe entering through the wrong bit of *Hades,* who needs ejecting? Or is this parable simply to teach us that we not only need to respond to being called as Christians but to genuinely put on the new clothes of 'chosenness' in Christ (see Ephesians 1:4 and Galatians 3:27)?

For statements like 'God changed his mind' or 'God is not willing that any should perish', while these are somehow 'metaphorical', we are adamant that they cannot be emptied of meaning. This, however, is a different issue from deriving major doctrines from incidental details rather than the main point of a parable.

In any event, these parables can tell us nothing about 'hell', by which we mean the final state of the unrighteous. It concerns *Hades/Sheol* the place where people await resurrection and judgement, not their ultimate destiny or fate. Whether in that 'sleep of death' there are any 'dreams' or not, does not affect this fact. If the view that people in *Sheol* are unconscious is true, then for Christians when we die the next thing of which we will be aware is the resurrection to incorruptible life with Christ. So when Paul's says:

> For to me, to live is Christ, and to die is gain... For I am hard pressed
> between the two, having a desire to depart and be with Christ, which
> is far better. (Philippians 1:21-24; also 2 Corinthians 5:8)

rather than meaning after death he will go 'straight to heaven' he is more likely to be referring to the resurrection out of the intermediate state.

There are a couple of other New Testament references that we should look at here. One is the Transfiguration where Jesus was seen by Peter, John and James as talking with Moses and Elijah on the mountain (Matthew 17:3, Mark 9:4, Luke 9:30). Was this a vision given to the disciples or were Moses and Elijah *really* there? Even if we assume that they were there it tells us nothing about what kind of experiential state God raised them from – maybe they were asleep, are awake for the Transfiguration, and then go back to sleep again? The stories of people who may never have died because God 'took them', such as Enoch and Elijah, likewise tell us nothing about what happens to us after death.

Then there's the reference to Jesus preaching to the 'spirits' in prison (1 Peter 3:18), but this refers to a specific group in the period of Noah (either humans or demonic spirits – see Genesis 6:1-4) and cannot tell us about the situation of the dead in general. Revelation 6:9 mentions the cries of the souls of the martyrs, but the revelation vision is symbolic so drawing definitive conclusions from this about the situation of the dead is difficult.

We also need to consider Jesus' promise to the thief on the cross in Luke 23:43. The common translation is 'Truly I tell you, *today* you will be with me in paradise'. But what is 'paradise' (*paradiso*)? The word only occurs three times in the New Testament and some 30 times in the LXX – particularly to refer to the garden of Eden, and sometimes (eg Ezekiel 28:13 and 36:35) to the future restoration of Israel. Kittel's *Theological Dictionary of the New Testament* (vol 5, p 767) says that in the later Judaism of the New Testament period:

> The site of the reopened Paradise is almost without exception the earth… The belief in the resurrection gave assurance that all the righteous, even those who are dead, would have a share in the reopened paradise.

Revelation 2:7 also promises feeding from the Tree of Life in the paradise of the future New Jerusalem. It is something we can experience now in part, and fully in the resurrection, just like we experience the Kingdom now in part (Romans 14:17), but will fully enter into it in the age to come (Acts 14:22).

The setting of the paradise as post-resurrection may well explain the great caution shown by Paul in the only other New Testament reference to it: in 2 Corinthians 12:4. In a context of 'visions and revelations' Paul speaks of someone (presumably himself) caught up into paradise to hear unutterable words, but warns 'whether in the body or out of the body I cannot tell'. Was this the real paradise, or was it a visionary experience?

The thief could presumably not have gone to be with Jesus that day in the post-resurrection paradise – even assuming that Jesus was there during his three days in the grave. This seems to make it more likely that the correct translation of Jesus' words should be: 'Truly I tell you today, you will be with me in paradise'. Either translation is linguistically possible, but the one we suggest is similar in structure to the use of 'today' many times in the LXX of Deuteronomy 11, (eg 11:13: 'I give charge to you today, to love the Lord your God…'). The 'today' belongs to the charge, not to the time when the command is to be fulfilled. The Latin *Codex Vaticanus* and *Syriac Curetonian* Gospels read this way (though other translations have the traditional punctuation). Could the thief have had some kind of intermediate taste of the paradise to come, as Paul did in his vision? Possibly. But to the thief whose view of 'paradise' would be a post-resurrection New Earth, he would more likely have taken it to mean that Jesus was speaking with authority like God in Deuteronomy 11, and that the promise related to a post-resurrection future.

Whether there are any 'dreams' in the sleep of death is not possible to determine with any certainty. Looking at Scripture overall, the most likely thing is that the dead are unconscious – like taking a general anaesthetic – and the next thing of which they will be aware is waking up to the resurrection and judgement. Any apparent exceptions are unique interventions of God.

Second Coming, Resurrection and Judgement

The Good News will be preached in all the world and then the end will come (Matthew 24:14), at which Jesus will come again (often called the *parousia*, 'presence' in Greek) as he promised (Matthew 24:36-37,44; 25:6; John 5:28-29; 21:22-23). After this Jesus says there will be Resurrection (Luke 14:14; 20:35; John 6:40; 11:23-25), followed by Judgement (Matthew 11:22,24).

The Bible doesn't say much about the process of resurrection or exactly what happens at judgement, and most of what we do read is written in symbolic and apocalyptic language, and therefore needs cautious interpretation. An in depth analysis of resurrection and judgement is beyond the scope of this book, however here we will briefly point out that in the New Testament there is a consistent theme that both the righteous and the unrighteous will be raised again and face judgement (eg Matthew 10:15; 25, Romans 2:5; 2 Corinthians 5:10; Hebrews 9:27; 2 Peter 3:7). Their judgement will be based on their faithful, or otherwise, lifestyles in this present life. The Bible is also clear that judgement will lead to life for the righteous and condemnation for those who were unrighteous.

Jesus himself speaks of 'hell' (*gehenna*) and 'eternal punishment' (*kolasin aionion*), as well as 'eternal life' (*zoe aionion*), so we need to take these seriously, and try to understand what he means by them.

Hell

Alternative Views of 'Hell'

The New Testament clearly speaks of a day of Judgement, and says that the unrighteous will be judged. But what will finally happen to them?

Historically there have been four main alternative suggestions about the eternal destiny of the finally unrepentant:

1) *Annihilation:* 'Eternal' is seen as meaning 'ultimate' or 'for the Age to Come' and this applies to eternal life. The 'Age to Come' punishment for the unrepentant is a painful process leading to total destruction in the fire of God's love.

2) *Hell With A Portal:* Hell's punishment can become corrective rather than punitive and God's grace allows people there to repent and be restored.

3) *Universalism:* This is a version of the 'Portal' view where eventually everyone will be saved because God's love will prevail. Ultimately God will get what he wants, which is that none will be lost.

4) *Endless Torment:* 'Eternal' is seen as non-stop time, and 'Eternal Life' is endless life, and so 'Eternal punishment' is never-ending torment.

Today, many ordinary evangelical Christians throughout the world simply assume that the Bible teaches the fourth view, endless torment, and that anyone who dissents is heretical or 'liberal' and denies the authority of Scripture. Whatever view is taken of the issue itself, this is simply not true. There are a number of books that make it clear there have been many mainstream Bible-believing Christian teachers who, over a long period of time, have basically believed 'hell' involves annihilation. They do and have done so because they believe this is what the Bible teaches, and that the 'timeless torment without hope' view has distorted the meaning of God's Word. In 2000 the Evangelical Alliance group ACUTE published *The Nature of Hell,* which has a long bibliography. Detailed studies are given in David Powys' 1997 book *'Hell' A Hard Look at a Hard Question,* as well as the 2011 3rd edition of Edward Fudge's *The Fire That Consumes.* This last book also disproves the suggestions made by some traditionalists that annihilationists (presumably starting with the 2nd century Irenaeus) are denying Scripture based on postmodern or liberal thinking. Annihilationist Christian scholars over the last 2000 years are doing no such thing, but are rather finding the basis for their beliefs in Scripture. We considered adding a more detailed section on this topic in volume 2, but there seemed no point given that all the study material is already in the books by Fudge and Powys.

Powys' book makes several things clear:

1. We need to look at what terms like 'hell' and 'eternal' meant to 1st century Jews – not just rely on traditional meanings ascribed in mediaeval theology, which had little understanding of 1st century Judaism.

2. The precise definition of what some of these terms meant cannot be known with certainty as the New Testament writers do not explain them, and the terms may not be used consistently in contemporary literature. We cannot tell what many Early Church teachers believed because they simply used the words of Scripture without further explanation.

3. The apparent dominance of 'endless torment' is due to what FW Farrar called 'the dark shadow of Augustine' who championed it in the 5th century (though some other Latin theologians had suggested it before him). The Early Church held diverging views, and over the last 200 years many orthodox, Bible-believing Christian scholars have held a view of annihilation, for example FW Farrar, Charles Gore, Basil Atkinson, GB Caird, HE Guiillebaud, John Stott, Philip E Hughes, John Wenham, Edward Fudge, David Powys, Stephen Travis, and Clarke Pinnock. There are many others.

Others with varying theologies have advocated a portal or universalist understanding of Scripture, for example Gerrard Winstanley, Richard Coppin, CS Lewis (?), Jürgen Moltmann, Gregory MacDonald, and more recently Rob Bell in *Love Wins*. We will not really consider this in the present work because the biblical term 'destruction' does not seem compatible with a universalist restitution.

Fundamentally, this is a discussion about the correct way to understand some of the concepts and teachings in the New Testament – we are *not* debating whether the New Testament is right in what it teaches. No one is attempting to 'put God on trial', as some have suggested, but there is an important question about the essential nature of the God of Jesus. When we try to decide on the interpretation of some ambiguous verses we all bring to this task other preconceptions. So here do we bring a Greek concept that humankind is inherently immortal, or a biblical concept that immortality is a gift of God? Do we bring an un-Hebrew idea of God's glory in retributive justice (extending this to a need for infinite punishment for finite sins), or the biblical idea of a God who is consistently love and takes 'no pleasure in the death of the wicked'? In either case where did these pre-concepts come from? We personally fully accept the authority of Scripture, but in the end faith is about knowing God. Men close to God, like the outstanding evangelical leaders John Stott and John Wenham, expressed moral revulsion at the idea of endless torment, not because they doubted Scripture but because they knew God and his character – and this made them all the more certain that where there was any linguistic ambiguity in the words of Scripture these should be understood in a way consistent with that character. But both these men were clear that Scripture was the inspired basis from which to get doctrine.

As we approach this issue there is a tension as to what sources best help us to determine the meanings of biblical terms. The Old Testament we take as inspired, and this is obviously a primary source. Other contemporary writings, however, may help us to understand the meanings of biblical terms used. As Powys shows, words and concepts developed in the period between the Old Testament and the 1ˢᵗ century, and Jesus and the apostles used contemporary language. The problem with this is that the meanings given to terms in Jewish literature outside the Old Testament varied.

The Historic Teaching of the Church

The Early Church universally believed that people had the freewill to reject or accept God's offer of free salvation (as we show in detail in chapter 7 of *Volume 2: Reconsidering Key Biblical Ideas*, see also chapter 16 of this volume) and this changed only with Augustine in the 5ᵗʰ century. On the nature of hell the situation is less clear, and all the above views can be found among early Christian writers. Many of them simply use the biblical language, like 'unquenchable fire', without making clear what they understood by it. For example, the 2ⁿᵈ century Justin Martyr says that there will be sensation after death and 'eternal punishment' and 'eternal fire' (*First Apology*), but these are just words of Scripture. In his *Dialogue*, however, he implies that only God is immortal, and commentators like Ellis see in this a corollary that 'eternal punishment' is that which is everlasting in its effect, ie the extinction of being (*Eschatology in Bible and Theology*, p 200).

The 2ⁿᵈ century Irenaeus also spoke of fire that is everlasting in his *Against Heresies*, but did not believe in immortality of the soul. Powys argues that he was an annihilationist. The late 3ʳᵈ century Arnobius in *Against the Heathen* 2:61, seems to imply that the unrighteous will not suffer instant annihilation but destruction by a painful process. None of the Church Fathers seem to have suggested that the wicked will not be punished at all after death. The immortality of the soul was advocated by 2ⁿᵈ century Latin Tertullian (who cited Genesis 2:6, ignoring the same phrase used of animals in 1:20-21). If the soul were immortal then of course the only conclusion would be either that sinners suffered for endless time or that at some stage they might be redeemed. The 3ʳᵈ century Origen speculated on the latter, though it was never part of his dogma. The late 4ᵗʰ century Gregory of Nyssa held more clearly to a view that hell was remedial and eventually all would be restored.

15 | Eternity

Augustine in the 5th century taught that hell was eternal torment, and his great influence led in 553 AD to any other view (like universalism) being declared heretical. So Augustine's view dominated the mediaeval period. Human immortality and torment without end became the orthodoxy of *Dante's Inferno* and the Reformation. However, this was seriously challenged with a rebirth of New Testament scholarship in the 19th century.

So What is 'Hell'?

The Bible uses a number of different descriptions of the final fate of the unrighteous, which help us to build up a picture of what people commonly refer to as 'hell'.

1) Destruction (Greek: *apōleia, appolymi*)

Colin Brown's *New International Dictionary of Theology* says:

> In the LXX *appolymi* represents 38 different Hebrew Words. Most frequently it stands for *'abad*, to be lost, perish or destroy. In non-religious contexts it is used variously of the destruction of a city, a group of people, or a tribe (cf Numbers 16;33; 32:39; 33:53)… *appolymi* (often used in the active) threatens the very existence of an individual or group… (Vol 1, p 463)

In the New Testament the noun or verb is used 108 times, and has a range of meanings: lost (eg Mark 9:41; Luke 15:4); to destroy/obliterate (eg Matthew 2:13; Luke 17:27); and to die or perish (in the 'middle voice' – see Mark 4:38; Matthew 26:52; Luke 11:51, 13:3, 15:17; 1 Corinthians 10:9).

So Jesus died 'that whoever believes in him should not perish (*apolētai*) but have eternal life' (John 3:15). Does 'perish' here and in similar verses mean extinction, or a state of continued existence but 'lostness'? Linguistically either could be argued for. Note that in Obadiah 16:15-16 the 'Day of the Lord' will make the nations opposed to God 'as though they had never been'. Malachi 4:1 likewise seems to say that the wicked will be 'burned up' leaving nothing. In general, when the term is used in judgement, it seems to us to imply obliteration rather than leaving in a state of prolonged pain.

2) Hell (Greek: *gehenna)*

This does not appear in Greek literature (or the LXX) but is a form of the

Hebrew *gē hinnōm*. This was originally a kind of rubbish dump south of Jerusalem. Here at one time Moloch had been worshipped in child sacrifice (see 2 Chronicles 33:6, Jeremiah 32:35). Jeremiah 7:32 and 19:6 make it a place of judgement. In Isaiah 66:24 God promises to make a New Heaven and New Earth and adds:

> And they shall go forth and look upon the corpses of the men who have transgressed against me. For their worm does not die, and their fire is not quenched. They shall be an abhorrence to all flesh.

Given that the men are dead, they don't feel anything, and the bodies, presumably, are totally consumed and destroyed. The worms and fire may be unquenched, but the bodies do not last forever.

In the New Testament *gehenna* is used once of the tongue in James 3:6, and only 11 times elsewhere – all by Jesus, in the synoptic gospels. Six of these are like Mark 9:43-44:

> If your hand causes you to sin, cut it off. It is better for you to enter into life maimed, rather than having two hands to enter *gehenna*, into the fire that shall never be quenched – where 'Their worm does not die, and the fire is not quenched.'

The comparison is for the hand to 'perish' or be destroyed, so that the whole body will not be. The reference to worms and fire is to Isaiah 66 above. The rubbish dump is a place where the fire and worms are continual, but the people are already dead and the bodies are consumed. It is not a place where torture continues indefinitely. Two of the other references are like Matthew 10:28:

> Do not fear those who kill the body but cannot kill the soul. But rather fear him who is able to destroy (*apolesai*) both soul and body in *gehenna*.

This links destruction (*appolymi*) with hell (*gehenna*). Paul says that if there is no resurrection then those who have 'fallen asleep in Christ have perished' (*appolymi*). Does Paul mean to imply that if there is no resurrection then dead Christians are suffering torture without end? Surely not? To Paul, the Messiah died for our sins, but our resurrected life is tied up with his resurrection. Without this, Christians would be in the state of godless non-existence pictured for the dead in the Old Testament. Then we might as well say 'Eat drink and be merry for tomorrow we die!' Those who say this believe death is extinction, not suffering for unlimited time. Powys (p 280) comments that this passage has 'a strong suggestion that the fate of the unrighteous may be destruction'.

Powys also points out that Jesus used *gehenna* rhetorically rather than to establish a doctrine of the fate of the unrighteous. His words were addressed to the 'righteous,' (either to his followers who were righteous or to the Pharisees who thought they were).

3) Eternal Punishment (Greek: *kolasin aionion*).

The word *kolasin* appears in Matthew 25 and in only one other place in the New Testament (1 John 4:18). The complete phrase 'eternal punishment' (*kolasin aionion*) appears *only* in Matthew 25, where Jesus connects it to 'eternal fire' which we discuss in our fourth point below:

> [41]Depart from me, you cursed, into the *eternal fire* prepared for the devil and his angels...
>
> [46]And these will go away into *eternal punishment*, but the righteous into eternal life. (Matthew 25:41,46)

So what does it mean and what is this whole picture in Matthew 25:31-46 about? It is worth looking at this, though it should be remembered that because such pictures and parables of Jesus are enigmatic it is hard to be sure what some of the details mean.

- The Sheep and the Goats

First we should ask, who are the sheep and the goats? Could it be that they are the visible Church, and that the judgement is based on whether or not the 'faith' of professing Christians is 'real'? Well Paul teaches that at some stage *everyone* (including the Church) *will* stand before the judgement seat to be judged on our lifestyles:

> For we must all appear before the judgment seat of Christ, that each one may receive the things done in the body, according to what he has done, whether good or bad. (2 Corinthians 5:10)

Some may argue that because both the sheep and the goats address Jesus as 'Lord' they are all part of the visible Church. However, to address him as 'Lord' would be natural whoever they were because he is clearly the King at a judgement scene. In an English court, for the accused to address the judge as 'my Lord' does not imply any previous knowledge or relationship.

There are also good reasons here to conclude that the sheep and goats are certainly not exclusively the Church, and, indeed, may not even include the Church. The first of these is that professing Christians would surely know that believers are the body of Christ and so to neglect them is to neglect him. But the impression one gets is that the sheep and goats are saying 'We never even saw or heard of you before, so when did we neglect you?'

The second reason the Church may be excluded is that the sheep and goats are designated in Matthew 25:32 as 'all the nations' (*panta ethnē*) When 'nations' is used in Matthew it generally means the Gentiles (4:14; 6:32; 10:5; 10;18; 12:18; 12:21; 20:19; 20:25). Matthew 24–25 form a discourse addressed privately to the 'disciples' (24.3) and in chapter 24 Jesus answers their questions about: i) the destruction of the Temple, and ii) the *parousia* or second coming. The destruction of the Temple will be in their generation, but the *parousia* at an unknown time. In this discourse, Jesus tells the disciples in 24:9 that they will be hated by 'all nations', but in 24:14 the gospel of the Kingdom is to be preached to 'all nations' before the end comes (a prophecy later changed to a commission in Matthew 28:19). The background, then, is that the gospel will be preached to all nations by Jesus' disciples, but that they will meet persecution and hatred. Maybe there is an echo, too, of Joel 3:2 where the Gentiles ('all nations') are gathered to be judged for their treatment of God's servant Israel.

The 'all nations' in Matthew 25:32 is therefore most likely to mean the Gentile world in general.

- The Least of These my Brothers

So who exactly are 'the least of these' (Matthew 25:35,44), the treatment of whom is the basis of judgement? Jesus does not say 'my followers' but 'my brothers' – so who are his brothers? Jesus defined his brothers as:

> For whoever does the will of my Father in heaven is my brother and sister and mother. (Matthew 12:50)

This obviously includes his explicit followers the Christians, but seems much wider than this. Elsewhere, again, Jesus speaks about the reception of his disciples, but widens it out to include any prophet or 'righteous' person:

> He who receives you receives me, and he who receives me receives him who sent me. He who receives a prophet in the name of a prophet shall receive a prophet's reward. And he who receives a righteous man in the name of a righteous man shall receive a righteous man's reward. And whoever gives one of these little ones (*Mikros*) only a cup of cold water in the name of a disciple, assuredly, I say to you, he shall by no means lose his reward. (Matthew 10:40-42)

These would include the righteous Jewish prophets in the Old Testament, but also the righteous Noah, Lot and others. It should also include any prophets amongst those Gentiles who, as we found in Romans 2, seek 'glory, honour and incorruption' and will receive eternal life (see chapter 13 above). They might have had amongst them prophets and righteous men like, Melchizedek in Salem, Epimenides in Crete/Athens, Lao Tzu in China and Pu Chan amongst the Wa tribe in Burma (as noted in chapter 13 above). Such prophets preach that there is one true God, and that faith in and relationship with him is paramount. To these, and those who honour and follow them, they may not have 'eternal life' now, but will be given it at the future judgement (Matthew 25:46; Romans 2:7).

However we interpret this passage, there may be no clear line between the sheep doing the visiting and the ones visited – but parables tend to have this kind of feature as in the earlier one in Matthew 25 where the wise virgins at the wedding are the Church but the Church is also the bride!

- The Basis of Judgement

It is useful here to note that those who read 'unending torment' into the phrase 'eternal punishment' seldom emphasize the basis on which Jesus says the righteous and the unrighteous will be distinguished. Their destiny is based on acts of compassion. Of course, these are not 'works of the Law', but Jesus says nothing about 'believing in Jesus', nothing even about faith. (Some branches of evangelical/Reformed faith, if they came across this passage and did not know it was in the Bible, would surely regard it as heresy!)

Moreover, it cannot be argued that the acts of compassion mentioned can be done only with faith and the power of the indwelling Holy Spirit – they are not miraculous healings or signs and wonders but simple acts of compassion that non-Christians can do.

So are the acts of compassion the basis or the sign of being a sheep? The word 'for' (*gar*) in vs 35 and 42 is overwhelmingly used to mean 'because' or 'since' but can be a bit vague. The only exact similar phrase in Matthew is 'for (*gar*) they say and (*kai*) they do not' (23:3), paralleling 'for (*gar*) I was hungry and (*kai*) you gave me meat' (25:36) – in Matthew 23:3 it clearly means 'because'. Very occasionally (as in Luke 8:46-47) it can mean the evidence for something or the way in which we know something is true. Maybe in Matthew 25 it could be stretched to mean that the acts of compassion are the evidence that they are 'the blessed of my Father' rather than the basis for it – though this would not be the most obvious linguistic meaning to take.

RT France (a conservative evangelical commentator and a renowned modern expert on the Gospel of Matthew) looks at the various attempts to reconcile the passage with common evangelical belief but concludes:

> So it does not seem to be possible to read this passage as expressing a 'Pauline' doctrine of salvation by an explicit faith in Jesus. (p 959)

Explicit faith *in Jesus* is simply not the basis Jesus states here – though a wider issue of reaction to the 'light that enlightens every man who come into the world' presumably could be. This is how it may be meant. Those with faith *in Jesus* have eternal life now. Those who do not know anything about Jesus but react positively (rather than with indifference) to those who carry a message about the one true God may be given eternal life at this judgement scene.

- So is this salvation by works?

No, forgiveness and acceptance by God are always a gift and never earned as a right. Jesus does not say that the sheep have earned eternal life, but that God gives it to them. But we should note that the New Testament usually speaks in terms of judgement according to lifestyles, not belief systems (for example John 5:28-29, 2 Corinthians 5:10 and Revelation 20:12-13). There is never, moreover, any indication that this is anything other than their own lifestyle, and not some quality of ethical perfection found in Jesus which is 'imputed' to them, as some Lutheran theologians have taught. But, as we have emphasized, the righteous lifestyle is one lived in relationship with God, and the pattern of loving and compassionate behaviour is a natural part of this. Our destiny is determined by a righteous lifestyle in this sense, but, to reiterate, our forgiveness and acceptance by God is a gift and is never 'earned'.

False religions may seek to earn the gods' favour through ritual or gifts, but true faith in the One God recognises that his favour is always a gift.

It should also be noted that the whole basis upon which God can forgive or 'pass over' former sins (Romans 3:25), is the faithfulness of Jesus the Messiah in his sacrificial death for those with faith. This, again, has been a major theme in this present book. No one can come to the Father except through Jesus, even though some of those who come to God (Old Testament Jews and the Gentiles in Romans 2) never heard of Jesus. Jesus died for the sins *of the world*, including those who never heard of him.

- Eternal Punishment

So what is the meaning of 'eternal punishment'?

Jesus promises his self-sacrificing followers 'in the age (*aioni*) to come eternal (*aionios*) life' (Luke 18:30). The word 'eternal' most basically means it concerns the age to come. It is also a *quality* of life, even though Christians have it in this present age (1 John 5:11). Its primary meaning is *not* non-stop time. So in the 'age to come' will time be like our present time? If we cannot really imagine what our 'spiritual body' promised by Paul will be like, and time is a property of space, imagining time in the age to come to be a never ending version of our present time may be presumptuous.

In a similar way, *kolasin aionion* means punishment that relates to the age to come rather than the present age. It reflects Jesus' contrast between destroying an eye now or being totally destroyed in that age. Critics sometimes argue that since 'eternal life' means life that lasts forever, so 'eternal punishment' must mean punishment that lasts forever. However, this misses the fact that lasting forever is not the primary meaning of *aionios*. Eternal life is primarily a quality of life, not a duration. Paul says:

> … we ourselves boast of you among the churches of God for your patience and faith in all your persecutions and tribulations that you endure, which is manifest evidence of the righteous judgement of God, that you may be counted worthy of the kingdom of God, for which you also suffer; since it is a righteous thing with God to repay with tribulation those who trouble you, and to give you who are troubled rest with us when the Lord Jesus is revealed from heaven with his mighty angels, in flaming fire taking vengeance [*ek dikesin* = judgement] on those who do not know God, and on those who

do not obey the gospel of our Lord Jesus Christ. These shall be punished with eternal (*aionion*) destruction from the presence of the Lord and from the glory of his power, when he comes, in that Day, to be glorified in is saints. (2 Thessalonians 1:4-10)

God's *judgement*, the *punishment* he gives, is eternal destruction. The judgement is on the narrower group of those who have heard and rejected the gospel, but also on the wider group of those who have had no relationship with God. Also in Jude 7, Sodom and Gomorrah are said to have been 'judged' (*dikē*) with 'eternal fire'. In context this really could not mean that the process of their destruction lasted for ever – you can visit the site today and there is no sulphurous fire and brimstone. It was the other-worldly quality of the fire.

RT France (a theologically conservative commentator) also insists:

In the debate among evangelical theologians on the issue of annihilation as against continuing punishment, the phrase 'eternal punishment' here in Matt 25:46 is commonly cited as a proof text for the latter position. But this is usually on the assumption that 'eternal' is a synonym for 'everlasting'. That assumption depends more on modern English usage than on the meaning of *aiōnios*, which we have seen to be related to the concept of the two ages. 'Eternal punishment', so understood, is punishment which relates to the age to come rather than punishment which continues forever, so the term does not in itself favour one side or the other in the annihilationist debate. Insofar as the metaphor may be pressed, however, it suggests destruction rather than punishment, especially if the imagery of the incineration of rubbish is understood to underlie the idea of hell (see on 5:22); the fire of Gehenna goes on burning not because the rubbish is not destroyed by it, but because more is continually added. The imagery of incineration in relation to the final destiny of the wicked also occurs more explicitly in 13:42: the weeds are destroyed, not kept burning forever. We have also noted the use of the verb 'destroy' in relation to hell in 10:28. These pointers suggest that an annihilationist theology (sometimes described as 'conditional immortality') does more justice to Matthew's language in general, and if so the sense of 'eternal punishment' here will not be 'punishment which goes on forever' but 'punishment which has eternal consequences', the loss of eternal life through being destroyed by fire. (p 967)

We agree with this. 'Eternal punishment' is a punishment relating to the age to come, and its consequences are for that age. It may also be painful, but it does not imply unending duration of pain. It is 'eternal *punishment*' not 'eternal *punishing*'.

4) The Lake of Fire

In Matthew 25, Jesus connects 'eternal punishment' (see point 3 above) with 'eternal fire', by doing this he is hinting at the concept of the Lake of Fire, that appears in Revelation:

> If anyone worships the Beast and his image, and receives his mark on his forehead or on his hand, he himself shall also drink of the wine of the wrath of God, which is poured out full strength into the cup of his indignation. He shall be tormented with fire and brimstone in the presence of the holy angels and in the presence of the Lamb. And the smoke of their torment ascends forever and ever; and they have no rest day or night, who worship the beast and his image, and whoever receives the mark of his name. (Revelation 14:9-11)

Revelation is packed with symbolism, but that does not mean that we can simply ignore this passage, as for example Rob Bell appears to do in his book *Love Wins*. Regarding the Lake of Fire:

> And fire came down from God out of heaven and devoured them. The devil, who deceived them, was cast into the Lake of Fire and brimstone where the beast and the false prophet are. And they will be tormented day and night forever and ever [for the ages of the ages]... The sea gave up the dead who were in it, and Death and Hades delivered up the dead who were in them. And they were judged, each one according to his works. Then Death and Hades were cast into the lake of fire. This is the second death. And anyone not found written in the Book of Life was cast into the lake of fire. (Revelation 20:9-15)

So what does it mean for 'Death' and 'Hades' to be cast into the Lake of Fire? Does it mean that they are *individuals* who will be tortured for limitless time? Or that they are phenomena that will be destroyed – extinguished so that there is 'no more death'?

What does 'the second death' mean? Life is an inherently continuous state. *Dying* may be a limited time process, sometimes painful, but *death* is an event. The 'first death' refers to the physical death we die at present. After death the body is then consumed until it no longer exists. Someone thrown into a physical fiery furnace would experience a brief but painful process of dying, then the event of death, followed by total destruction of their body. So what is the 'second death'? Is it a process in which a being itself is destroyed/extinguished? Then those who follow Satan are 'consumed' by the fire of God, whereas Satan and the false prophet seem just to suffer in it. Is the 'false prophet' really an individual – or is it like Death and Hades a phenomenon (in this case the lies of Satan)? Is Satan immortal, and so will always feel pain in the presence of God's manifested *Love*? It is difficult to be definitive.

For those deepest in evil, with the mark of the Beast, there will be torment as they enter the Lake of Fire, *the smoke of which* will last 'for the ages of the ages'. Supposing for now that this means endless time, then is the smoke the evidence or memory of the torment, or their actual continuing suffering?

Smoke going up forever is also mentioned in Isaiah 34:10, which talks about the destruction of Edom: 'Its land shall become burning pitch. It shall not be quenched night or day; its smoke shall ascend forever'. However, in the next verse Edom is apparently to be inhabited by a whole menagerie of animals and birds, so this description does not represent unending retributive suffering for the Edomites, but irreversible destruction. So the more natural reading is that the smoke going up forever in Revelation 14 represents the memory or consequences of the suffering in the Lake of Fire.

(For more on interpreting resurrection, judgement and the Lake of Fire see Roger Forster's forthcoming book on Revelation.)

5) Weeping and Gnashing of Teeth and Outer Darkness

The phrase 'weeping and gnashing of teeth' is used 6 times in Matthew and once in Luke. What does it signify? Psalm 112:10 says:

> The wicked will see it [the honour of the righteous] and will be grieved; he will gnash his teeth and melt away; the desire of the wicked shall perish.

This seems to indicate a sense of loss and frustration before annihilation or perishing. In Lamentations 2:16 the phrase seems to indicate anger. In Job 16:9, Psalm 35:16 and Psalm 37:12 it indicates the anger of the unrighteous against the righteous. In none of these Old Testament uses does 'gnashing of teeth' ever indicate physical pain. Matthew 13:42 and 50 have 'weeping and gnashing of teeth' as the wicked, in contrast to the righteous, are thrown into the blazing furnace. This seems to be rage and anguish at their impending destruction.

Elsewhere 'weeping and gnashing of teeth' is linked with exclusion – which Matthew pictures as 'outer darkness'. Key verses are:

o   *Matthew 8:12*. Jesus laments the lack of faith in Israel and says that many Gentiles will come and take places in the kingdom feast: ... but the sons of the kingdom will be thrown outside, into the darkness, where there will be *weeping and gnashing of teeth*.

o   *Matthew 22:13*. The wedding feast parable, says that the king finds a man without a wedding garment: ... 'bind him hand and foot, and take him away, and cast him into outer darkness'; there will be *weeping and gnashing of teeth*, for many are called but few are chosen. (Maybe this is why Peter tells us to make our calling and election sure (2 Peter 1:10)).

o   *Matthew 24:45-51*. The parable of the wicked servant who behaves badly and whose master will: ... cut him in two and appoint him his portion with the hypocrites. There shall be *weeping and gnashing of teeth*.

o   *Matthew 25:14-30*. The parable of the three servants, each given some money while their master is away. On his return the first two are found to have used it well, but the third did nothing with it. The master denounces him as wicked and lazy, and ... casts the unprofitable servant into outer darkness. There will be *weeping and gnashing of teeth*.

o   *Matthew 25:1-13*. Immediately before the parable of the three servants, we find the parable of the ten virgins, and this seems therefore to be speaking of a similar theme. The five foolish virgins are excluded from the feast, and in Luke 13:22-30 we find those who thought they knew Jesus trying to get in through the narrow gate and also being excluded.

In all these references, the people involved are 'insiders' – servants or subjects of the kingdom, or someone who is called to the kingdom but is improperly dressed. One theme is that the Kingdom must be properly entered before the *parousia* (or second coming), at which time the opportunity is lost. The 'gnashing of teeth' is not pain but anger and a sense of loss (though perhaps the virgins are too ladylike to gnash teeth!). So is this 'outer darkness' to be identified with the fiery destruction of *gehenna*?

Is it a place of teeth gnashing for unending time? None of the Matthew texts state either way, and the central concept is not the punishment of judgement but the exclusion from the kingdom, because they seem not to be genuinely acting as part of the family. So much in such parables of Jesus cannot be interpreted with certainty. Are the five virgins those who have genuinely been believers but lost the oil of the Holy Spirit? Can we really imagine someone sneaking unsuitably dressed into the Kingdom, only to be spotted as God walks around the guests? Can outer darkness or obscurity (as it could also be regarded) really be the same as the fiery lake? Someone who is 'cut in two' cannot gnash his teeth, and in the Old Testament to be cut in pieces means destruction (eg Daniel 3:29).

All this means that we cannot be definitive about the meaning of the 'outer darkness'. It may be that these insiders are some of those who are going to be 'saved but as through fire' (1 Corinthians 3:15), and that the outer darkness and sense of loss are relative. Although the language Jesus uses is parabolic (eg 'cut in two') – nonetheless it is extreme ('wicked' and 'lazy') so it would be foolish to presume upon being saved in this way. Another obvious meaning seems to be that those who thought they were insiders are in fact not, because their lifestyles (like the goats in Matthew 25) were not righteous, and for them there will be anguish and anger at their sense of loss, before they meet their final punishment.

Conclusions on Hell

The New Testament does not teach the Greek philosophical idea that humans are inherently immortal. Eternal life is a quality of life given now, and 'incorruption' will be a gift when we rise again. If the unrighteous continue to exist this will be because God chooses to give them continuing existence.

The Bible is plain that God does not want anyone to 'perish' so he sent his Son to die for the sins of the world so that anyone who has faith will not perish, but have eternal life. Plainly the experience of the second death, of 'perishing', is painful, but is it a process finishing in time, or is it going to go on for unending time? If it finishes, then will this be with the extinction or the redemption of those in it?

Most New and Old Testament passages seem to indicate the final fate of the unrighteous is extinction. One or two passages in the apocalyptic vision of

Revelation could be read otherwise; so, as we interpret these, it makes sense to try to do so consistently with what we know of God from elsewhere. We know that God is Love. We know that he would rather everyone repent. But is he also bound by his own retributive justice? Does it work to suggest that someone who has sinned against an infinite God just once, has to suffer purely punitive retribution without hope for unending time? The fact that this kind of thinking has been prevalent since Augustine does not make it a biblical concept.

God as judge features highly in the Old Testament, but Powys says:

> The early traditions do not indicate a strong association between punishment and judgement in the functions of Israel's judges. (p 73)

> Vengeance... is not a major theme anywhere in the Old Testament, and in no case is there any suggestion that any will experience God's vengeance after death. (p 82)

> Punishment in the Old Testament is rarely if ever an end in itself. (p 176)

Throughout the Old Testament punishment was either corrective or to 'put away the evil from among you' by destroying its agents. So we need to be very careful if we import into God's justice ideas of indefinite suffering.

The Morality of Hell?

Some theologians portray God as a kind of split personality. On the one hand God is 'love' – so he picks out some people to show this to. On the other hand God is 'just' – so he picks out the rest to allow (or maybe even cause) to sin and then put in pain forever to show this 'justice'. We cannot accept that this is the God of Jesus and the Bible.

If someone rejects God, then does God still love them? God commends his love for us in that while we were still sinners Jesus died for us (Romans 5:8). Even sinners, Jesus says, love their friends, but:

> ... love your enemies, do good, and lend, hoping for nothing in return; and your reward will be great, and you will be sons of the Most High. For he is kind to the unthankful and evil. Therefore be merciful, just as your Father also is merciful. (Luke 6:35-36)

Is Jesus asking us only to arbitrarily pick out a minority of our enemies to love? Surely not. As sons of God we will love *all* our enemies – as he does. So we ask those who believe in hell as torment for unlimited time, could God not make these sufferers cease to exist if he chose to? If he cannot then he must be weak. If he can and will not then he cannot love them. We find the claim of Habermas and Moreland quite bizarre:

> ... it is clearly more immoral to extinguish humans with intrinsic value than to allow them to continue living in a state with a low quality of life. (*After Death*, p 173)

Having a 'low quality of life'?! Suffering the supposed pangs of extreme torment with *no hope* of ever experiencing relief? Would they really rather that someone they loved ceased to exist or lived in non-stop, *without hope*, torment forever? What a strange idea of what is immoral. Were there any hope of eventual redemption this might make sense, but not otherwise. This is not to 'judge God' but to judge the strange ideas of some theologians about God.

We do not believe that God is a split personality. We should not *contrast* God's love with his wrath or justice. God is *love* (1 John 4:8,16), God is *light* (1 John 1:5), God is a *consuming fire* (Hebrews 12:29). These are all the same. God's love/light exposes evil for what it is and consumes it. Those who reject and resist it will ultimately be consumed by it in judgement – and this experience will be painful. But God will not override their freedom to choose.

In Exodus 24:17:

> The sight of the glory of the LORD was like a consuming fire on the top of the mountain in the eyes of the children of Israel.

In Exodus 33, even Moses could not see the pure face of God, and when he saw just part of this then his own face shone with God's glory so that he had to veil it from the other Jews.

The same *fire* of the *love* of God will engulf believers on the *Day*, ie the judgment day as in 1 Corinthians 3:12-17. The righteous saints are building the Temple of God, the Church. On the *Day* each person's work in this regard will be tried by the fire. Wood, hay and straw will be consumed and only precious materials survive. Anything you and I build into the Church will be tested against this *fire* of God's love. Hear O Israel, the Lord your God is *one*! He is a Trinity but not a split personality. He is consistently *love* but it is the effects of his pure love that differ.

There are also some questions about the experience of the righteous in this age to come. If you are a Christian then think of someone you loved dearly in this life, but who never became a Christian. Would you feel happy to be in a New Heaven and New Earth where there was 'nothing to hurt or destroy' but you knew that this loved one was suffering, without hope, for unlimited time? To suggest that we will all be so busy having a good time that it will not bother us, or that somehow we will feel it 'serves them right', seems to sit ill with the kind of righteous, loving people Jesus wanted us to become. Mercifully few, even amongst traditionalists, may follow the ideas of Jonathan Edwards' disciple John Gestner, who pictures the righteous as *enjoying* seeing the time-unending hopeless sufferings of the sinners (unlike their God who 'delights not in the destruction of the wicked') – possibly including John Stott, whose salvation Gestner seems to question.

These types of question do not *prove* that hell is not suffering for unlimited time, but they should at least make us hesitant to interpret the few ambiguous biblical verses in this way.

Having said this mysteries concerning time and eternity will always remain in this age. We have one final thought to add in here from theoretical physics. A person falling into a black hole would appear to a distant observer to slow down and hover just above it. But from the point of view of the person, he or she would fall in and get crushed by the singularity at the centre of the black hole in a finite time. If this works in physics, then could it be possible that in the process of spiritual judgement the person being judged experiences a process which takes a finite time, whereas to other observers it would appear timeless? Could this help us to understand the idea of the smoke of their torment going up forever?

Hellfire and Evangelism

One criticism of annihilationism puzzles us: we have heard it said that without the threat of unending suffering Christians may not bother to evangelise or listeners respond.

Well, firstly, as evangelicals our focus is on what the Bible teaches – what is the truth about the God of Jesus. Whether it is *convenient* or not seems irrelevant. But even in its own terms this criticism is puzzling. As far as concerns motivation for evangelism, surely we are motivated by the love of God flowing into and out through us, and our love for others makes us want to share God's love with them? As far as concerns response, suppose we meet someone who is touched by the words of Jesus about loving enemies and dying for the sin of the world, and wonders if it is true. So he comes and asks us this. 'I know of a little girl in my non-Christian culture who grew up being continually abused by her stepfather, was always hungry and eventually died of malnutrition and neglect. For sins committed in her brief sad life is she to be tortured for unlimited time to glorify the justice of God?' How an affirmative answer could be thought to encourage people to accept the truth of Christianity and become Christians mystifies us. In any event the annihilationist Christian leaders listed above have been at the forefront of evangelism.

Hell with a Portal/Universalism

Finally, a word about the portal and universalist views. Universalists and annihilationists both believe in a God of Love. The difference is that annihilationists believe that Love will not override freewill, and so those who ultimately reject the Love of God will be destroyed by it. Universalists believe that ultimately all human freewill will be overcome by God's sovereign Love and everyone will be redeemed. The language of Scripture seems to us to indicate that destruction will be a final reality for those who continue to reject God's free offer of forgiveness and salvation – so we are not universalists.

Could there be any 'second chance' after death to repent, or even a continuing chance over extended time? We are not speaking here of those (Romans 2) who throughout life sought 'glory, honour and immortality' without hearing of Jesus, and will be given eternal life through him at judgement. We speak about those who did know about and reject in this life the 'light that enlightens everyone who comes into the world'. Could there be any second chance for them? Well, we may remember that when God sent Jonah to Nineveh there was no mention of any chance to repent – but God changed his mind (3:10)! The *Living Bible* pithily puts it:

> And when God saw that they had put a stop to their evil ways, he abandoned his plan to destroy them and didn't carry it through.

Jonah was angry and complained to God that he knew God was: 'a gracious and merciful God, slow to anger and abundant in lovingkindness, one who relents from doing harm'. God is not fickle and has never failed to fulfil a promise to those who continue in steadfast love to him, but Jonah knew that God could change his mind if he saw an opportunity to show mercy. Jonah was not mandated to declare the possibility of repentance and forgiveness, but he knew it was always possible. We are not mandated to declare that there is any second (or even third, or fourth...) chance after death, but it would be a bold theologian who told God that he could not change his mind if there were an opportunity to show mercy. Not even Jonah did that, but he was angry when it happened.

We do not like being labelled 'annihilationists' (or indeed any kind of 'ists') because we seek only to be true to Scripture and the God and Father of our Lord Jesus the Messiah. But we will continue to declare what God has mandated us to declare:

> 'For behold, the day is coming, burning like an oven, and all the proud, yes, all who do wickedly will be stubble. And the day which is coming shall burn them up', says the LORD of hosts, 'That will leave them neither root nor branch. But to you who fear my name, the Sun of Righteousness shall arise with healing in his wings'. (Malachi 4:1-2)

New Heaven and New Earth

So we have looked at the ultimate destiny of the unrighteous, but what happens to the righteous in eternity? God's ultimate strategy is to have a New Heaven and a New Earth in which there is no hurt and no pain. Can we imagine this? Probably not, but what do we know from Scripture?

Resurrection Bodies

In the resurrection we will have new 'resurrection' bodies:

> But someone will say, 'How are the dead raised up? And with what body do they come?' Foolish one, what you sow is not made alive unless it dies. And what you sow, you do not sow that body that shall be, but mere grain... But God gives it a body as He pleases, and to each seed its own body. All flesh is not the same flesh... There are also celestial bodies and terrestrial bodies; but the glory of the celestial is one, and the glory of the terrestrial is another... So

also is the resurrection of the dead. The body is sown in corruption, it is raised in incorruption. It is sown in dishonour, it is raised in glory. It is sown in weakness, it is raised in power. It is sown a natural body, it is raised a spiritual body. There is a natural body, and there is a spiritual body... And as we have borne the image of the man of dust, we shall also bear the image of the heavenly man. (1 Corinthians 15:35-49)

Looking at a daffodil bulb would give you no idea of what a daffodil would look like! The physical body 'sown' gives us no idea what the spiritual body will be like. The term *soma pneumation* (spiritual body) is a strange one – appearing nowhere else other than here. But when we say that we believe in the 'resurrection of the body' we need to be careful. Our beings (Greek – *psyche*) at that time will be given immortality to go with the eternal life we already have. It is some kind of a 'resurrection' of a spiritual *body*.

For our citizenship is in heaven, from which we also eagerly wait for the Saviour, the Lord Jesus Christ, who will transform our lowly body that it may be conformed to his glorious body. (Philippians 3:20-21)

But a spiritual body may differ a lot from our present physical bodies. Presumably we will recognise people, although relationships like marriage will be transcended – and *in this respect* we will be 'like the angels' (Matthew 22:30). Our bodies will be like that of the 'heavenly man', Jesus, but John hints to us that what Jesus *will be* is not yet fully revealed:

Beloved, now we are children of God; and it has not yet been revealed what we shall be, but we know that when he is revealed, we shall be like him, for we shall see him as he is. And everyone who has this hope in him purifies himself, just as he is pure. (1 John 3:2-3)

Transformation

In verse 5 John accepts that Jesus has been 'revealed' to take away our sin, but that we do not really know yet what he *will be* when he returns and we are raised to be like him. But the conclusion he draws is that our hope should make us purify ourselves. His letters are full of warnings that the righteous person is the one who *practices* righteousness – real faith produces a holy lifestyle, and a holy lifestyle is one which has the love and compassion about which Jesus spoke in Matthew 25:34-37.

Paul is clear that not only is our initial forgiveness through faith, but that living a righteous lifestyle is not done by gritting one's teeth and keeping regulations, but by faith – this is the core message of Galatians. We are 'transformed by the renewing of our minds' (Romans 12:2) – an inside change that affects our behaviour as he goes on to say. Our 'salvation' does not mean merely a ticket to a spiritual heaven, but the process of redeeming and transforming us – and we are to 'work out our own salvation with fear and trembling for God energizes in us to will (*thelō*) and to energize of his good pleasure' (Philippians 2:13, our own translation). It is *God's* power but *we* have to set our minds on the Spirit (Romans 8:5). We are together building the *Church*, the body of Christ and Temple of the Holy Spirit. How far we succeed in this will determine the degree of our joy in the presence of the love/fire/light that is God. How far we kept 'works of the law' or any other regulations is irrelevant, but 'each one's work' in respect of God's great project of a love-bound Church will be tested by this fire, as we have already indicated:

> For no other foundation can anyone lay than that which is laid, which is Jesus Christ. Now if anyone builds on this foundation with gold, silver, precious stones, wood, hay, straw, each one's work will become clear; for the Day will declare it, because it will be revealed by fire; and the fire will test each one's work, of what sort it is. If anyone's work which he has built on it endures, he will receive a reward. If anyone's work is burned, he will suffer loss; but he himself will be saved, yet so as through fire. Do you not know that you are the temple of God and that the Spirit of God dwells in you? (1 Corinthians 3:11-17)

This is not necessarily a matter of doing great deeds, eloquent preaching, having faith to move mountains, or even being martyred. All these things without love are nothing, as Paul goes on to say in 1 Corinthians 13. Jesus said love would be the first commandment and main distinguishing point of his Church – so is this what we are building? The lake of fire of the purity of God's love will light up our life's work, and only what is built of precious metals in love will survive. But 1 John 4:18 assures us that if we have the love of God in us now, burning through us to produce the love for others, then we need have no fear in that day of judgement. The fire of God's love will bring delight, not pain or loss. John is clear throughout his works that loving one another is the key commandment, and anyone who says he loves God and does not love his brothers and sisters is a liar – however good his theology is. Jesus' picture in Matthew 25 is similar. This does not mean that good theology is unimportant, but that in the ultimate fire of God's love it is not head knowledge, but knowledge of God that counts.

So, God's plan is finally achieved – his great project is accomplished. God has three things in the glorified Church. He has a love-filled bride to reciprocate his love (Revelation 21:2). He has a 'tabernacle' or 'city' in which to dwell (v3,10). And he has many sons (male and female) with whom he can share his life and character (v7).

We find that things are restored to something like the situation in the garden of Eden (see above in chapter 7). There is a river, but now it proceeds out of the throne of God and contains water of life (Revelation 22:1; Genesis 2:10). The tree of life is there, but now its leaves may be used for the healing of the nations (Revelation 22:2; Genesis 2:9; 3:22). The precious things which were raw materials in Eden have been built up into something beautiful and everlasting (Genesis 2:11,12; Revelation 21:18-21). They have been built into a dwelling place for God, so that the intermittent communion he had with man in the garden of Eden is exchanged for continuous and clear communion (Genesis 3:8). There is no mention of the tree of the knowledge of good and evil, for those who dwell in the new world have the Lamb of God to enlighten them (Revelation 21:23). No one needs to lust to 'become like gods' for they see what the God of the Lamb is really like – and they themselves are already in his image (Revelation 22:4). There is no serpent there, for nothing unclean may enter (Revelation 21:27) and so there is no curse (Revelation 22:2). Those who overcame in the battle have inherited these things (Revelation 21:7), and shall reign with the Lamb for ever and ever (Revelation 22:5).

Hallelujah the Lord Almighty reigns, and the throne of God and of the Lamb shall be for evermore!

16

Key Concepts and Definitions

Tradition

In Luke 24:27 Jesus teaches the need to carefully 'interpret' the Scriptures, applying good principles of exegesis to see how all of Scripture points to God's Messianic plan to save humanity and the world. Part of this is to look at the way in which other Christian scholars have looked at various passages. But there is also a danger. The Pharisees had an extremely high view of Scripture and studied it avidly, but Jesus said that some of their traditions 'made the word of God of no effect' (Matthew 15:6). We need to beware that our own evangelical 'traditionalism' does not do the same thing. Paul likewise warns us to:

> Beware lest anyone cheat you through philosophy and empty deceit, according to the tradition of men, according to the basic principles of the world, and not according to Christ. (Colossians 2:8-9)

Where some overriding philosophical principle distorts understanding of any central teachings of Jesus then this is a bad tradition.

Augustinian Innovations

One of the greatest philosophical thinkers in human history was Augustine of Hippo, whose theological innovations form the basis of many traditions amongst both Catholic and Protestant denominations today. Some of the new ideas Augustine introduced into Christianity have been touched on in this volume, and we will look at these in detail in chapter 7 of *Volume 2: Reconsidering Key Biblical Ideas.*

Here is a summary of some of Augustine's main theological innovations.

1) Irresistible Grace

In the preceding four centuries, and in Augustine's own earlier teaching, there was a universal belief in the Church that God freely offered undeserved forgiveness and right-standing with him, and 'was not willing that any should perish, but rather they turn and repent'. The Early Christians believed that human 'freewill' did not enable anyone to live a life without ever sinning, but did enable them to decide whether to accept or reject God's free offer of salvation.

Augustine changed this. He took the phrase 'compel them to come in' (Luke 14:23), to mean that God literally compels people to become Christians – ignoring (as we noted on p 154) the parallel Matthew passage in which 'call' or 'invite' is used both for the original guests and the ones who came. Along with this he formed a new interpretation of 'election' as being individual rather than 'in Christ', and 'predestination' as concerning who should become Christians. Everyone (except the 'ever-virgin' Mary who was sinless) was so corrupt that only if God forced them to would they become Christians. 'Irresistible grace' means that God arbitrarily chooses some to force to become Christians, and leaves the others to go to hell.

2) Legitimatising Torture

Since Augustine thought that God 'compelled' people to become Christians, he thought that the Church should do the same. So he was the first theologian to advocate the use of 'fear of punishment and pain' to compel nonconformist Baptists to become Roman Catholics. Since his concept of *Amor Dei* involved God using compulsion, he also said that the best way to love such nonconformists was to torture them to save their souls.

3) The All-Determining God

Augustine introduced a novel idea of the sovereignty of God, which meant that absolutely everything that happened was what God really wanted, so that when Jesus gave his famous lament over Jerusalem (Matthew 23:37) 'how often would I have gathered – and yet you would not', in fact, in not being gathered the people were doing exactly what God *really* wanted.

4) Original Sin and Infant Baptism

Augustine advocated an idea that we all inherited the guilt of Adam's sin, supplemented by the shame of all sex, including marital sex, so that even children of Christians were born guilty. This was based on a Latin mistranslation of *eph ho* in Romans 12:5, and a single Old Testament verse (Psalm 51:5) which was taken out of context.

Augustine taught that the ceremony of infant baptism washed away the guilt of this 'original sin' even if performed by a drunken heretic, and indeed the involuntary nature of infant baptism illustrated the doctrine that God himself compelled people to become Christians.

5) Righteousness, Justification and Faithfulness

Augustine changed the meaning of 'justification' from its meaning in the Greek of the New Testament, to a Latin-influenced meaning of 'Being made right with God'. Augustine obliterated the key phrase 'the faithfulness of Jesus the Messiah', by interpreting it as an 'objective genitive' – though he admitted that his study of Greek was unenthusiastic! Augustine reinterpreted the phrase 'the righteousness of God' to no longer mean that God is righteous.

6) Marriage and Celibacy

In his personal life, at the time of his conversion he had a son and a longstanding devoted 'common law wife' who had also now become a devout Christian – but he refused to formalise their relationship in marriage. Instead he ditched her, and opted for a woman of higher social standing.

Because he thought sex was always shameful he advocated marital celibacy in direct contradiction to 1 Corinthians 7 and Hebrews 13:4. He thought that the only purpose of sex should be to produce children – which is probably where the current Roman Catholic ban on contraception owes much of its force.

7) Eternal Conscious Torment

Augustine's influence had a lot to do with the suppression of any view on 'hell' other than of unending conscious torment, which held sway for centuries.

So why does any of this matter? Because unfortunately the traditionalism which stems from Augustine still infects much of the Church. Luther began as an Augustinian monk and Calvin continually quotes Augustine, so much of his innovation also passed through them into Protestantism. The Protestant reformer Ulrich Zwingli was carrying on the tradition when he had the Anabaptist scholar Balthasar Hubmaier racked to make him a 'good Protestant' after losing a theological debate with him. Anabaptists were more usually drowned by Protestant state churches, Catholics tended to burn them.

Today, good evangelicals (who would never in their wildest nightmares imagine beating or torturing Baptists to make them become Roman Catholics or join a Reformed church) inherit some of the baggage of Augustine's philosophical theology – often without even knowing it.

Some traditions can be good (1 Corinthians 11:2); but we need to be wary that these are really in accord with the word of God and teachings of Jesus – and in particular the New Testament as given to us in Koine Greek. This is why, in *Reconsidering Key Biblical Ideas* there is a chapter detailing some of these ideas of Augustine, so that modern readers can assess them biblically.

Reconsidering Key Biblical Ideas

In *Volume 2: Reconsidering Key Biblical Ideas,* we look at six key areas of related concepts for understanding God's strategy in human history, and also why wrong ideas about them have arisen in the Church. However, we thought it would be helpful here to list some of the key ideas in short easy reference summaries, useful for discussion, small group work, or personal study.

The six key subject areas (corresponding to the chapters in *Volume 2: Reconsidering Key Biblical Ideas*) are:

1) Wills, Plans and Sovereignty
2) Justification and Righteousness
3) Works and Faithfulness
4) Chosen and Elect
5) Foreknowledge and Predestination
6) Hardening and Unbelief

1) Wills, Plans and Sovereignty

Augustinian and Reformed traditions teach that God's will is always done as his plan is absolute. God would then overrule all moral decisions, and it would be purely God's decision that certain people become Christians an are saved, while others do not and so go to hell. There are two problems with this: 1) everything that happened would be directly God's will – including suffering, evil and the sin in your life; 2) God directly says that he does not always get what he wants – which some try to get around by suggesting God has a 'secret' will, which is different from what he says he wants.

Question

Is God's will always done? If not, how can he be 'sovereign' or 'almighty'?

Keywords

• **Will:** [Greek – *thelēma, thelō*]

Thelēma means a will or a desire. God has a will, and each human has a will, which may agree with God's will, or go against it.

- Jesus said that God's will was to gather Israel, but it did not happen because their will was against this (Matthew 23:37; Luke 13:34).

- John 7:17 says that if someone aligns his will with God's will then he shall know the truth. Those who do God's will are Jesus' brothers (Matthew 12:50; Mark 3:35), enter God's kingdom (Matthew 7:21) and live forever (1 John 2:17).

- The Early Church noted all this and coined the term 'freewill' to express that God allows humans freedom to go against his will for them.

- The Bible says nothing about any kind of 'secret' or 'effectual' will of God that is always done.

• **Plan:** [Greek - *boulē, boulomai*]

Boule means a deliberate plan. In the New Testament, both God and humans are said to have plans.

- Luke often applies *boule* to God's plans (Luke 7:30; 23:51; Acts 2:23; 4:28; 5:38 13:36; 20:27; 27:12), including plans for individuals, as well as more general plans and purposes for humanity.

- Luke 7:30 says that a person can reject God's plan (*boulē*) for them.

- God's plan (*boulōmenos*) is that none should perish because he wants all to repent (2 Peter 3:9, see also John 3:16). So it must be possible to reject God's plan for them, otherwise why is not everyone a Christian?

• **Sovereignty**

This is a popular word with some Christians, but for example the NKJV nowhere describes God as 'sovereign' nor is the 'sovereignty of God' mentioned.

185

- God is proclaimed to be a great king (eg Psalm 47:2) and 'king of kings' (1 Timothy 6:14; Revelation 17:14; 19:16) though this same title is also used of Artaxerxes (Ezra 7:12) and Nebuchadnezzar (Ezekiel 26:7).

- Like earthly kings, God is powerful, defeats his enemies and protects his subjects – but doesn't necessarily always get what he wants.

• **Almighty:** [Hebrew: *El Shaddai*, Greek: *pantokrator*]
Many modern versions render *El Shaddai* as 'almighty'. The only reason for this (according to *Van Gemeren's Dictionary of Old Testament Theology and Exegesis* vol 4 p 401) is that this was an 'educated guess' by the translators of the Greek LXX who rendered the term as *pantokrator*.

- In Hebrew, *El* means God, *shad* is a female breast (eg Isaiah 66:11) and *dai* means 'enough' (eg Exodus 36:7). '*The all-sufficient God*' would be a more natural translation of *El Shaddai* – as reflected in Genesis 49:25: '*the Almighty (shaddai)* will bless you… Blessings of the breasts (*shaddaiyim*) and of the womb.' It seems odd to render *shaddai* as 'almighty' here, when the Hebrew is effectively 'enough-breast' .

- In reality there is no word for 'almighty' in the Hebrew Old Testament.

- The Greek word *pantokrator* seems to mean 'ruler of all' as the word *kratos* in the New Testament implies 'strength' (Acts 19:20) or 'dominion' (1 Peter 4:11 and 5:11, Jude 25 and Revelation 1:6) – and in 1 Timothy 6:16 different versions take it as either!

- The LXX also often uses *pantokrator* to translate the Hebrew 'LORD of hosts' (probably explaining Paul's loose quotation in 2 Corinthians 6:18).

- *Pantokrator* is used 9 other times in the New Testament, all in Revelation which is where we most clearly see spiritual forces opposing God.

Conclusion

o   God has a will and deliberate plan for humanity, but this also depends on the freewill of each human, so God's will may be rejected.

o   No one can thwart God's overall plan for a coming Kingdom in a New Heaven and Earth, but they can personally opt out by refusing to repent and put their faith in God's Messiah who died for their sins.

o   God is sovereign in that he is 'King of kings' but this doesn't mean his will is always done, or that he determines everything that happens.

o   God has 'all dominion' and is rightfully ruler of all, but the Bible is clear that he does not always get what he wants – however, we can be confident that he will ultimately triumph and evil will be destroyed, because he is able to use even the rebellious plans of others to further his cause.

2) Justification and Righteousness

Romans 3 says 'all have sinned and fall short of the glory of God' but that there is a 'righteousness of God' through which we can be 'justified'. There is much debate as to exactly what 'righteousness' and 'justification' mean.

Question

What does 'justification' mean? What makes someone 'righteous'?

Keywords

• **Righteous/Righteousness:** [Hebrew – *ṣaddîq*, Greek – *dikaios dikaiosynē*] Righteous does not mean sinless or ethically perfect or keeping all of God's laws, but being in a right-standing with God, and living a life that reflects this. In the Bible 'the righteous' are often contrasted with 'sinners' (see below).

– Being 'righteous' *may* reflect a covenant relationship with God but *doesn't need* to be bound to any specific 'covenant': eg Noah (who wasn't sinless) was 'righteous' (Genesis 6:9); Abraham was looking for 10 righteous in Sodom (Genesis 18); Lot is referred to as righteous (2 Peter 2:2-9) and is contrasted with 'the wicked'.

– Psalm 14:1 says 'none is righteous no not one' and refers to workers of iniquity who 'eat up God's people' – in contrast Psalm 14:5 promises that 'God is with the generation of the righteous' (see also Psalm 32:11, 33:1, 55:22).

– Paul's loose quotation of Psalm 14:1-3 in Romans 3:10-12 is not an out-of-context quote to 'prove' there are no righteous people on earth – he himself refers to 'righteous' people in Romans 5:7 and 1 Timothy 1:9. Rather Paul is asking 'Are we (Jews) any better than they (Gentiles)?', concluding that overall Jews were little better if at all because of the 'workers of iniquity' in their society.

– Jesus uses the Greek word 'righteous' (*dikaios*) in the same way (Matthew 10:41, 23:39, 25:37) to mean those in right-standing with God. In Luke 6:32 he contrasts his disciples with 'sinners'. In Matthew 23:28 Jesus speaks of Pharisees who *outwardly appear righteous to men*, but speaks in the same passage of Old Testament prophets who really were righteous. Pharisaic 'righteousness' was based on the wrong things – ritual and ceremony.

– To Jesus the 'righteous' are those whose lives show spontaneous acts of love to others that indicate real relationship with God (Matthew 25:46). Christians have to do better than the Pharisees (Matthew 5:20) because we should avoid anger and wrong thoughts, not just acts of murder, lust, adultery, etc.

– Throughout the Bible the 'righteous' are a real group living in relationship with God *and acting accordingly*, and are contrasted with 'sinners' whose lifestyle is in rebellion against God. 1 John 3:7-8 also makes this contrast: 'He who practices righteousness is righteous, just as he [Jesus] is righteous. He who sins is of the devil, for the devil has sinned from the beginning'. We need to confess our sins as we walk in the light, but if we really are 'righteous' this is reflected in a lifestyle which loves God and others – and if someone says he loves God but hates his brother then he is a liar (1 John 4:20).

– God is also called 'righteous' in both Old and New Testaments. This righteousness of God fundamentally relates to his justice and faithfulness in relationship. Romans 3:1-5, 21-26 particularly links these ideas, remembering that 'just' and 'justify' and 'righteous' and 'righteousness' all come from the same Greek word. For Israel this relates to faithfulness to covenant, but in Genesis 18:25 Abraham implies the judge of all the earth will 'judge right' in regard to any 'righteous' found in Sodom, who are clearly not part of any covenant. Judgement and righteousness are also linked in John 7:24 and Revelation 19:11.

• **Justification**: [Greek – *dikaiōsis*]
Most evangelicals have been raised to believe that 'justification' means 'being *made* right with God'. Alister McGrath in his book *Iustitia Dei* shows that this meaning was mistakenly invented by Augustine because of a Latin mistranslation.

– *Dikaiōsis* does not mean to 'make righteous', nor does it refer only to the initial time when people are forgiven and restored to relationship with God. It means to be 'vindicated' or to be 'shown to be righteous'.

– In Romans 3:4 God himself is said to be 'justified' or 'vindicated' when he is shown to be rightdealing in judgements!

– Abraham was 'justified' when he had faith in God 'and it was accounted to him for righteousness' (Romans 4:3). This was *not* his conversion as he went out in faith decades earlier (Hebrews 11:8): it was when he was *shown to be* in right-standing with God, and was *before* his circumcised so wasn't a work of the Law.

– Abraham's faith was both tested and demonstrated when he was told to sacrifice Isaac (Hebrews 11:17). There is a further sense in which he was 'justified' when this incident proved the reality of his faith – this is the point in James 2:21. If 'justify' really meant to 'make righteous' at initial conversion, then James would contradict Paul. James' point is that simple belief *about* God isn't real faith, because real faith leads to action – so Christians are 'justified', ie *shown to be* in right relationship with God, when their righteous lifestyle follows their faith.

– Galatians 2:15-16 explains how we are demonstrated to be in right-standing with God not by 'works of the law' (ie circumcision, diet, Sabbath) but by the *faithfulness of* Jesus Christ effective to us because we have faith. Without his sacrificial death we couldn't have forgiveness nor be pronounced in a right relationship.

– The truth that we receive unmerited forgiveness and restoration based on what Jesus as done on the cross is certain and not at issue. But understanding the true meaning of the term 'justification' is a paradigm change which radically affects the way in which texts containing it are read.

- **Accounted to him** [Hebrew – *va-yahsheveha*, Greek – *logizetai*]
Romans 4:3 says (quoting Genesis 15:16): 'Abraham believed God, and it was accounted to him for righteousness', but what does 'accounted to him' mean?
  - In Psalm 106:30 almost the same phrase is used of the righteous judgemental act of Phinehas which stayed God's hand of judgement on his people. Numbers 25 says it was Phinehas' zeal for God and not the act itself that was crucial.
  - Some theologians suggest it is Jesus' ethical qualities of sinless perfection that are 'counted' for righteousness for believers. This is wrong – 'righteousness' is not an ethical quality but about right-standing, and there is no indication for either Abraham or Phinehas that ethical qualities were 'imputed' from someone else.
  - We know that God has forgiven the sins of Abraham, Phinehas and ourselves because of what Jesus did on the cross. But it is a person's own faith/zeal that is graciously accounted by God as right-standing.
- **Sinners/Wicked** [Hebrew – *rāšā'/ḥaṭṭā'*, Greek – *harmartoloi*]
The Hebrew *rāšā'* means the 'wicked' and *ḥaṭṭā'* are 'sinners'. The Old Testament *ḥaṭṭā'ym* is translated (eg in Psalm 1:1,5) using *harmartoloi* in the LXX, and the New Testament uses the word in the same sense.
  - A 'sinner' isn't *anyone* who *has sinned* (because we all have: Romans 3:23) but one who is in rebellion against God, leading a sinful lifestyle (Matthew 9:10).
  - In both Old and New Testaments 'sinners' are contrasted with the 'righteous' (eg Psalm 1:5, Luke 5:32). In Luke 6:32 Jesus contrasts his disciples with 'sinners'.
  - Romans 5:8 that 'while we were yet sinners Christ died for us' but in the same verse Paul mentions a 'righteous' man, and the implication of 'yet' is that after spiritual rebirth and entering relationship and right-standing with God we are no longer 'sinners' in the biblical sense but 'righteous'.
  - If a preacher looks round and says 'we are all miserable sinners' that preacher is not using the term in a biblical sense. We all *were* miserable sinners, but hopefully some of the congregation are now 'righteous'

Conclusions

- o All of us have sinned, but this does not make us 'sinners' in the biblical sense because a 'sinner' is someone living a godless lifestyle.
- o Righteous doesn't mean 'never sinned', but being in a right-standing with God and so living a lifestyle of loving God and others. True Christians are therefore 'righteous' and not 'sinners' in this biblical sense.
- o Justification means being *shown* to be in right-standing relationship with God, *not* being *made* right with God. Christians are justified by a faith that shows results, though God's forgiveness and acceptance of them is based on the faithfulness of Jesus the Messiah in his sacrificial death for the sins of the world.

3) Works and Faithfulness

So justification means being *shown* to be in a right-standing relationship with God, but what is the basis of this justification? Romans 3:28 says we are 'justified by faith apart from the deeds of the law', but James says we are 'justified by works, and not by faith only' (2:24), and that 'faith without works is dead' (v26).

Question
Are we justified by faith or by works?

Keywords

• **Works of the Law/Works**: [Greek – *ergōn nomou/ergōn*]

'Works of the Law' doesn't mean general good deeds, but ritual observances that distinguished Jew from Gentile, especially: circumcision, diet, Sabbath-keeping. The Jews believed having the Law marked them out as a holy people living in right-standing with God.

- If 'justification' meant being made right with God (ie at the initial act of conversion) then James and Paul would contradict each other because clearly the faith must predate any resulting works. Paul is saying that we are shown to be in right-standing with God through faith. James is saying this faith is shown to be real by the acts of compassion that it leads to. There is no contradiction.

- Recent scholarship highlights some serious misconceptions about the Pharisees:

  i) Paul did not have to 'prove' to them that we have all sinned (cf also John 8:7) and all need God's forgiveness – they already knew this.

  ii) They did not think that by doing good works they could 'earn' forgiveness.

  iii) They did think they were 'justified' by works of the Law. Put another way, they thought that meticulous Law keeping was the key sign of holiness.

- Christians in Galatia were clear that they had been forgiven and received the Spirit by faith (Galatians 2:2-3). The issue with them was not how to 'get right with God' but how to be 'justified' – ie to *be shown* to be living in a right relationship with God. They were trying to do this through circumcision (the sign of the Abrahamic covenant) and ceremonial observance (4:11).

- Richard N Longenecker (in *Galatians*, p 81) translates accurately what Paul says in Galatians 2:16: 'a person is not justified by the works of the law but by the faithfulness of Jesus Christ (Jesus the Messiah), even we have believed in Christ (Messiah) Jesus in order that we might be justified on the basis of the faithfulness of Christ and not on the basis of works of the law'. The ultimate vindication of us as in right-standing with God is based on what Jesus did for us, and God raising him from the dead (Romans 4:25).

- Ephesians 2:8-10 is about being *saved* not about justification: 'For by grace you have been saved through faith, and that not of yourselves; it is the gift of God, not of works, lest anyone should boast'. The context is of God elevating us to sit 'in Messiah' in the heavenly places and to fight in his armour. This positioning is not because of any kinds of works we have done (ritual or otherwise) but because of God's gracious undeserved response to our faith.

• **Faith / Faithfulness:** [Greek – *pistis, pisteuō*]
The word *pistis* carries a range of meanings including 'belief about', 'faith/trust in' and 'faithfulness towards'.

– To Jesus, faith not ritual was the mark of being in right-relationship with God. But this faith would *lead* to right-living, ie loving God and others.

– In John 6:29 they ask Jesus what they should be doing to be doing the 'work of God'. He tells them to get their priorities right – the first thing is to have faith in God and his Messiah. But John 14:12 shows that he *does* expect his followers to do 'mighty works' *when* they have the power of the Spirit within.

– The demons 'believe in God' (James 2:19) but it is not faith. Faith in God is not intellectual belief but a trust in God that leads to a particular lifestyle.

– John's letters also emphasize that to claim to love God but to show no effect of this in love and care for others marks someone as a liar (1 John 2:4, 4:20).

– We noted Longenecker's translation of Galatians 2:16 involving the key phrase *pisteus Iēsou Christou* – 'the *faithfulness of* Jesus the Messiah'. Romans 3:20 says: 'by the works of the Law no flesh will be justified in His sight; for through the Law comes the knowledge of sin' (NASB). Then it too uses this key phrase: 'But now God's righteousness has been revealed apart from the law – though the law and the prophets bear witness to it: it is God's righteousness through the *faithfulness of Jesus the Messiah* to those who believe' (NT Wright's translation).

– This, Paul says, is how God could forgive sins throughout history (v25), and is now shown to be both righteous/just but declaring people righteous out of the *faithfulness of Jesus* (v26). Thus those *throughout history* who had real faith in God have been forgiven and justified out of the *faithfulness of Jesus the Messiah*. No one comes to the Father except through him

Conclusions

o We are justified, or shown to be in right-standing, by our faith-relationship with God, which results in acts of love and compassion for others. 'Works of the Law' do not indicate holiness, nor does any kind of Christian 'legalism'.

o Those who have faith in God have their sins forgiven based on the faithfulness of Jesus the Messiah in dying a sacrificial death, and receive their right-standing with God as an unmerited gift of grace.

4) Chosen and Elect

The word 'elect' in this context is not to do with voting, but just means a choice. Since Augustine, various theologians have viewed 'election' as God's irresistible choice of some people to receive a ticket to individual blessing, rather than as the bestowal of an office. In these traditions, 'You have not chosen me but I have chosen you' has been made into an assertion that God selects who should become Christians and so be saved. The Early Church before Augustine believed that humans have 'freewill' which enables everyone to decide whether to accept or reject God's free offer of salvation.

Question

Has God 'chosen' only certain people to become Christians and go to Heaven? If not then what does 'chosen/elect' actually mean?

Keywords

• **Elect / Chosen:** [Greek – *eklektos*]

The primary New Testament meaning of *eklektos* is bestowal of a particular office, ie being given responsibility and a task to perform, without implication of unmerited privilege. *Eklektos* is applied in different contexts: to the 12 disciples, to Israel and individuals within Israel, to Christ and the Church in Christ.

- 'You did not choose Me, but I chose you and appointed you that you should go and bear fruit' is said by Jesus specifically to the 12 disciples (John 15:27), and refers to his choice of them as apostles, not their election as believers (Luke 6:12-13; Mark 3:13-14). This passage only directly applied to the disciples for this task, not to every believer.

- Judas was chosen as one of Jesus' special witnesses: 'Did I not choose you the twelve, and one of you is a devil?' (John 6:70,71).

- In Acts 2:21-22,36 the 11 chose a replacement for Judas who was chosen with them for apostleship but had 'by transgression fallen' from this ministry (v25). Jesus' choice was about their role not their eternal destiny.

- There are parallels here with the election of Israel. Israel was chosen as a nation to prepare the way for the Messiah through whom all nations would be blessed (Genesis 12:3; 18:18; 22:18). While some of Israel were faithful, others fell away from God's purposes for them.

- God's choice of Israel was not about heaven and hell, but purely a result of his own strategy. God was also with Ishmael who was not part of the chosen line of Israel (Genesis 21:20).

– Paul not only regarded Israel chosen as a nation, but in Romans 11 speaks of a remnant within the nation who are 'elect according to grace'

– Jesus himself was the 'chosen one' (Luke 9:35; 23:35; 1 Peter 2:4; 2:6; Isaiah 42:1) not in some sense of selection, but because he was the special one of God.

– At the Transfiguration Jesus being 'chosen' is equated to being 'beloved' in Matthew 17:5 and Luke 9:35.

– Christians are also 'elect': Romans 8:33 (16:13); Ephesians 1:4; Colossians 3:12; 1 Thessalonians 1:4; 2 Timothy 2:10; Titus 1:1; 1 Peter 1:2; 2:9; 5:13; 2 Peter 1:10; Revelation 17:14. (Matthew 24:22-31; Mark 13:20-27; [Luke 18:7?]).

– Ephesians 1:3-4 says God 'chose us in [Christ] before the foundation of the world, that we should be holy and without blame before him in love'. When we become part of the body of Christ, the Church, we share in his election. We also share in his work and place in the heavenlies which is not a place of repose but spiritual warfare (see Ephesians 6:12).

– Jesus died for the sins of the whole world (1 John 2:2) and 2 Peter 3:9 says that the Lord is 'not willing that any should perish but that all should come to repentance'.

– God chose us *in* Christ, not to be *put into* Christ.

Conclusions

o *Ekletos* means 'chosen/elect', which primarily refers to being given a responsibility to perform a task, eg the 12 Disciples. However, God's choice never overrules the moral choices of individuals, eg Judas.

o The New Testament never says that God chose anyone to *become* Christians, but that as Christians we are chosen to take up the functions of being Christ's body.

5) Foreknowledge and Predestination

The traditionalist view of 'predestination' in Augustinian/Reformed theology is that God has predetermined everything that happens, including who will and who will not become Christians. 'Foreknowledge' in this context is commonly taken by traditionalists to mean 'to choose beforehand'.

Question

What does predestination really mean?

Keywords

• **Foreknowledge:** [Greek – *proginoskō*]

The word 'know' (*ginoskō*) means to recognise, understand, acknowledge, or have a relationship with – it never means to 'choose'. Accordingly the word *proginoskō* (*pro* = before) means to know in advance, to foreknow. It does not mean to choose in advance or foreordain as some translations have it.

- Peter warns against those who 'twist' Scripture, saying 'since you know this beforehand (*proginoskō*), beware lest you also fall from your own steadfastness, being led away with the error of the wicked.

- *Proginoskō* means to foreknow in secular works, eg Plato (Rep. iv 426c), Aristotle (N Ethics 6.2), in the LXX, Apocrypha and the writings of many Early Church leaders like Justin and Clement. It can also mean prognosis in the medical sense.

- In the New Testament in Acts 2:23; Romans 8:29; 11:2 and 1 Peter 1:2,20 *proginoskō* means 'to know about in advance'.

- The only other New Testament use is in Acts 26:5, where Paul tells Agrippa that the Jews 'knew me from the first' (NKJV) / 'have known about me for a long time' (NASB).

- If God is 'outside time' foreknowledge would mean he knows all that is going to happen. If God is 'inside time' it means he knows about the aspects of the future he has purposed to do, as well as all possible outcomes.

- Romans 8:29 links foreknowledge and predestination: 'For whom [God] foreknew, he also predestined to be conformed to the image of his Son, that he might be the firstborn among many brethren.'

• **Predestination:** [Greek – *prohorizō*]

The word 'predestine' or 'foreordain' is made up of two Greek words: *pro* (= in advance) and *horizō* (=boundary/designate). The term *horizō* is used in the LXX to mean 'mark off boundaries' and from it we get our word 'horizon'.

- *Prohorizō* is translated as 'predestination' or 'predestined' in the KJV, NKJV, NASB, NIV and ESV; the RV uses 'foreordained'; the RSV uses 'predestined' or 'destined and appointed'.

- *Horizō* can be used with a human subject without connotations of inevitability, see for example Acts 11:29.

- In the New Testament *prohorizō* appears 6 times, used only of God.

- Acts 4:27-29 links God's purpose (*boulē*) with predestination (*prohorizen*), describing God as a master strategist – he does not determine how people will use their freewill to make moral decisions, but he knows all the possible outcomes and plans accordingly.

- The other five uses of *pro-horizō* concern the future destiny and tasks of the Church, *not* with how any individual *came to be* a Christian (Romans 8:29,30; 1 Corinthians 2:7-9, Ephesians 1:5; Ephesians 1:11)

- Ephesians 1:11 shows we are predestined to have an inheritance in Christ. 1 Corinthians 2:7-9 says that 'our glory', or the horizon God has set out for those 'in Christ' (the Church), is our destiny as those who will restore creation (Romans 8:18-19).

- Ephesians 1:4-6 links being our being 'chosen', (see study 4 above) with our predestination to 'adoption as sons'. This is a future event when we will be fully conformed to the image of the Son (who will be firstborn of many brothers and sisters), that is, we shall be like Christ.'

Conclusions

o *Proginoskō* means to know about beforehand. It does not mean to 'choose' beforehand.

o Predestination does *not* concern who should, or should not, *become* Christians, but rather their future destiny *as* Christians. God may have predestined us for adoption as sons, but it is our freewill choice whether to accept or reject God's plan for us (Luke 7:30).

o The predestiny of the Church is to be revealed when Jesus returns and we are placed-as-sons in our redeemed bodies for the praise of God's glory.

6) Hardening and Unbelief

In the story of Moses and Pharaoh in Exodus the 'hardening of Pharaoh's heart' has sometimes been a source of confusion to people who believe in a God who gives people freewill to make their own moral choices, and who loves everyone and has compassion wherever he can.

Question

Why did God 'harden' Pharaoh's heart? Is this consistent with a God of love? Can a just God punish someone for something he made them do?

Keywords

Three distinct Hebrew words are used in Exodus in connection with the 'hardening' of Pharaoh's heart:

- **Stubborn:** [Hebrew – *qashah*]
  - God predicts he will harden (*qashah)* Pharaoh's heart in Exodus 7:3
  - Exodus 13:15 says Pharaoh is *qashah.*
  - *Qashah,* as opposed to *kabed* and *chazaq,* which we cover below, seems to refer to the overall process of hardening, not to any specific instance.

- **Heavy/immovable/stubborn:** [Hebrew – *kabed*]
  - Obduracy and refusal to change (*kabed*) is something over which someone has a moral choice
  - The word *kabed* appears Exodus 8:15, 8:32, 9:34 and in 1 Samuel 6:6, where Pharaoh makes his own heart 'hard' or 'stubborn'
  - Only after Pharaoh has made his own heart *kabed* 3 times does God says he has made Pharaoh's heart *kabed* in Exodus 10:1
  - Also Exodus 7:14 and 9:7 both say that Pharaoh's heart is stubborn / hardened, but do not indicate an agent.
  - In general Pharaoh makes his own heart hard, with God acting on it in a kind of confirmatory judgment only at the end of the process (10:1).

- **Strengthen/make firm:** [Hebrew – *chazaq*]
  - Strength of resolve (*chazaq*) is either just there in a person, or God can act to provide it.
  - Pharaoh's heart is described as *chazaq* in Exodus 7:13; 7:22; 8:19; 9:35
  - The word chazaq is used for these incidents of God strengthening Pharaoh's

196

resolve in Exodus 4:21; 9:12; 10:20; 10:27; 11:10; 14:4; 14:8; 14:17; Joshua 11:20.

– Chazaq refers to Pharaoh being made firm in his resolve and having courage to follow his inclinations.

Conclusions

o The use of *qashah* in Exodus 7:3 and 13:15 refers to the overall process of hardening in summary, not to any specific instance.

o *Kabed* refers first to Pharaoh's obduracy in hardening his heart and later to God confirming Pharaoh's choice. It is as if the Lord says: 'Very well, if he is determined to be hard and unrepentant then I will make his heart hard, just as he wishes'.

o It's Pharaoh who throughout chapters 7:13-9:11 makes his heart hard (*kabed*) and has firm resolve (*chazaq*), breaking his word in 8:28.

o God's first act is in 9:12 – a strengthening of Pharaoh's resolve.

o God's actions on Pharaoh stimulated not so much impenitence as foolhardiness. When any normal person would have given in due to fear, Pharaoh received supernatural strength to continue with his rebellion.

o God does not interfere with Pharaoh's basic moral alignment and choice to make him bad. Pharaoh had chosen his path of rebellion and oppression before any action of God on him.

o This is not about God deciding Pharaoh's eternal destiny, but about his place in God's strategy in plans on this earth.

o God's motives in this are actually stated:

   i) That Israel should clearly understand who had delivered them (Exodus 6:6-7; 10:2; 13:14-15)

   ii) That they should carry possessions with them away from Egypt (Exodus 3:21-22)

   iii) That God might multiply his signs and bring them forth in great acts, so that the Egyptians should know that he was the true God (Exodus 7:3-4; 11:9; 14:4,17,18)

   iv) That his name might be declared not only in Egypt but in the whole earth (Exodus 9:14-18, 15:13; Joshua 2:10-11; 1 Samuel 8:8).

Going Deeper

We hope that these short studies have whetted your appetite to get deeper into God's word. Our own personal study of Scripture started many years ago, but we are still discovering new things, new depths and details that inspire us to keep on studying the Bible even more. You are never too young, or too old to start!

There are a range of resources we should mention here:

- First, as previously mentioned *Volume 2: Reconsidering Key Biblical Ideas* looks in much greater depth at the key concepts covered in the summaries above.

- Please do also follow up particular topics by reading other books. We have listed the books we refer to in the *Bibliography* (p199-201).

- On pages 202-3 we include a *General Index* of this book so you can quickly look up people or topics of interest.

- Following this there is an *Index of Verses Cited*, so that if you wish to follow up a particular verse or passage, you can see at a glance if and when we refer to it in this book. (NB *Volume 2: Reconsidering Key Biblical Ideas*, will contain a separate list for that volume).

We would love to encourage you to get stuck into the study of Scripture – to read it, meditate upon it, pray about it, but most importantly we encourage you to get out there and live it...

In this book we have given you the foundations of how God interacts with us, his creations – from the background of the spiritual battle we all face as believers, to the history of how God has been working in history. So now it is up to you to apply what you have read to your lives.

If you are reading this book then *you* have an individual part to play in God's strategy and plan for humanity... now it's up to you to discover what that is, and start living it!

Roger Forster & Paul Marston, July 2013

Bibliography

Abbot-Smith (1991) Abbot-Smith *A Manual Greek Lexicon of the New Testament*

ACUTE (2000) *The Nature of Hell*

Atkinson (1969) Basil Atkinson *Life and Immortality*

Augustine (424-426) Augustine *Enchiridion*

Barnes (1843) Allen Barnes *Notes on the New Testament: Romans*

Bell (2011) Rob Bell *Love Wins*

Blanchard (1971) John Blanchard *Right With God*

Boyd (2003) Gregory A Boyd *Is God to Blame?*

Brown (1986) Colin Brown (trans/ed) *The New International Dictionary of New Testament Theology [4 vols]*

Bruce (1958) FF Bruce *The Spreading Flame*

Bruce (1963) FF Bruce *Epistle to the Romans*

Brueggemann (1982) Walter Brueggemann *Genesis*

Brunner (1961) Emil Brunner *The Letter to the Romans*

Caird (1966) GB Caird *The Revelation of St John the Divine*

Carter (1964) WN Carter *The People of the Book and Their Land*

Clines (1989) David JA Clines *Job [2 vols]*

Cole (1973) Alan Cole *Exodus*

Craigie (1983) Peter C Craigie *Psalms 1-50*

Cranfield (1979) CEB Cranfield *A Critical and Exegetical Commentary on the Epistle to the Romans*

Davies (1948) R Davies *Paul and Rabbinic Judaism*

Doddridge (1831) Philip Doddridge *The Family Expositor*

Douglas (1980) JD Douglas (ed) *The New International Dictionary of the Christian Church*

Douglas (1980) JD Douglas (ed) *The Illustrated Bible Dictionary [3 vols]*

Dummelow (1993) JR Dummelow *The One Volume Bible Commentary*

Dunn (1988) James DG Dunn *Romans 1-8, Romans 9-16*

Dunn (1990) James DG Dunn *Jesus, Paul and the Law*

Durham (1987) John I Durham *Exodus*

Edersheim (1890) Alfred Edersheim *Bible History*

Ellis (1997) in Kent E Brower & Mark W Elliott *Eschatology in Bible & Theology*

Ellison (1959) HL Ellison *Jesus and the Pharisees*

Ellison (1966) HL Ellison *The Mystery of Israel*

Ellison (1982) HL Ellison *Exodus*

Farrar (1889) FW Farrar *Lives of the Fathers*

Fee & Stuart (2003) Gordon D Fee & Douglas Stuart *How to Read the Bible for All Its Worth*

France (2007) RT France *The Gospel of Matthew*

Fudge (2011) Edward William Fudge *The Fire that Consumes*

Fudge & Petersen (2000) Edward William Fudge & Robert A Petersen *Two Views of Hell*

Garvie (?) Alfred E Garvie *The Century Bible: Romans*

Gestner (1990) John Gestner *Repent or Perish*

Gifford (1886) EH Gifford *The Epistle of St Paul to the Romans*

Gillebaud (1964) HE Gillebaud *The Righteous Judge*

Gore (1912) Charles Gore *St Paul's Epistle to the Romans [2 vols]*

Gore (1916) Charles Gore *The Religion of the Church*

Habermas & Moreland (2004) Gary R Habermas & JP Moreland *Beyond Death: Exploring the Evidence for Immortality*

Hagner (1993) Donald A Hagner *Matthew 1-13*

Hartley (1988) John F Hartley *The Book of Job*

Helm (1993) Paul Helm *The Providence of God*

Hughes (1989) Philip E Hughes *The True Image: The Origin and Destiny of Man in Christ*

Ironside (1928) HA Ironside *Romans*

Josephus (c 94) Flavius Josephus *The Antiquities of the Jews*

Justin Martyr (c114-175 AD) Justin Martyr *Dialogue*

Kidner (1967) Derek Kidner *Genesis*

Klein *et al* (1993) William W Klein, Craig L Blomberg, Donald L Hubbard Jr *Introduction to Biblical Interpretation*

Lewis (1940) CS Lewis *The Problem of Pain*

Lewis (1961) CS Lewis *Mere Christianity*

Lincoln (1990) Andrew T Lincoln *Ephesians*

Bibliography

Longenecker (1990) Richard N Longenecker *Galatians*

Luther (1543) Martin Luther *On the Jews and their Lies*

McGrath (1986/1998) A McGrath *Iustitia Dei: A History of the Christian Doctrine of Justification*

Morris (1988) Leon Morris *Romans*

Moule (1887) HCG Moule *The Epistle to the Romans*

Nanos (1996) Mark D Nanos *The Mystery of Romans*

Neil (1885) James Neil *Everyday Life in the Holy Land*

Osborne (1991) Grant R. Osborne *The Hermeneutical Spiral*

Pinnock (1996) in John F Walvoord *Four Views on Hell*

Pinnock *et al* (1994) Clark Pinnock et al *The Openness of God*

Piper (2007) John Piper *The Future of Justification: A Response to N.T. Wright*

Powys (1997) David Powys *"Hell": A Hard Look at a Hard Question*

Richardson (2006) Don Richardson *Eternity in their Hearts*

Roberts & Donaldson (repr 1986-7) A Roberts & J Donaldson *The Ante-Nicene Christian Fathers vol 2*

Sanday & Headlam (1902) W Sanday & AC Headlam *The Epistle to the Romans*

Smith (1971) MA Smith *From Christ to Constantine*

Stewart (1961) RA Stewart *Rabbinic Theology*

Stott (1988) in David L Edwards & John Stott *Evangelical Essetials*

Thomas (1946) WH Griffith Thomas *St Paul's Epistle to the Romans*

Travis (1982) Stephen Travis *I Believe in the Second Coming of Jesus*

VanGemeren (1996) William A VanGemeren (ed) *New International Dictionary of Old Testament Theology & Exegesis [5 vols]*

Watts (1985) John D Watts *Isaiah 1-33*

Wenham (1974) John Wenham *The Goodness of God* (later title *The Enigma of Evil*)

Wenham (1987) Gordon J Wenham *Genesis [2 vols]*

Wesley (1755) John Wesley *Predestination Calmly Considered*

Wittmer (2011) Michael E Wittmer *Christ Alone*

Wright (1997b) Tom Wright *What St Paul Really Said*

Wright (2002) NT Wright *The Letter to the Romans* in *The New Interpreters Bible vol X*

Wright (2009) NT Wright *Justification: God's Plan and Paul's Vision*

General Index

Abraham – 10, 12, 19, 33, 54, 61-2, 63-4, 68, 71-6, 83, 86, 87-9, 95, 97, 105, 107, 109, 110, 112, 118, 120, 187-9, 190

Accounted to him – 188-9

Adoption – 67, 129-37, 139, 195

Almighty – 14, 16, 22, 41, 55, 185-2

Annihilationism – 157-60, 168, 170, 175-7

Armour of God – 7, 10, 35-6, 39-40, 44, 121, 191

Augustine – 18, 25, 49, 53-4, 66, 77, 87, 126, 134, 142, 154, 158, 160, 173, 181-4, 185, 188, 192, 194

Baptism – 8, 96, 116, 183

Calling – 8, 123, 137, 171

Destruction – 16, 44, 53, 104, 120, 139, 157-9, 160, 161, 162, 167-8, 170-2, 175-6

Early Church – 18, 26, 53, 63, 68, 127, 132, 158-9, 160, 185, 192, 194

Egypt – 86, 94, 104, 109,196-7

Election – 39, 63, 89, 100, 106, 122-3, 134, 171, 182, 192-9

of Israel, 64-5, 66, 77, 80, 95

Esau – 77-81, 108-9

Eternity – 119-21, 123 125, 138, 141-6, 157-8, 160, 161, 163, 165-9, 172, 175, 177-8, 183

Eternal destiny – 78, 80, 89, 92, 94, 99-100, 127, 157, 192, 197

Eternal life – 60, 75, 112, 114, 141-2, 145-6, 153, 157-8, 161, 163, 165, 166-8, 172, 176, 178

Eternal punishment – 119-21, 123, 141, 142, 157, 158, 160, 163, 165, 167-9, 183

Faith/faithfulness – 1, 9-11, 13, 15, 17-18, 20, 29, 33, 40, 44, 48, 51-3, 63-7, 72-3, 75-6, 84-5, 88, 98-99, 101, 105-7, 109,10, 111-3, 116-20, 122, 130, 133, 136-7, 150, 157, 159, 163-7, 167, 172, 178-9, 183, 186, 188-5, 190-7, 192

Foreknowledge – 61, 109, 122, 126, 128, 142, 194-5

Freewill – 17-8, 53, 89, 127-8, 142, 156, 172, 182, 185-2, 192, 195, 196

Gehenna – 157, 161-3, 168, 171

Gentiles – 46-7, 63, 65, 66, 72, 101-3, 105-8, 111-2, 114-7, 126-7, 130, 164-5, 167, 171, 187, 190

Glory – 24, 35, 45-8, 53, 67, 86-8, 102-4, 109, 111-2, 114, 116-7, 128, 131, 135, 137-40, 149, 159, 165, 168, 174, 176, 177-8, 187, 195

God
- changes his mind – 50, 86-9, 99, 143, 154, 176
- motives with Pharaoh – 92-4,104-5, 196-7
- plan/strategy of – 1, 7, 26, 33, 34, 52-4, 59-60, 62, 64-5, 66, 72-3, 86, 90, 92, 95, 97, 99, 101, 103, 107, 109-10, 119-20, 122, 128,133, 143, 176, 180, 181, 185-2, 195, 197, 198
- will of – 7, 11, 37, 49, 50, 52-4, 56, 59-61, 98-100, 102, 108, 110, 127, 129-30, 138, 149, 164, 182, 185-2, 193

Hades (Sheol) – 141, 147-54, 169

Hardening – 92-4, 196-3

Hated (as opposed to 'loved') – 77-81, 108

Heaven/Heavenlies – 7, 10, 31, 35-7, 39-40, 43, 46, 47, 64, 84, 104, 113, 121-3, 125, 130, 141, 155, 162, 167, 169, 174, 175, 191, 192-9

Hell – 80, 122-3, 141, 154, 157-77, 182, 183, 185, 192

Holy Spirit – 27, 36, 41, 42-3, 66, 128, 135, 139, 165, 172, 179

Immortality – 112, 114, 146, 152, 159-61, 168, 170, 172, 176, 178

Imputed righteousness – 13, 166, 189

Isaac – 19, 54, 71-6, 77, 97, 109, 188

Ishmael – 73-6, 78, 109, 192

Israel – 1, 32, 34, 48, 52, 53, 62, 63-9, 71-2, 74, 76, 77-81, 83-9, 91-2, 94-6, 97-8, 100-10, 120, 122-3, 127, 150, 155, 164, 171, 173-4, 185, 188, 192, 197

Jacob – 40, 67-9, 77-81, 83, 89, 95, 97, 100, 108-9

Jesus
- ascension of – 46

General Index

- Christ/Messiah – 9, 34-6, 40, 41, 44, 45-8, 52, 53, 61-2, 63, 66, 67, 72-4, 76, 84, 107-8, 109-10, 111-2, 116-9, 120, 121, 128, 129, 130, 131, 152, 154-5, 162-3, 167, 178, 183, 186, 189, 190-7, 192
- crucifixion of – 46, 48, 66, 72, 110, 111, 119-21, 128, 143, 155, 158, 165, 188-5
- faithfulness of – 52, 66, 112, 117-8, 167, 183, 188-5, 190-7
- resurrection of – 47, 121, 131, 137, 151
- second coming of – 141, 155-6, 164, 171, 195
- teaching of – 8-9, 13, 28-9, 35, 36, 42-3, 46, 50-1, 53, 54, 80, 85, 93-4, 103, 107, 115, 118, 145-6, 150, 152-6, 161-7, 171-2, 173, 179-80, 181, 184, 185, 187, 191, 192
- temptation of – 8, 9, 43, 126
- transfiguration of – 122, 155,193
- victory of – 33, 39, 42, 45-8, 56, 61, 103, 119, 121, 131, 145, 151-2, 167-8, 178

Job – 7, 10-1, 14-25, 28-30, 31, 36-7, 41-2, 45-7, 98, 126, 149, 170

Judas – 8-9, 192-3

Judgement – 33, 93, 112-6, 141, 151, 153, 156-7, 161-2, 163-8, 170, 171-76, 180, 188-9

Justification – 72, 76, 112-4, 117, 187-5, 190-7

Lamb – 8, 43-4, 45, 47, 60-2, 96, 111, 120-1, 139-40, 169, 180

Law (*Torah*) – 10, 32, 63-5, 67, 76, 84-5, 98, 102, 106, 111, 114, 116-7, 136-7, 153, 187-9, 190-1

Lot – 12, 71, 73, 87, 89, 109, 118, 165, 187

Melchizedek – 71, 73, 109, 118, 165

Moses – 83-90, 91, 94, 96, 97, 98, 106, 109, 110, 147, 153, 155, 174, 196

New Heaven and New Earth – 52-3, 139-40, 141-3, 157, 162, 175, 177-80, 186

Omniscience – 17-9, 143

Open Theology – 19, 143

Paul – 11, 12-4, 25, 27, 35, 39, 40-3, 47, 50-1, 55, 63-9, 72, 74-6, 77-8, 80-1, 83-4, 87, 89-90, 91-2, 94-5, 97-109, 111-8, 130, 132, 135-8, 146, 149-52, 155, 156, 162-3, 166, 167, 179, 181, 186, 187-5, 190-7, 192, 194

Pharaoh – 91-6, 97, 104-5, 110, 196-3

Pharisees – 13, 53, 76, 99, 106, 150-3, 163, 181, 187, 190

Portal view of Hell – 157-9, 172

Predestination – 66, 77, 89, 126-34, 138, 182, 194-5

Reformed theology – 13, 87, 108, 126, 134, 154, 161, 165, 184, 185, 194

Relational theology – 19, 143

Repentance – 87, 92-3, 104-5, 108, 110, 112-4, 116, 143, 177, 193

Resurrection – 36, 48, 96, 121, 131, 137, 141, 146, 148, 149-52, 154-57, 162, 177-8

Righteous/Righteousness – 11-4, 15, 19-24, 27, 36, 37, 40, 45, 47-853, 61, 64-5, 71, 83-5, 87-9, 95, 97-8, 106, 111-119, 141, 148-9, 152-3, 155, 157, 163, 164-7, 170-2, 174-5, 177, 178-9, 183, 187-5, 191

Satan/the devil – 7-11, 14-22, 24-7, 30, 31, 39, 41-3, 48-9, 51, 56, 59-62, 96, 119-21, 123, 125-6, 138, 139-40, 141, 149, 163, 169, 187, 192

Sheol (*see Hades*)

Sinners/Wicked – 12-5,21-3, 41, 44, 45, 47-8, 88-9, 103, 111-2, 115, 119, 160-1, 168, 170-2, 175-7, 187-9, 194

Sovereignty – 45, 49-50, 52-6, 87-8, 109, 176, 182, 185-2

Spiritual battle – 7, 8-9, 14-5, 24, 25, 30, 31, 34, 35-6, 37, 39, 40, 43-4, 47, 49, 55, 56, 61-2, 63, 66, 72, 74, 89-90, 96, 108, 119, 121-2, 125, 138-9, 180, 198

Temple – 33-4, 62, 67, 95, 103, 144, 164, 174, 179

Traditionalism – 15, 19, 46, 51, 62, 66, 73, 77, 108, 111, 116, 126, 156-8, 173, 175, 181, 184, 185, 192, 194

Universalism – 157-9, 160, 176

Unrighteous – 48, 56, 83, 95, 97-8, 104, 112-4, 141-2, 148, 152-53, 154, 157, 160-1, 162-3, 170, 172, 177

Vessels for honour/no honour – 101-3, 105-6

Vessels of mercy/wrath – 103-5, 108, 110

Works of the Law – 13, 64, 66, 76, 81, 84-5, 165-6, 179, 188, 190-7

Yahweh – 10-11, 18, 23, 45, 55, 85, 110, 142

Index of Verses Cited

This index lists verses cited in this volume, grouped by Bible book. Chapter and verse are listed numerically, followed by the page numbers on which they appear. Please note some verses may be cited individually and also as part of longer passages.

Genesis
2:7 – 146
3:4-5 – 10,60
3:15 – 120,149
5:24 – 61
12:1-3 – 71,120
18:23 – 89
22:2 – 54
22:17-18 – 63
27:36 – 68
35:29 – 147

1 – 51
2:9,10,11-2 – 180
3:6 – 51
3:22 – 180
6:1-4 – 155
15:6 – 72
18:25 – 83
22:8 – 62,120
25:9 – 73
29:30-31 – 79
49:25 – 55

1:20-21 – 160
2:16-7 – 51,60,147
3:8 – 180
4:4 – 120
6:6 – 86
16:10,13 – 73
21:12,13 – 73-4
22:12 – 19
25:8,17 – 147
32:28 – 67
49:33 – 147

2:6 – 160
3:1 – 8
3:14-15 – 8,61
4:10 – 148
6:9 – 12,61
18:20,21 – 87
21:20 – 73
22:14 – 62,73
25:23 – 78
33:3-13 – 78

Exodus
4:21 – 93,94
7:3-4 – 92-94
8:32 – 92
9:34,35 – 92,93
11:10 – 93
14:4,8 – 93-4,105
15:15 – 95
29:9 – 144
33:5,7-11 – 88
34:29-35 – 85,88

3:6 – 150
4:22 – 67
7:13,14,22 – 93
9:7,12 – 93
10:1,2 – 93,94
12:4 – 120
14:13 – 96
19:5,6 – 67,84,107
29:45 – 85
33:11,12-13 – 85
36:7 – 55

3:18,19 – 109
5:21,22 – 110
8:15 – 92
9:14-18 – 91,94
10:20,27 – 93
12:14 – 144
14:17,18 – 93,94
21:6 – 144
32:9,14 – 86
33:15-19 – 83,88
40:34 – 67

3:21-22 – 94
6:6-7 – 94
8:19,28 – 93
9:15 – 104
11:9 – 94
13:14-15 – 92,94
15:13 – 94
24:17 – 174
32:32-34 – 87
34:8-9 – 85,88

Leviticus
1–16 – 67
19:18 – 85
26:27-33 – 103

Numbers
16:33 – 161

10:8 – 144
32:39 – 161
13–14 – 95
33:53 – 161
15:15 – 144

Deuteronomy
11:13 – 156
33:15 – 144

4:8 – 67
15:17 – 144
4:25-27,29 – 103
30:14-20 – 84
6:5 – 85
32:50 – 147

Joshua
2:9-11 – 94-5,105
11:20 – 93
24:15 – 51

1 Samuel
15:11,29,35 – 86
1:22 – 144
16:7 – 109
6:6 – 93
28:9-19 – 148
8:8 – 94

2 Samuel
7:12-16 – 144
24:1 – 126

1 Kings
21:1-35 – 87
2:10 – 141,147
8:11 – 67
8:13 – 144

2 Kings
20:2-5 – 87
22:20 – 147

1 Chronicles
21:1 – 126
23:13 – 144
28:4 – 144

2 Chronicles
3:1 – 62
32:24-26 – 87
33:6 – 162

Ezra
6:3-5 – 33
7:12 – 55

Index of Verses Cited

Job
1:9-10 – 14	1:1 – 10	1:5 – 10	1:8 – 20,21
2:7 – 22	1:8 – 11	1:11 – 10	2:3 – 16,20,21
5:8 – 45	2:9 – 15	4:7-9 – 15,20,21	4:17-18 – 15,20
8:4-6 – 15,20,21	5:17 – 16,22	5:18 – 15,22,45	8:2 – 23
10:15 – 14	8:8-20 – 15	8:20 – 20	10:7 – 14
11:14 – 15	10:21 – 147	11:2 – 23	11:4-6 – 15,21,22
15:5 – 15,23	14:16-17 – 11	14:16 – 14	15:4 – 21
16:9 – 170	15:10 – 15	15:14 – 21	15:15,16 – 15
22:4-5 – 15,21,22	18:2 – 23	19:25-7 – 149	22:2-3 – 14-5,20
33:5-12 – 21,23	25:4,6 – 15,21	26:5 – 147	32:1 – 15
35:7 – 20	34:5-11 – 22	34:7-11 – 15,21	34:35-37 – 15,23
36:16-17 – 22	35:16 – 23	36:5-6 – 22	36:7 – 15
42:8 – 31	38:1 – 10	40:7 – 30	42:7 – 23
	42:10 – 28,30		

Psalm
15:17 – 149	5:12 – 12	6:5,6 – 141,147	14:4-5 – 12
37:12 – 170	16:9-11 – 149	30:9 – 147	35:16 – 170
51:7 – 52	41:13 – 144	47:2 – 55	51:5 – 183
103:19 – 55	62:12 – 114	88:5,11-2 – 147-8	90:2 – 144
137:9 – 147	110:4 – 144	112:10 – 170	115:17 – 147

Proverbs
	1:12 – 147	13:24 – 79,80	27:20 – 147

Ecclesiastes
	1:4 – 144

Isaiah
11:4 – 41,42	5:14 – 147	9:7 – 144	11:1-9 – 140
26:19 – 150	11:6-9 – 34,96	14:8-9 – 148	14:12-13 – 125
39:1-8 – 87	34:10 – 170	38:1-6 – 87	38:18 – 147-8
53:10 – 47	44:28 – 100	45:1,4,9 – 100	53:8 – 34
65:25 – 34	56:4 – 51	59:16-20 – 40	65:12 – 52
	66:11 – 55	66:24 – 162	

Jeremiah
18:8,10 – 87	7:32 – 162	8:6 – 87	18:6-7 – 101
26:3,13,19 – 87	19:6 – 162	20:16 – 87	23:41 – 92
	31:19 – 87	32:35 – 162	42:10 – 87

Lamentations
	2:16 – 170

Ezekiel
26:7 – 55	12:3 – 87	14:14,20 – 14	18:23 – 88
33:11 – 88	28:3 – 32	28:13 – 155	32:21 – 148
	36:35 – 155	37:11-14 – 150	42:5 – 35

Daniel
3:28 – 33	1:17 – 32	2:17,22-23 – 32	3:25 – 32
5:11,14,24 – 36	3:29 – 172	4:1-3 – 33	4:34-37 – 33
7:21,22,27 – 35	6:10-11 – 33	6:23 – 33	7:13,18 – 35,144
12:1 – 34	9:20,26 – 34	10:2-12,26 – 34	10:13,20,21 – 34
	12:2 – 36,150	12:13 – 36	

Hosea
	1:9,2:23 – 105	12:4,5 – 68

Joel
	3:2 – 164

Amos
	3:7 – 32	7:3,6 – 87

Obadiah
	16:15-16 – 161

Jonah
	2:2 – 148	3:10 – 87,176	4:2 – 87

Habakkuk   1:2   –   97   1:6   –   92   1:11   –   48
2:1,2   –   97   2:4   – 48,51,113   2:14   –   96   3   –   98

Zephaniah   3:7   –   143

Zechariah   3:1   –   11,126

Malachi   1:2-3   –   78-81   1:6-14 –   81   4:1-2 – 161,177

Matthew   2:1   –   32   2:13   –   161   4:4   –   41
4:6,7   –   42   4:9   –   126   4:10   –   9   4:14   –   164
5:22   –   168   6:24   –   79,80   6:32   –   164   7:21   –   53
8:12   –   171   9:10   –   13   9:24   –   9   10:5   –   164
10:15   –   157   10:18   –   164   10:25   –   157   10:28 – 162,168
10:37-38 –   80   10:40-42 –   165   10:41   –   13   11:22,24 – 157
12:18 – 122,164   12:21   –   164   12:28   –   36   12:32   –   145
12:34   –   9   12:50   – 53,164   13:32   –   145   13:42 – 168,171
13:49   –   145   13:50   –   171   15:6   –   181   16:18   –   152
16:23   –   9   17:3   –   155   19:16   –   145   20:19   –   164
20:22,25-28 – 46 20:25   –   164   20:28   –   131   22:8-9 –   154
22:13   –   171   22:29-32 – 150,178   22:44   –   144   23:3   –   166
23:28   –   13   23:37   – 52-4,182   23:35   –   13   24:3,9,14 – 164
24:14   –   157   24:36-37 –   157   24:44   –   157   24:45-51 – 171
25:1-13 – 171   25:6   –   157   25:14-30 –   171   25:31-46 – 163
25:32   –   164   25:34-37 –   179   25:35   –   164   25:35-6 –   166
25:37   –   13   25:42   –   166   25:44   –   161   25:46 –13,141,165-8
26:52   –   161   27:52-3 – 151,2   28:19   –   164   28:19-20 – 120
28:20   –   145

Mark   3:35   –   53   4:3   –   29   4:19   –   145
4:38   –   161   8:33   –   9   9:4   –   155   9:41   –   161
9:43-44 – 162   10:30   –   145   10:42-45 – 46,131   12:28-34 –   85
16:20   –   27

Luke   4:8   –   9   6:32   –   13   6:35-36 –   173
7:30 – 52-3,99,143 8:46-47 –   166   8:52   –   151   9:30   –   155
9:35   –   122   11:20   –   36   11:51   –   161   12:50   –   121
13:3   –   161   13:22-30 –   171   13:34   –   53   14:14   –   157
14:23 – 154,182   14:26   – 79,80   15:4   –   161   15:11   –   152
15:17   –   161   16:1   –   152   16:8   –   145   16:13   –   79
16:14   –   153   16:19   –   152   17:27   –   161   18:30   –   167
20:35   –   157   22:24-27 – 46,131   23:43   –   155   24:27   –   181

John   1:1   –   41   1:4   –   145   1:9   –   118
1:12   –   52   1:14   –   48   1:29   –   111   3:15   –   161
3:19   –   42   4:22   – 108,118   5:28-29 – 157,166   6:40   –   157
6:63   –   41   6:70   –   8   7:17   –   53   7:18   –   139
7:27   –   29   8:44-45 –   8,42   8:50   –   139   8:56   –   62
9:1-3   –   28   10:10-11 –   145   10:28   –   146   11:11   –   141
11:11-13 – 151   11:21-27 – 150,157   12:23-32 –   46   13   –   131
13:2   –   9   13:13   –   46   13:31,32 – 46,139   14:6 – 111,119
14:13   –   139   16:14   –   139   17:1   –   139   17:22   –   139
21:22-23 – 157

Index of Verses Cited

Acts
2:24 – 152
2:34-5 – 144
10:34,35 – 65
13:45 – 98
14:15-17 – 98
18:6 – 65
26:17 – 65

1:8 – 120
2:27 – 149,152
4:27-28 – 127
11:29 – 127
13:46-47 – 65
14:22 – 156
22:21,22 – 65

2:17 – 36
2:31 – 141,149
7:6 – 151
13:25 – 149
13:50 – 98
17:28 – 118
23:6 – 150

2:22-23 – 47,127-8
2:32 – 152
9:5,15 – 65
13:34-7 – 147,151
14:2 – 98
17:22-31 – 98
24:15 – 141

Romans
1:18 – 104,111
2:5 – 141,157
2:29 – 67
3:21 – 10
3:22-3 – 52,111
5:1-2 – 51,116
6:1 – 98
8:1 – 116
8:15-17 – 135
8:19-21 – 131
8:28-30 – 129-34
9:1-26 – 105
9:10-13 – 77-81
9:16 – 109
9:20-1 – 99-102
9:31 – 84,106
10:12 – 106
11:5 – 106
11:25 – 102
11:32 – 108
14:17 – 36,156

1:4 – 121,131
2:1-4 – 113
2:7 – 146,165
3:2 – 102
3:19-20 – 117
3:25 – 167
5:3-4 – 24,138
6:2-5 – 116
8:4 – 63
8:17 – 131
8:23 – 130,135-6
8:29 – 140
9:4,5 – 95,102
9:14 – 83
9:17-8 – 91
9:22-23 – 102-4
10:1 – 63
10:14 – 95
11:13-24 – 107
11:26-31 – 94
11:33 – 110
16:25 – 145

1:14-18 – 113
2:4-5,9 – 104
2:17 – 100,115-7
3:3-8 – 97
3:23 – 12,52
3:31 – 98
5:8 – 173
6:1,15 – 98
8:5 – 179
8:18-19 – 128,132
8:26-28 – 25-6,90
8:38-39 – 138
9:6-7 – 67,74
9:14-19 – 94,98
9:18 – 95,99
9:26 – 106
10:5-8 – 106
10:20 – 106
11:13 – 65
11:28 – 108
12:2 – 179

1:16 – 112
2:5-16 – 114-6
2:24 – 103
3:9-19 – 111-2,116
3:21-26 – 112,6,8
4:19-20 – 75
5:12 – 149
7:1-14 – 75
8:15 – 130
8:19 – 140
8:28 – 25,110,143
9:1-5 – 63,74,87
9:7-9 – 76
9:15-16 – 83,89
9:19 – 97,99,101
9:30-33 – 106
10:6 – 84
11:1-2 – 63
11:17 – 102
11:30 – 105,108
12:5 – 183

1 Corinthians
3:10-15 – 140
9:24,26 – 89,109
13 – 47,179
15:35-49 – 177-8

1:20 – 145
3:11-17 – 174,9
10:1,2 – 96
14:1,26 – 23
15:52-55 – 146,152

2:7-9 – 128
3:15 – 172
10:9 – 161
15:18,20 – 151,2

3:9 – 27
7 – 183
11:2 – 184
15:23 – 141

2 Corinthians
4:16-18 – 138
6:1 – 27

3:14-4:6 – 103
5:8 – 155
6:18 – 55

3:18 – 137
5:9 – 14
12:4 – 156

4:14 – 48
5:10 – 141,57,63,66
12:7 – 25

Galatians
3:8,14 – 72
4:3 – 136
4:21-31 – 75

1:15 – 65
3:14-16 – 74
4:5 – 136
5:7 – 89

2:2 – 89
3:24,25,26 – 136
4:6-7 – 137
5:22,23 – 103

2:8 – 65
3:26-28 – 130,154
4:15 – 24

Ephesians
1:5,6 – 132
1:11-12 – 129-32
2:2 – 26
3:20 – 26

1:3 – 35,39,121
1:7 – 121
1:13,14 – 132,135
2:6 – 35,121
4:30 – 135

1:3,4 – 122,154
1:10 – 125
1:20 – 121
3:8 – 65
5:26 – 41

1:3-6 – 129-30
1:11 – 26,131
1:20-21 – 35,39
3:12 – 121
5:27 – 129

6:4 – 24	6:11 – 7	6:10-12 – 39,120	6:12 – 31,35,122
6:13 – 96	6:13-18 – 35,40	6:13,17 – 41-3	
Philippians	1:21-24 – 155	2:9-10 – 45	2:10 – 125
2:13 – 179	2:16 – 89	3:10-14 – 137	3:20-21 – 178
4:13 – 40			
Colossians	1:10 – 14	1:18 – 125,131	1:20 – 125
1:22 – 129	1:24 – 138	2:8,9 – 51,181	2:14-15 – 119
1 Thessalonians	2:16 – 103	4:13,15 – 151	4:16-17 – 141
2 Thessalonians	1:4-10 – 167-8	1:7-9 – 141	2:8 – 42,140
1 Timothy	2:4 – 52	3:11 – 8	6:15 – 55
6:16 – 146	6:17 – 145		
2 Timothy	1:10 – 142	2:20-21 – 102	2:26 – 9
3:3 – 8	3:16 – 24	4:7 – 109	
Titus	1:2 – 54	1:12 – 118	2:12 – 145
Hebrews	1:2 – 125,131	1:3 – 7,46,51	1:13 – 144
2:10 – 132,137	6:18 – 17	7:3,7 – 71	7:15-24 – 144
8:13 – 145	9:12,22 – 84	9:14 – 119	9:22 – 84
9:27 – 141,157	10:1,4 – 84	10:22 – 24	11:3 – 51
11:7 – 64	11:8 – 72	11:13-16 – 150	11:31 – 105
12:1 – 24,109	12:5-11 – 24	12:29 – 174	13:4 – 183
James	1:13 – 16	1:14 – 9	2:14 – 13
2:25 – 105	3:6 – 162	4:7-8 – 9,13,120	5:15 – 29
5:16 – 13,26	5:16-18 – 37		
1 Peter	1:2 – 122	1:3-5 – 36	1:20 – 47,61
2:9-10 – 107	3:9 – 53	3:12 – 27	3:18 – 155
4:11 – 55	5:8 – 43	5:11 – 5	
2 Peter	1:10 – 123	2:2-9 – 12,71	3:4 – 151
3:7 – 157			
1 John	1:1-2 – 146	1:5 – 129,140,174	1:9 – 13,52
1:10 – 12,52	2:17 – 53,60	2:29 – 13	3:2-3 – 178
3:5 – 178	3:7 – 13	3:8 – 9	3:9 – 13
4:8,16 – 129,174	4:18 – 163,179	5:11 – 167	
Jude	1:7 – 168	1:9 – 34	1:25 – 55
Revelation	1:6 – 55	1:16 – 41,139	1:18 – 152
2:7 – 156	2:12,16 – 41,139	5:3,4 – 43	6:8 – 152
6:9 – 155	12:7 – 120-1,139	12:7-11 – 10,43	12;11 – 119
12:12 – 139	14:9-11 – 169	16:6 – 44	17:6,14 – 44,55
17:16 – 139	18:24 – 44	19:13,15 – 41	19:15-21 – 139
19:16 – 55	20:2-3 – 9	20:9-10 – 140	20:9-15 – 165-6
20:12-13 – 166	20:13-15 – 141,152	21:1 – 52,140	21:2-10 – 180
21:4 – 152	21:17-21 – 180	21:23 – 140,180	21:27 – 180
22:1-5 – 180	22:2,3,14 – 60		